TESSA NEWCOMB
WHERE I BELONG

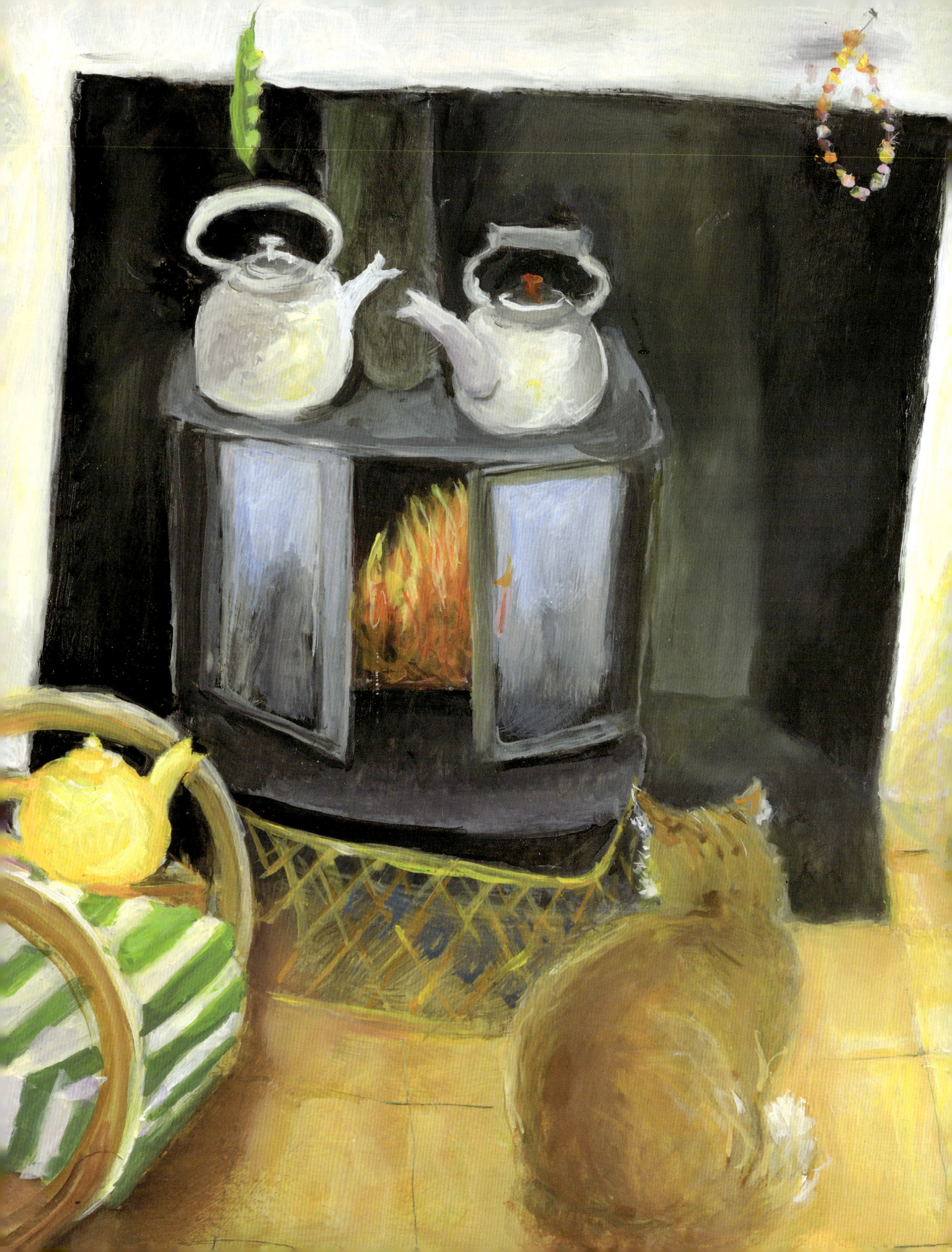

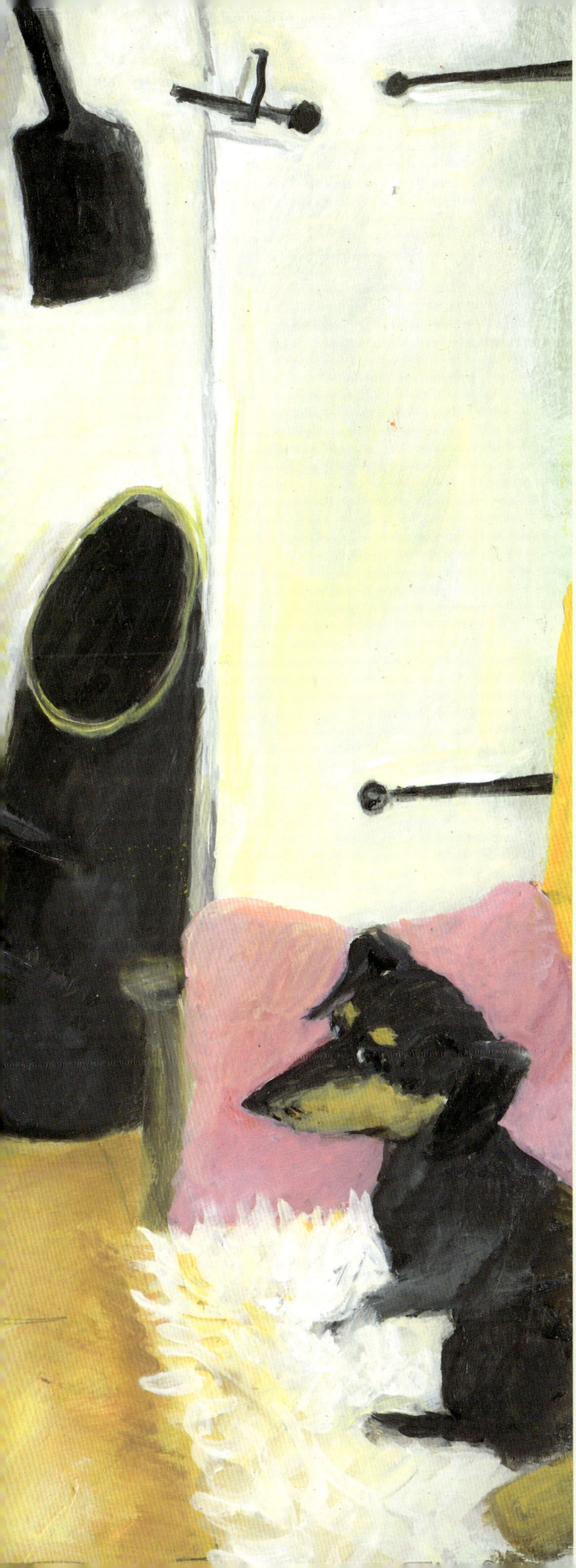

TESSA NEWCOMB

WHERE I BELONG

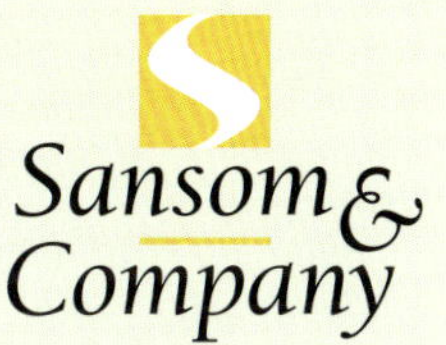

Sansom & Company

First published in 2021 by Sansom & Company Ltd.,
81G Pembroke Road, Bristol BS8 3EA

info@sansomandcompany.co.uk
www.sansomandcompany.co.uk

© Tessa Newcomb

ISBN 978-1-911408-77-2

British Library Cataloguing-in-Publication Data:
A catalogue record for this book is available from
the British Library

Design and typesetting by E&P Design, Bath

Printed and bound by Cambrian Printers Ltd, Wales

Cover: *Target Hill* (detail)
2020 · oil on board · 42 x 46 cm / 16½ x 18 in
Frontispiece: *The Stove*
2020 · oil on card · 23 x 26.5 cm / 9 x 10½ in

FOREWORD

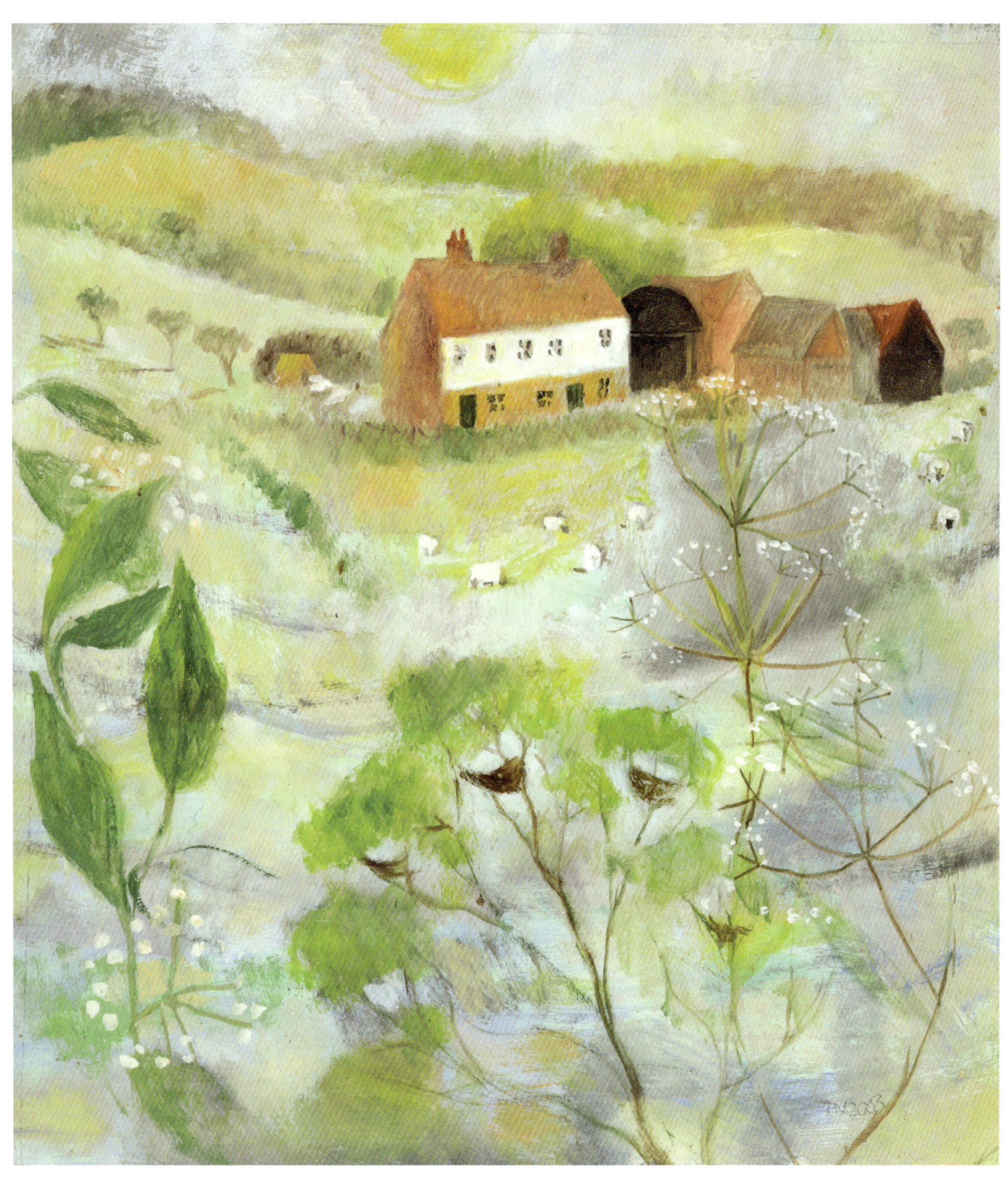

White House Farm
2006 · oil on board · 42.5 x 37 cm / 16¾ x 14½ in

FOREWORD

As a child, growing up in Great Glemham, Suffolk, I had a recurrent dream. It focused on an oak tree in the corner of a large, rising field. The soil was soft and sandy; and the crop was thin — it may have been barley. Small wildflowers and weeds were also scattered across otherwise bare earth. It was a beautiful view: the mighty oak, the soft soil and the ascendant land. But what made the dream so memorable and exciting was an additional detail. Amid the barley shoots and weeds was another crop. Poking up through the sand were dozens, perhaps hundreds, of small metal Dinky toys: cars, jeeps, lorries, trucks and fire engines. Heaven!

The waking moments that followed were tantalising. At first I would sleepily think that the dream was real: that I could locate the field in my mental map of our farm — and what treasures awaited! But as sleep receded, that sureness slipped away. I would go through the field names: New Road, Kiln Piece, Dairy Maid, Bachelors. They all felt nearby, close. But as my eyes opened, it became clear that the field would not fit amongst them. It had gone again. But the possibility that it did exist or that next time I might really find it was deeply inspiring. It left me with a feeling that if I just walked a little bit further or turned another hedgerow corner, I might find the oak, the field — and the toys.

I mention this memory because it sums up what I think, personally, is so captivating about Tessa Newcomb's paintings. They invite the viewer to take a step or two in the reverse and slightly more magical direction: from reality to the imagined. For the subjects of Tessa's work — the local river valleys, the fens, village scenes, people out walking with pets, gardens, seashores, allotments, cafés, fishing boats, markets and home — are simultaneously reassuringly familiar but also distinctly different from the viewer's own reality. They are brought to life by Tessa's imagination and invite the viewer to step inside her world: East Anglia as she experiences it.

Being able to collaborate with Tessa over the past decades has been one of the great pleasures of my life in the arts. We first met through a commission to paint murals in a cottage next to Great Glemham Church — including an oil painting on board of my home farm. This led to a small exhibition in 2003 of works by Tessa, myself and my late grandmother, Fidelity Cranbrook. This, in turn, became the seed that grew into the Alde Valley Spring Festival. Tessa's paintings have been at the heart of the Festival and life at the farm for over fifteen years as it has grown into a painters' place: a home for the arts as well as for myself and many guests — and a surprisingly large number of chickens, ducks, sheep, cats, dog and pigs. A recent painting, *Everything You Need*, summed this up beautifully.

I think that the secret of Tessa's work is that it is so deeply and personally true to place. She catches the subtle and elusive sense of belonging that many of us quietly seek or hope for. In beholding Tessa's paintings, the observed and imagined become intertwined and we step into her world. And in doing so, for a few moments, we gain Tessa's special sense of belonging.

Jason Gathorne-Hardy
White House Farm, Great Glemham, 5 March 2021

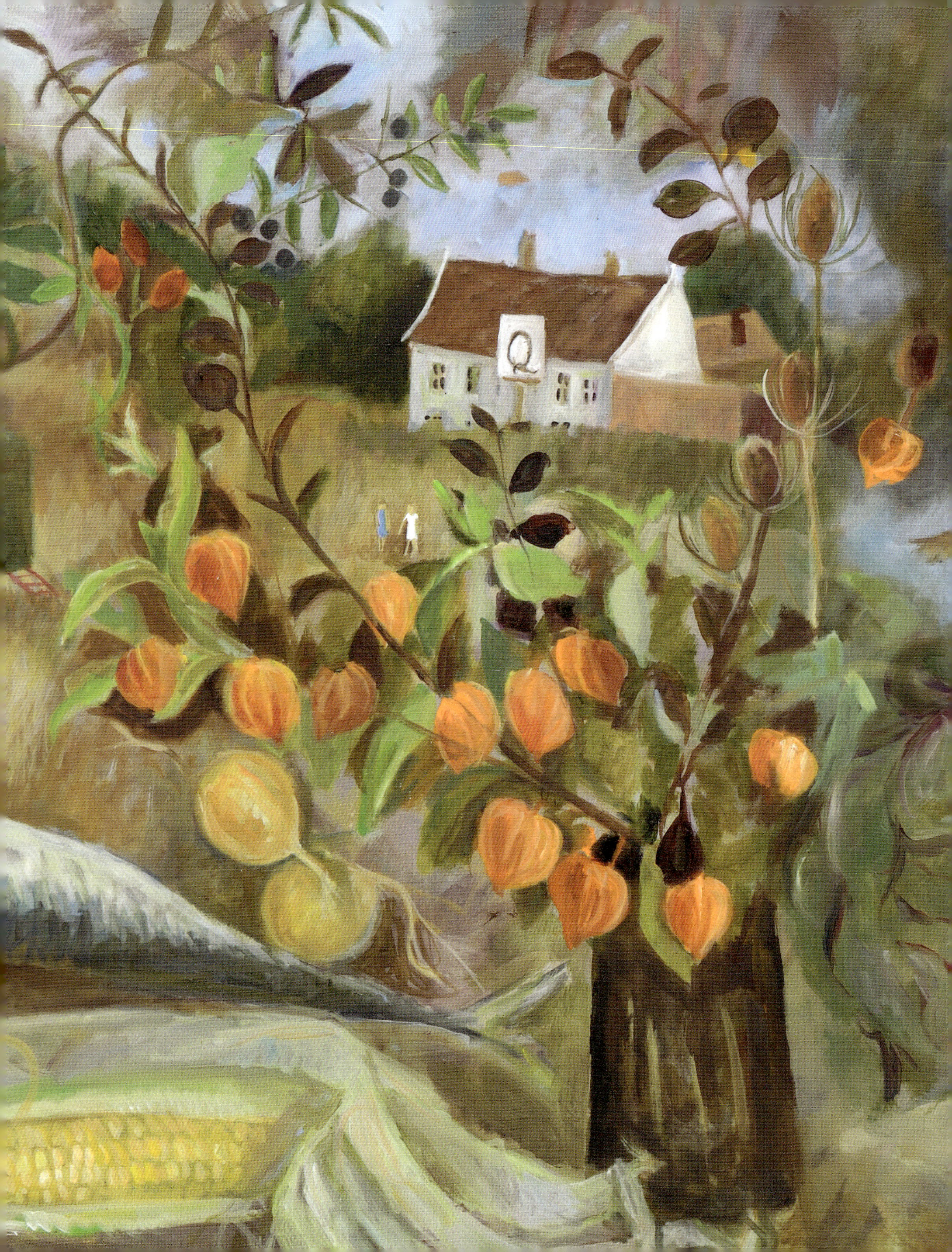

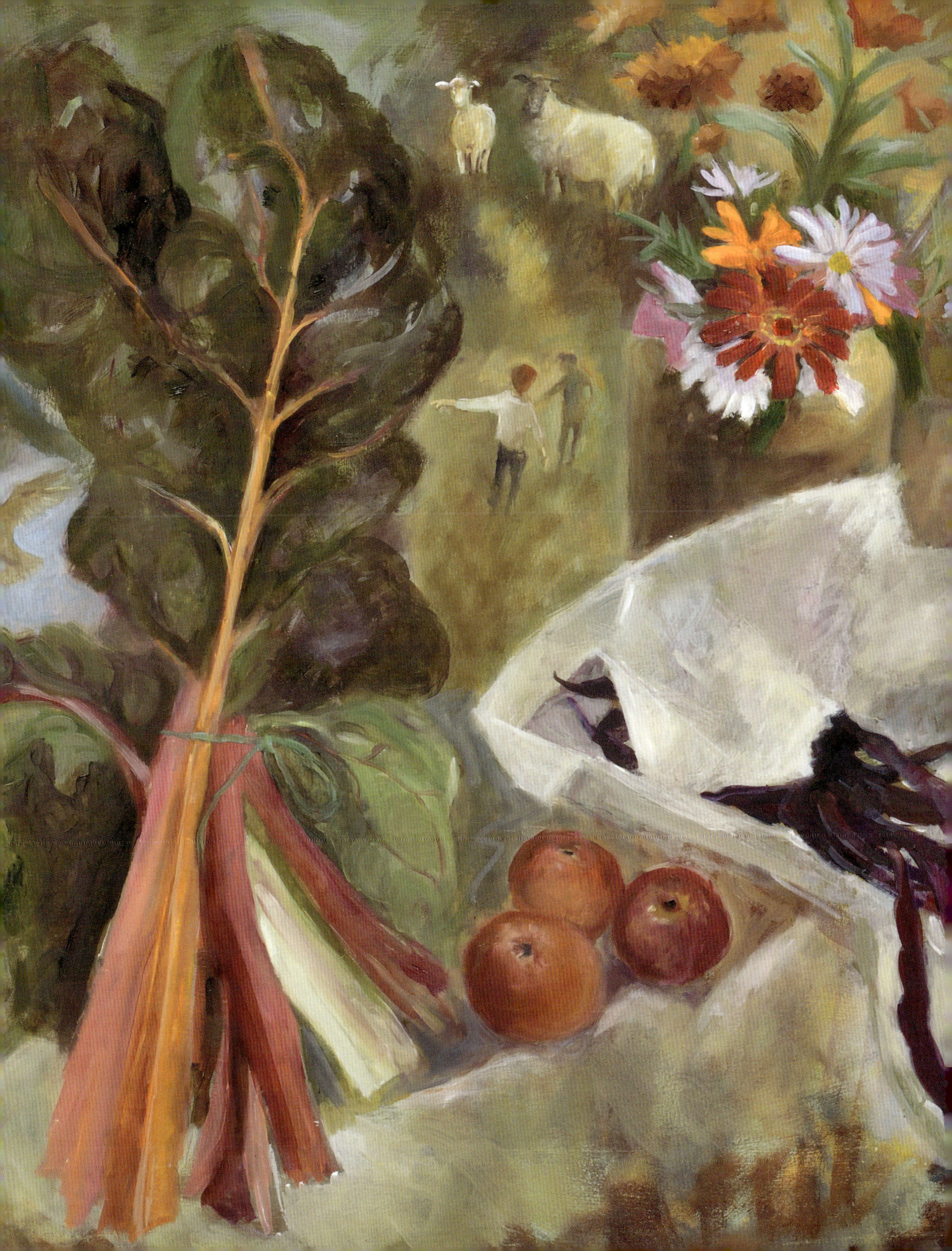

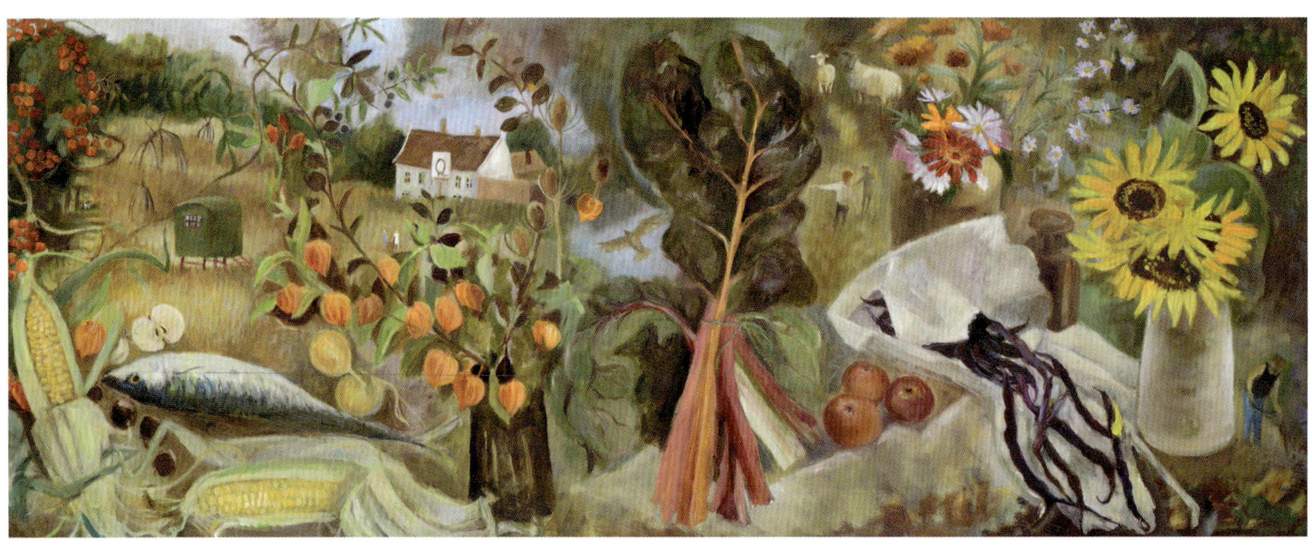

Everything You Need
2019 · oil on board · 61 x 152.5 cm / 24 x 60 in

INTRODUCTION

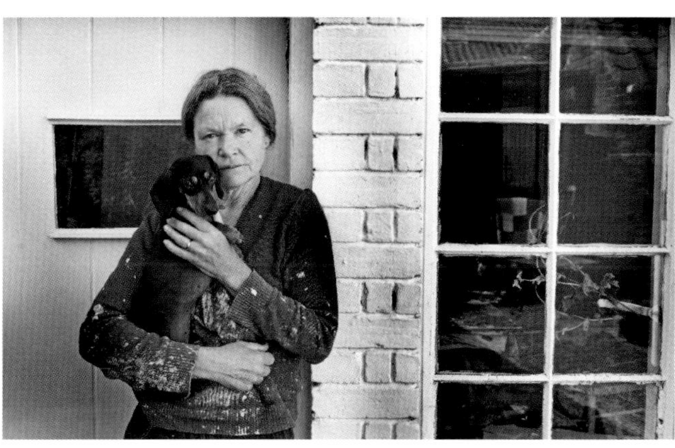

We all have places we are attached to. Some people can't get to theirs. When I have been away, or something has happened, and every day when I'm at home, I go for my usual walk. I see what changes have taken place. I want to feel safe; I want to belong. I call it 'the beating of the bounds'.

Peter: *I am native, rooted here.*
Balstrode: *Rooted by what?*
Peter: *By familiar fields, Marsh and sand, Ordinary streets, Prevailing wind.*

From libretto by M. Slater for Benjamin Britten's *Peter Grimes* (1945)

In this book I start in the Waveney Valley, where I lived until I was sixteen. We visit the Fens when I have just left school, biking out into the unknown. It was foggy. Then up to 'the high plateau of Suffolk': here we walk the roadside and I can feel as my mother felt as I look at the same plants. We go to the coast where the petals of yellow horned poppies shake in the North Sea wind. We walk on the cobbles of Elm Hill in Norwich, visit a dog show and go to the farmers' market.

Some places are humble, like my home and allotment, known from being worked; and some are 'thin' places, like Holy Trinity Church in Blythburgh, 'The Cathedral of the Marshes' — places where there's not much between you and the eternal world. We meet people who are connected to the places and have given me more understanding of them. All happen to be in East Anglia.

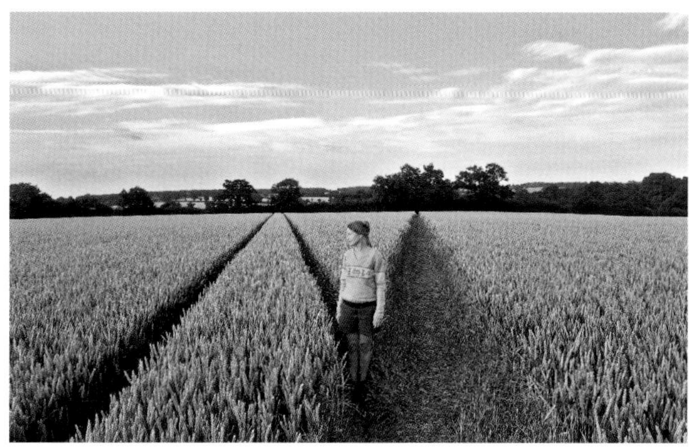

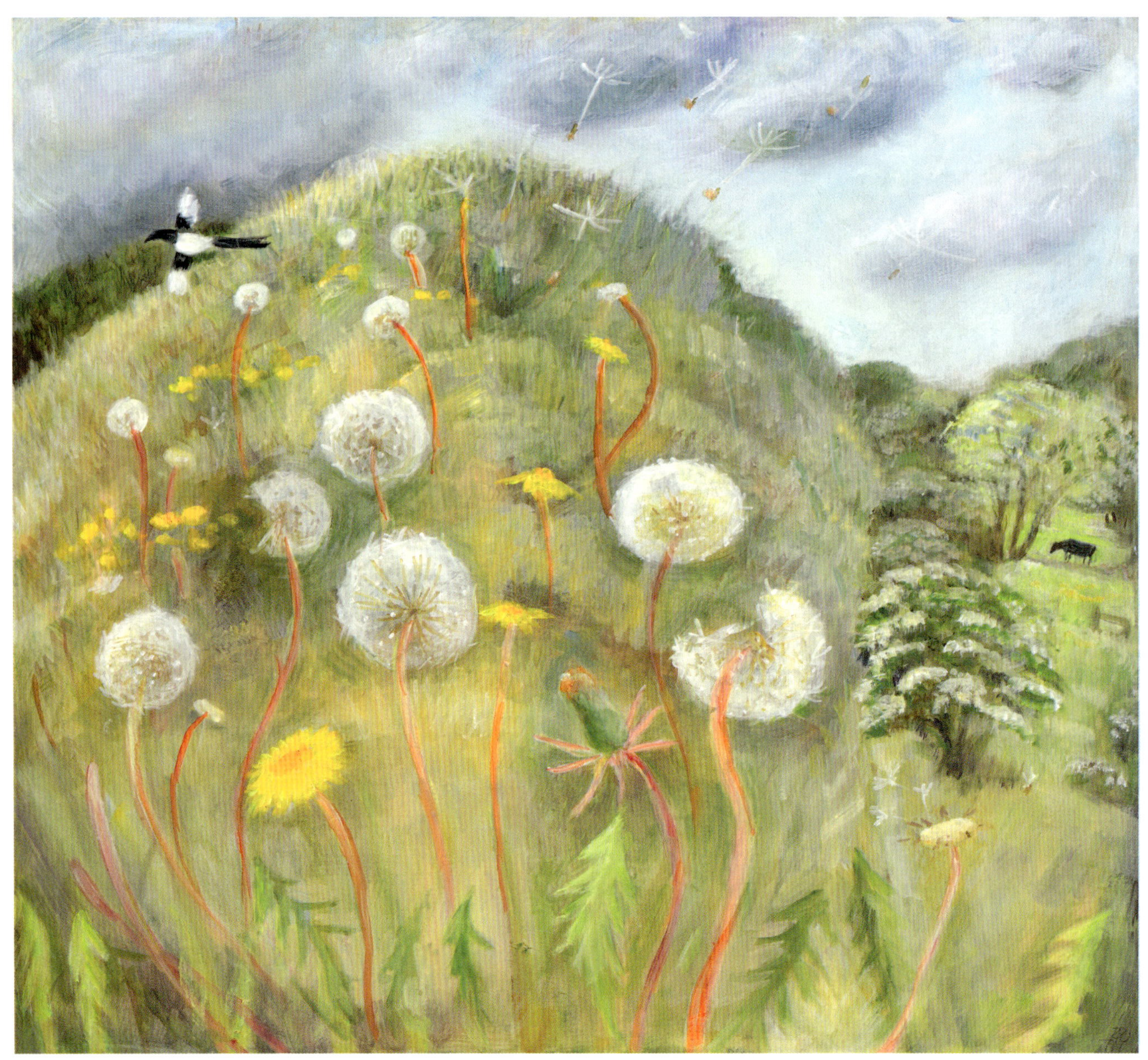

Target Hill
2020 · oil on board · 42 x 46 cm / 16½ x 18 in

1 · THE WAVENEY VALLEY

We often return to places we have known as children. They are and are not the same. In our minds we have crystallised the place, the time and the feelings, while the actual place flows on, moves, changes. We recognise some parts, while others are nothing to do with us. An old house might have been gutted and rebuilt, changing its status with its shape, and we can let it go, but are floored on recognising a gatepost, and want to shout out that we know that gatepost, that it's ours — which it is and it isn't. You left the land, but it remained faithful as much as it could. It expects you to come back, to know it. It has waited for you like an old dog. As much as you would like not to hear its voice, not to mind, you do.

THE RIVER AND THE VALLEY

The river Waveney runs from its western end at Redgrave, on the Suffolk/Norfolk border, to the Broads in the east. It's fed by the river Dove and Gold Brook then slides along its valley through Diss, Harleston, Bungay, and to Beccles, where it becomes something else — the Norfolk Broads, which is not my country. It eventually joins with the river Yare and goes out into the sea at Great Yarmouth. I know the bit between Diss and Bungay, having lived there until I was sixteen.

My parents had a smallholding and were some of the first people to try to live off their land and the things they made. When I returned to Needham, in Norfolk (where I was born), after my mother Mary died in 2008, I stood at the top of the hill overlooking the Waveney Valley and looked down to what had been their farm and land. We had a cottage with its farm buildings, a large tithe barn, fifty acres of arable and fifty acres of marsh-land bordering the river. I thought of how their

lifestyle had affected many people and future generations. How the things they made have now become collectors' items. Godfrey's pots of rich slipware are now being appreciated and have recently been collected together into a book, and Mary's much sought-after paintings have long been out in the world, far from their subjects.

The Waveney divides the counties of Norfolk and Suffolk. We lived in Norfolk and swam in the river to Suffolk, then back. It's not very wide or imposing, but brown — slow and sure, a friendly river. It is said by some that the name Waveney comes from waving waters. The reeds wave. I thought all rivers were like that until, on various holidays, I discovered others that were stony — fast and clear.

Anyone who has swum in the Waveney will know that you have to get in first, usually down a muddy bank where there are patches you can stand on. You can find a few places where there is a gravelly bottom, but mostly it is muddy, which gets softly between your toes; then it's the reeds. The reeds wind themselves around your legs, the swans can break your arms, and the pike — the pike can bite your bottom when it's wedged in the centre of a tractor inner tube that you use to paddle upstream over the deep bits. And once pike bite they can't let go because their teeth point inwards. But we were brave at ten. I rode my ponies bareback, rubbed myself with dock leaves after I fell into nettles, and stood in warm cowpats. The marshes were my country, the ditches very dangerous.

SWANS

The landscape seems to be dominated by swans. A family are grazing, the big adolescents tearing at the lush grass. The parents need them to be moving and glide impatiently on the ice-water.

When the family has assembled, glowing pink
in the setting sun, they all glide magnificently
upstream. As I leave the valley in the come-early
dusk, one big swan stands out, a white in the
disappearing landscape.

LUCKS MILL

At the top of the hill is Bobby's house. She looked
after the sheep at the Big House and would walk
back to her solitary cottage in rubber boots with
two collies. My mother liked her. You can sense
these things when you are young.

Turn off the ridge and go down, very steep for
Suffolk. Rolling hills overlooking the Waveney
Valley. Put your boots down sideways, it's slippery.
Over there is a sandy place with scrubby trees.
It was said there were badgers there. I knew when
I was young that I would be going out in the dark
to meet badgers.

The grass is lively and green for midwinter.
The cows have been moved off now. Down to
Lucks Mill which isn't there. You can see where
it was. It had been a small flax mill until 1890.
In my childhood in the early '60s there were the
remains of a mill and of cottage life, with the
apple tree still fruiting in the orchard. The well's
still there, and two mill stones, and the mill pond
where my mother once painted a single swan on
its purple-brown water. I don't know where the
painting is, or the swan, or my mother, but the
pond is still there.

EDDIES AND FLOODS

The Waveney is great. Lovely to see it working well
when it's rained all through the night. The river has
eddies, foaming bubbles, reeds caught in low alder
branches and my Pooh stick.

It's good to find the river doing the same things
as when we were young. The trees are in the same
places, the paths more trampled.

Over one particular Christmas, we did not have
snow, but rain. Rain fell on already wet land. The
ditches came alive. Our ditches are normally deep
but impassive. They now ran fierce with loud noise.
The Waveney swelled and the marshes took the flood
water as they are meant to, but then more water
came. By Christmas Day most of the small roads in
the valley were blocked, some houses sadly flooded.

Our cottage was on the edge of the marshes that
lead down to the river. Each year as a child I would
watch our land being submerged. We woke to look
over a bright expanse of water, but it stopped,
always, at the ditch at the bottom of the garden.
They knew where to build houses.

By New Year the waters had receded. We had to
go and see. The grass was a rolled green, the valley
alive with birds and walkers. Canada geese loved the
patches of lying water. Gulls sharp against the trees
were happy. So much sand on the road, it had to be
scooped up by a tractor. Odd things were retrieved
from the hedges. The reeds were still plastered
down from the force. A man was making young
willow trees planted along the bank stand up
again, securing their footing.

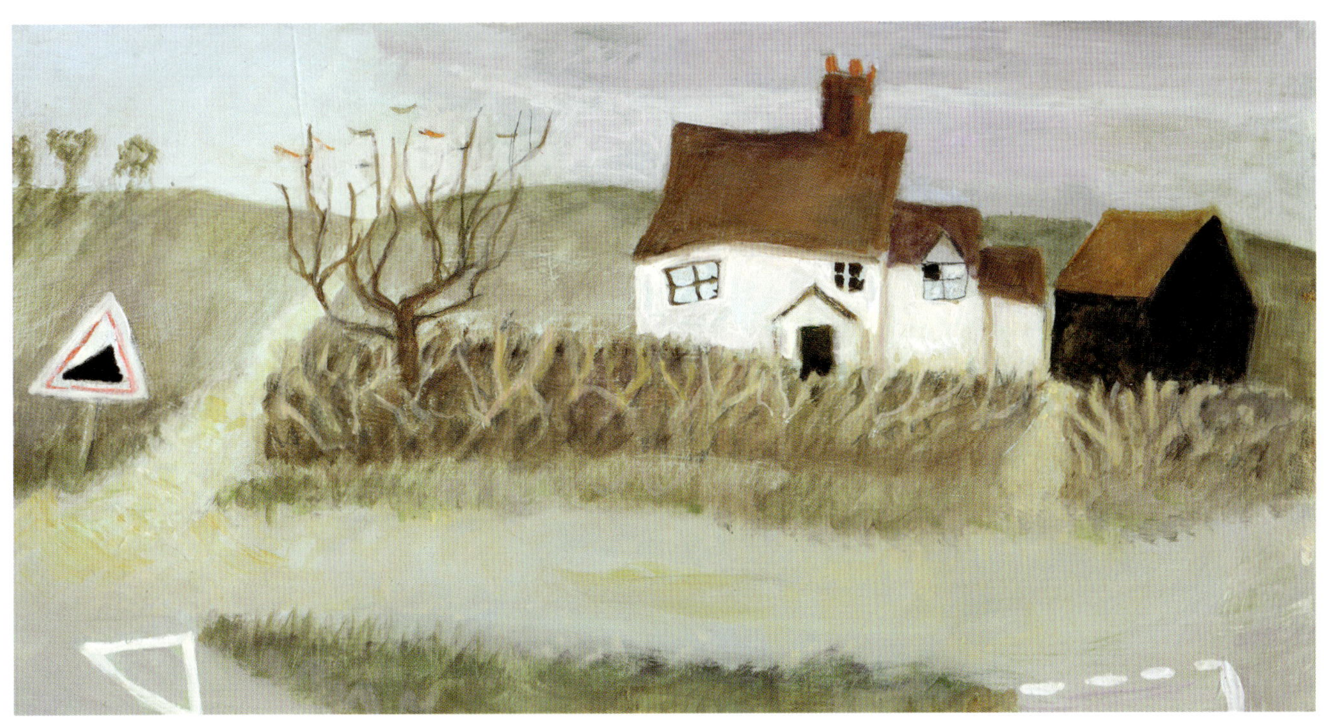

Up
2015 · oil on board · 14.5 x 27.5 cm / 5¾ x 10¾ in

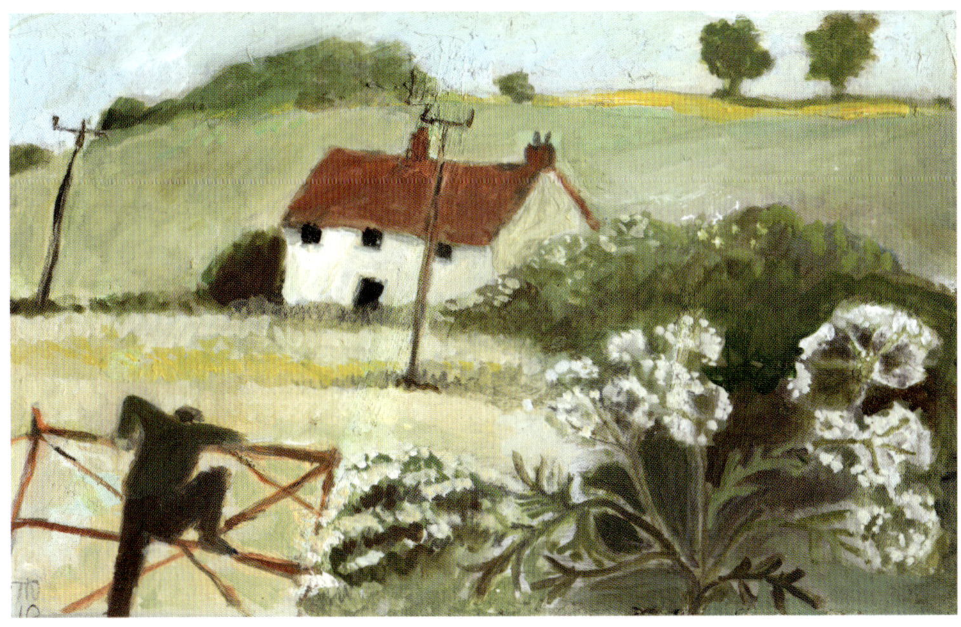

Climbing over the Gate
2010 · oil on board · 9 x 14 cm / 3½ x 5½ in

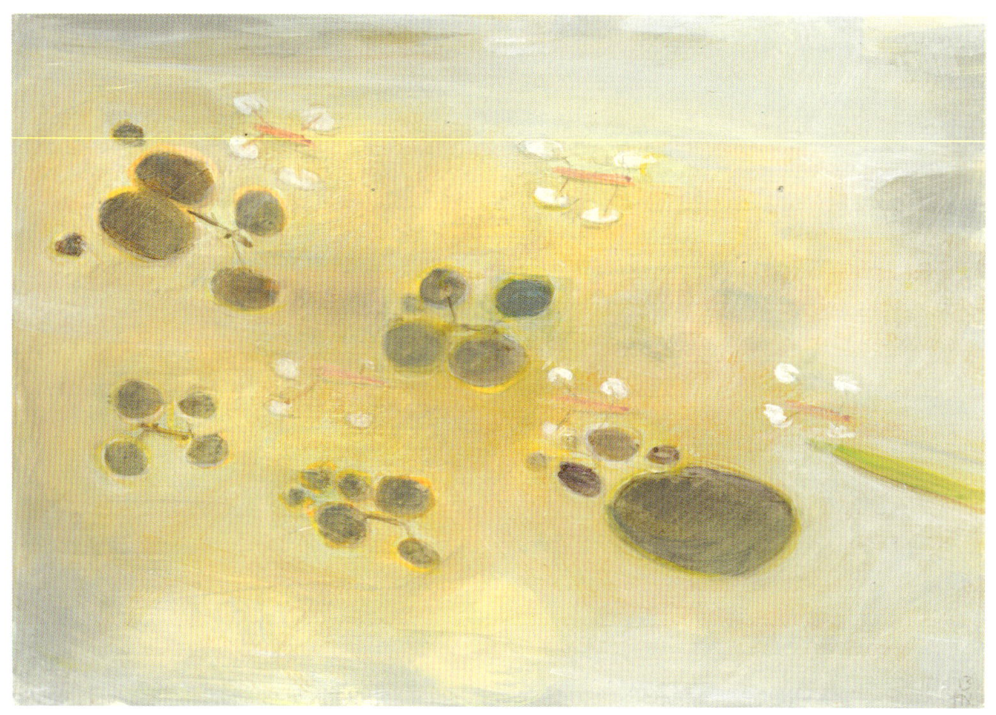

Shadows of Lesser Water Boatmen
2013 · oil on card · 19 x 26.5 cm / 7½ x 10½ in

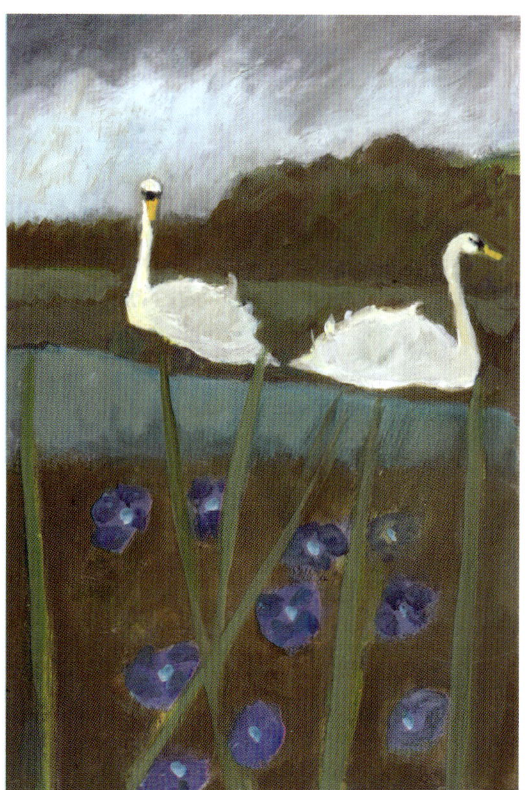

Rain-torn Clouds
2019 · oil on board
20 x 13.5 cm / 7¾ x 5¼ in

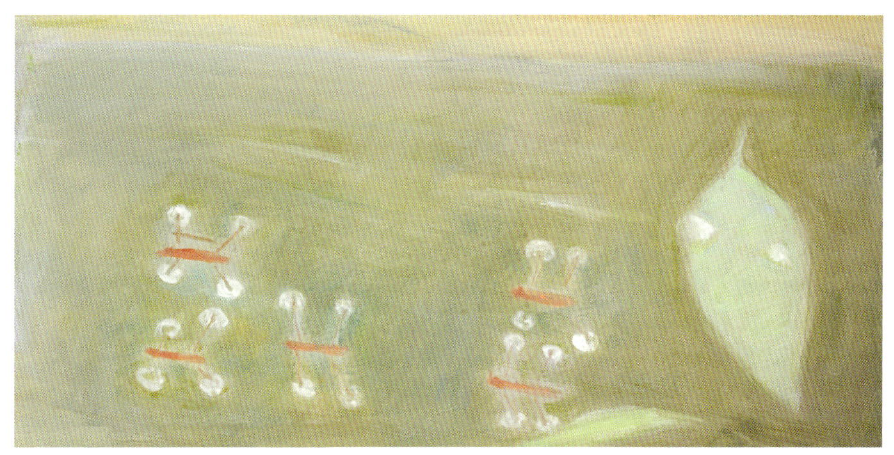

Lesser Water Boatmen
2013 · oil on board · 11.5 x 23 cm / 4½ x 9 in

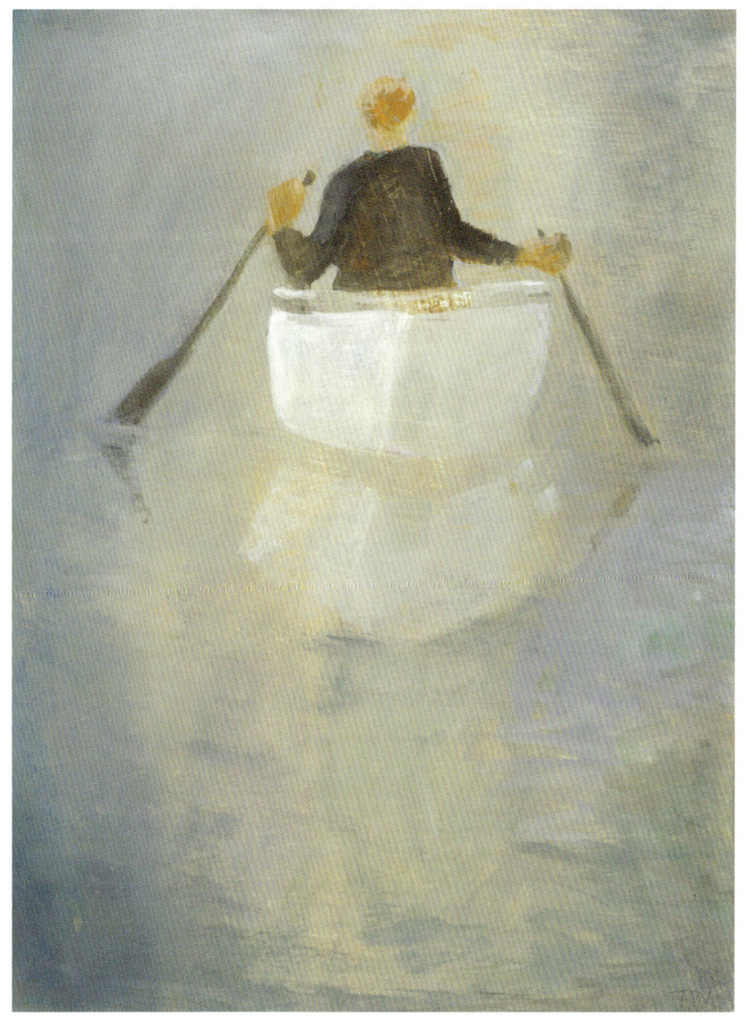

Boy in Boat
2013 · oil on board · 25.5 x 18 cm / 10 x 7 in

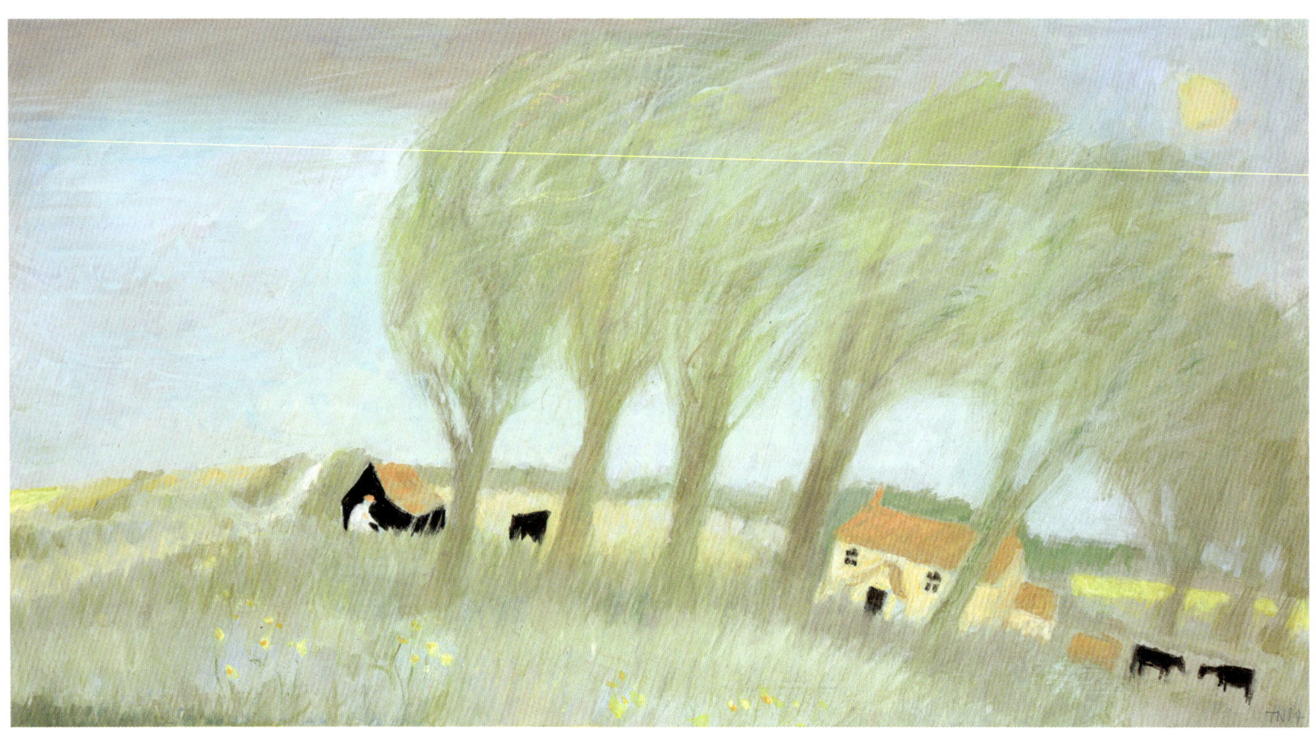

Low Road
2014 · oil on board · 18 x 33 cm / 7 x 13 in

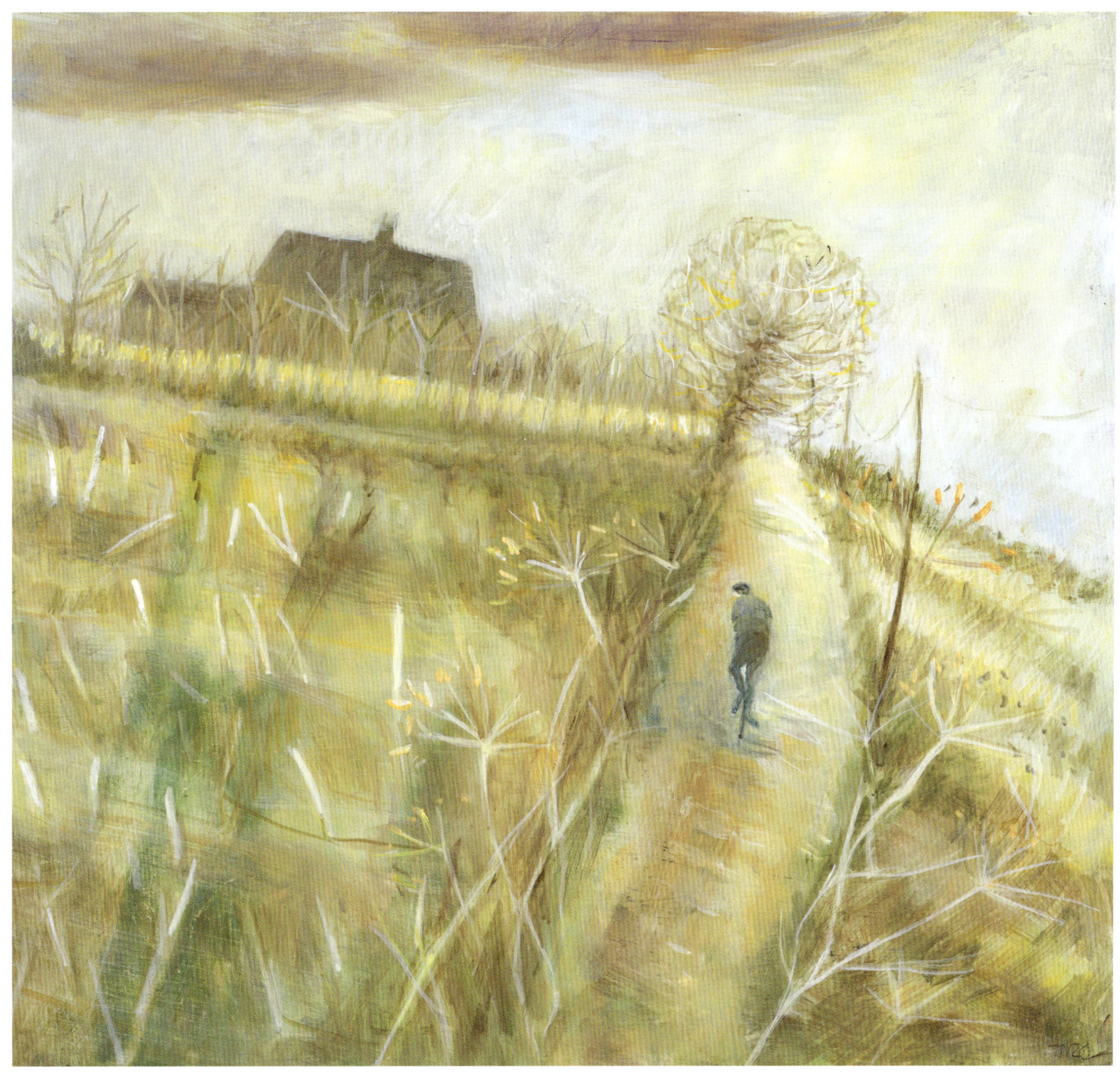

The Land Falls away to the Right
2020 · oil on board · 35 x 36 cm / 13¾ x 14¼ in

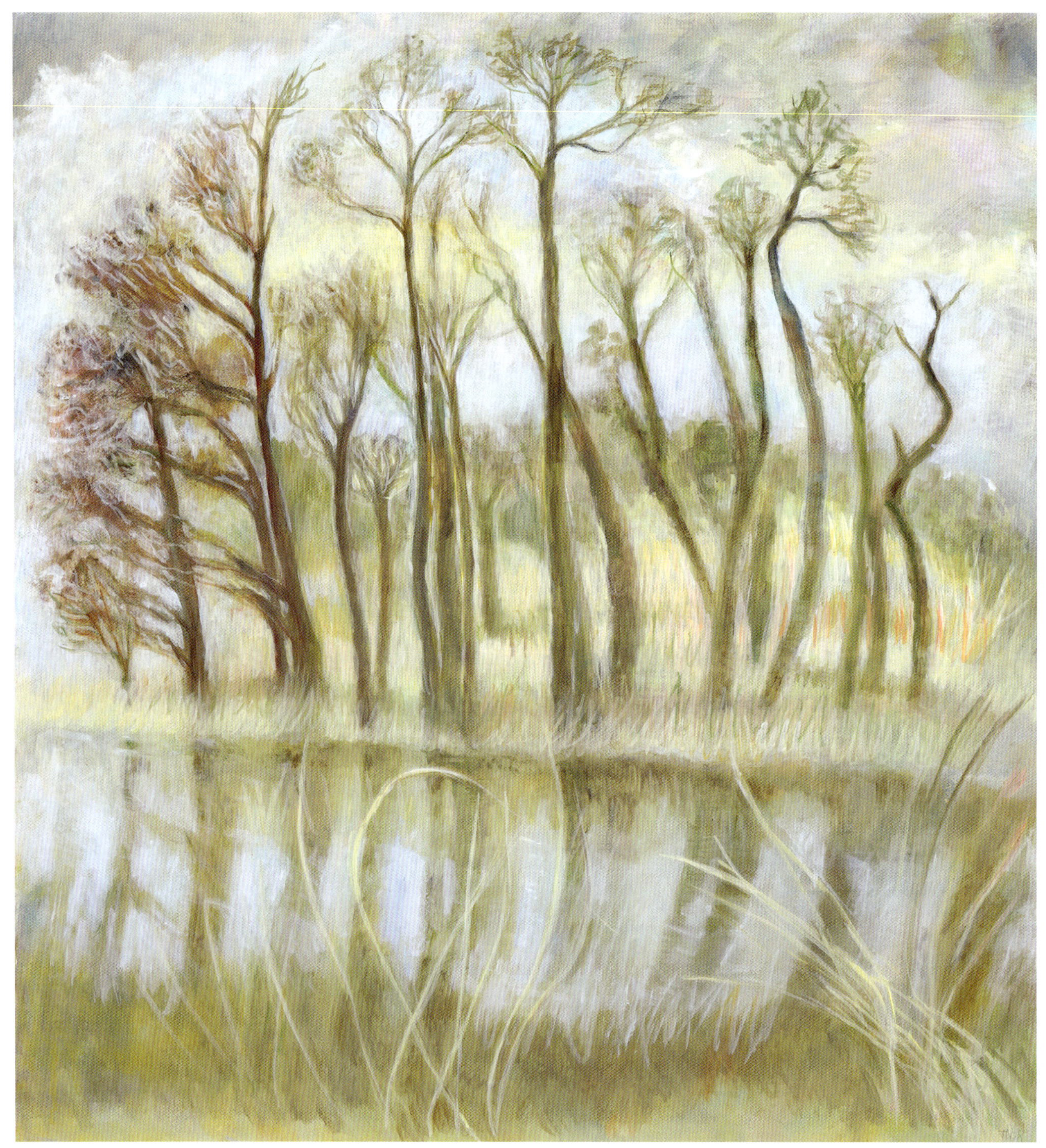

Alders
2018 · oil on board · 63.5 x 57 cm / 25 x 22½ in

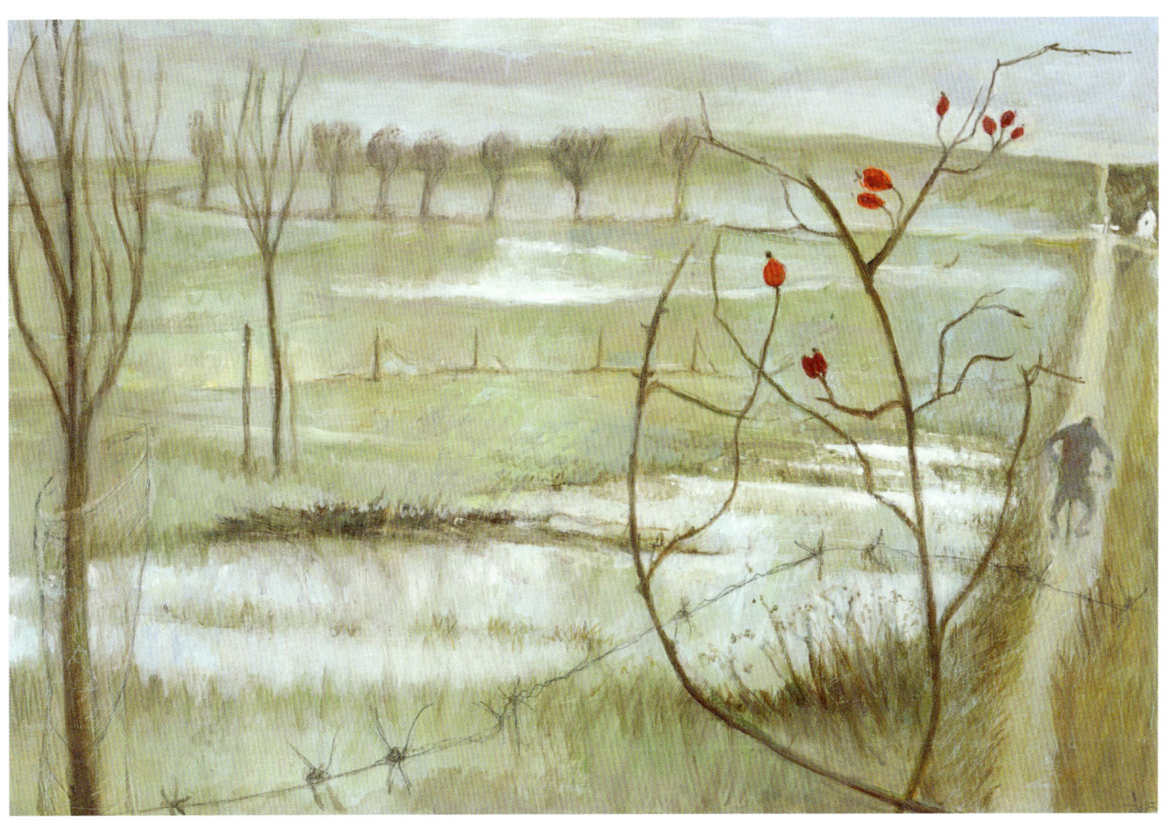

Floods
2015 · oil on board · 30.5 x 44 cm / 12 x 17¼ in

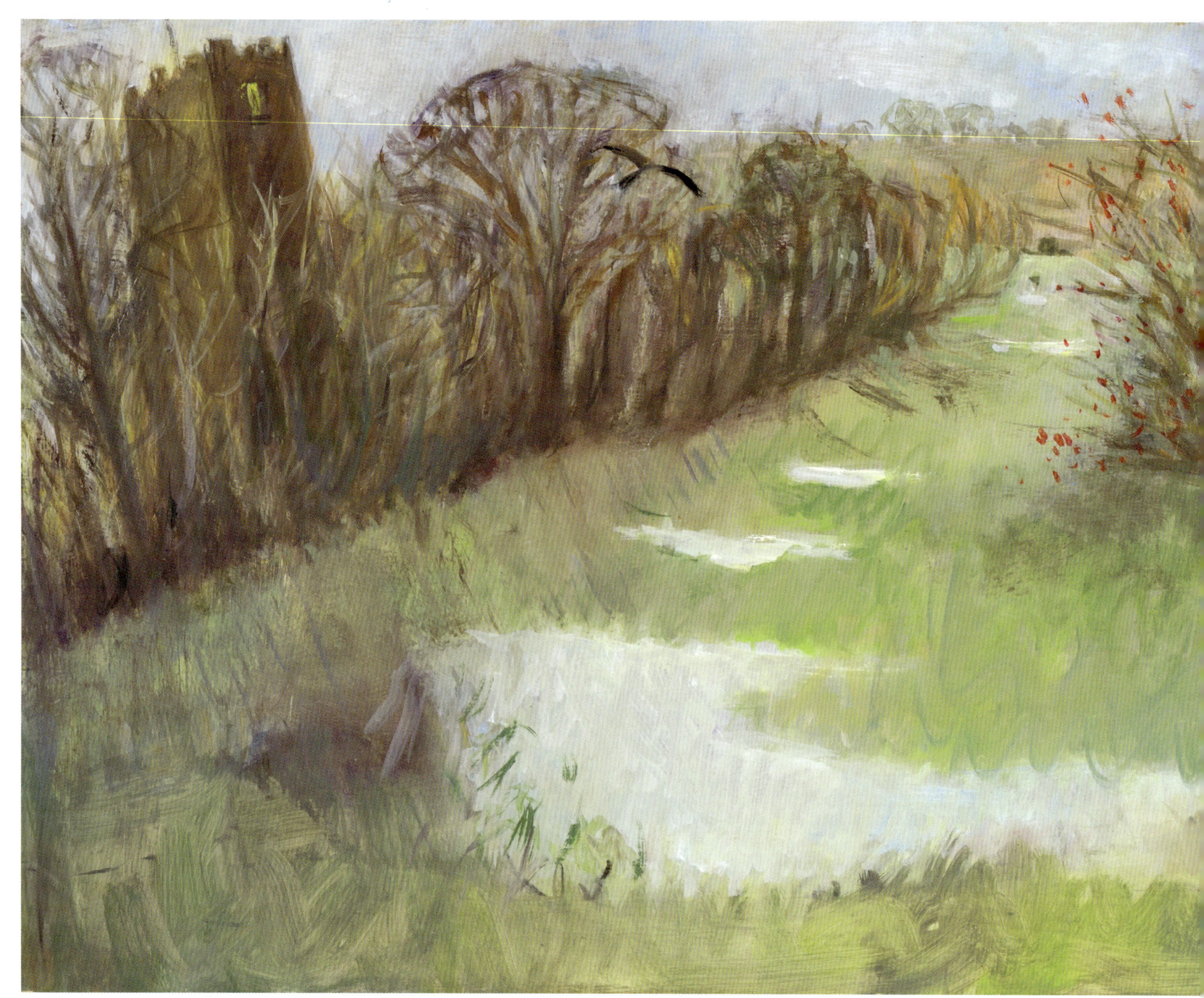

Taking the Water
2020 · oil on board · 25.5 x 63.5 cm / 10 x 25 in

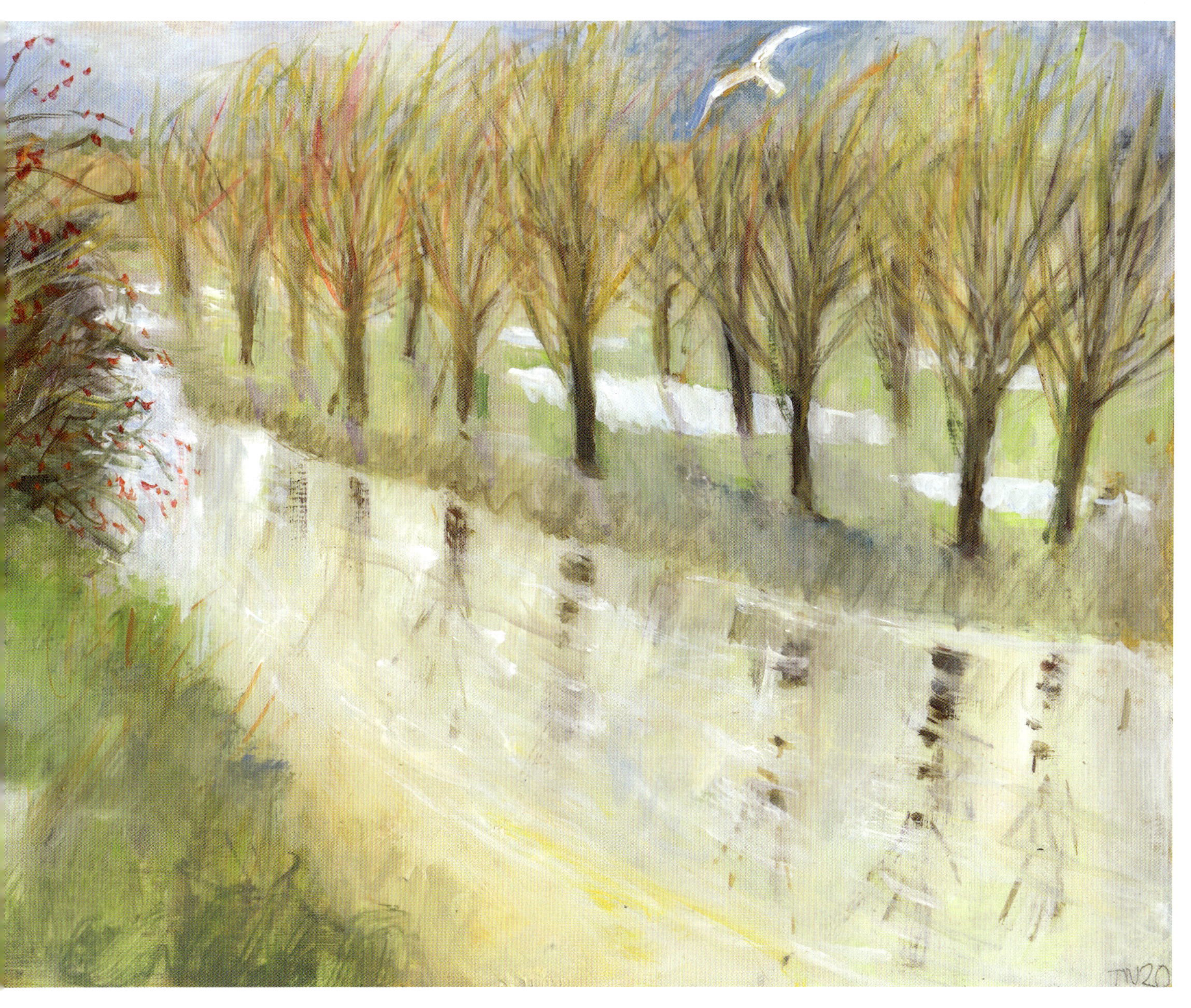

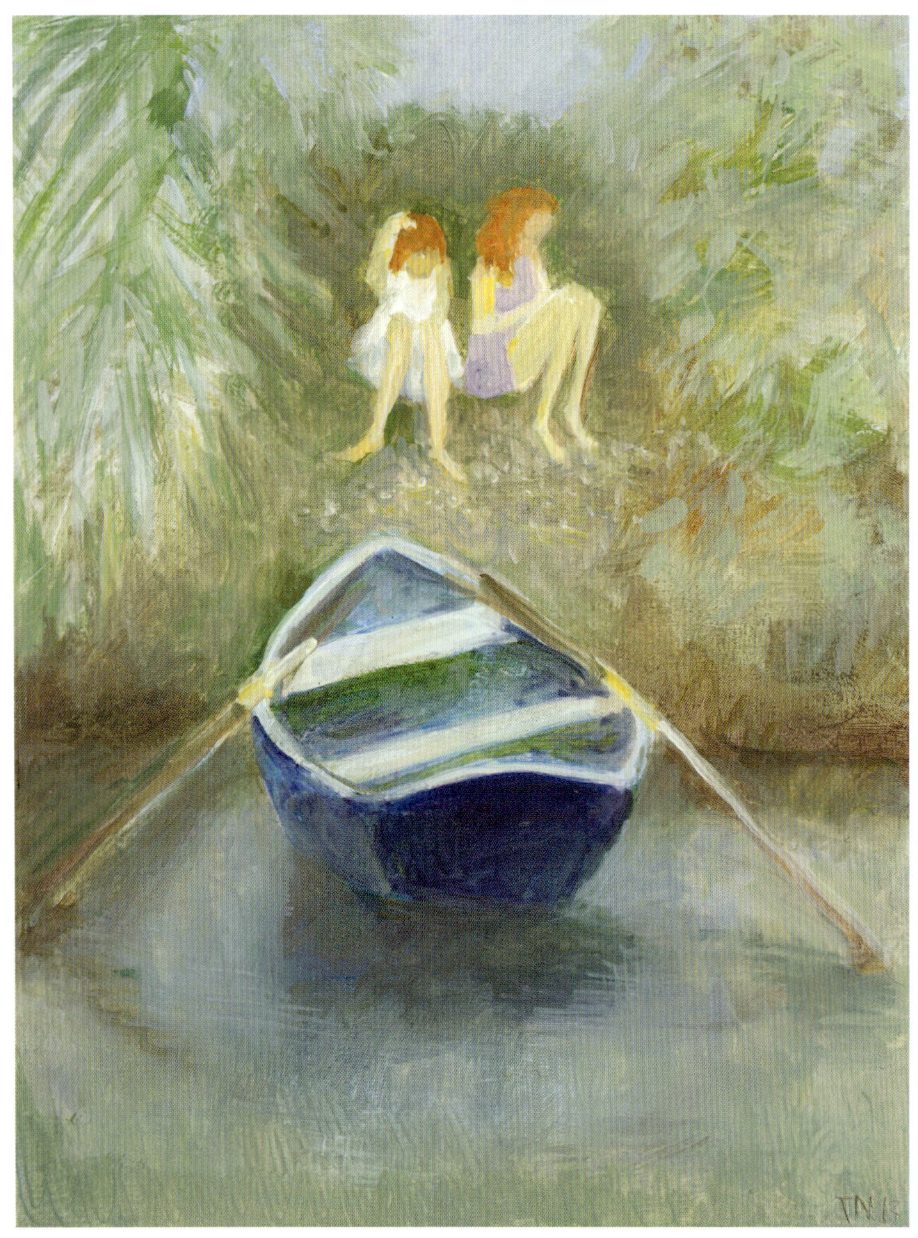

We Were Girls by the River
2013 · oil on board · 20.5 x 15 cm / 8 x 6 in

2 · THE FENS

SWIMMING IN OUR KNICKERS

Susan lived just this, the Norfolk side, of the railway line that goes from King's Lynn to Ely, and just this side of the Great Ouse and the New Cut, which are those straight stretches of water that divide the Norfolk countryside and the Fens. It's where one launches out into the Fens, where the soil sinks — drained, black, flat, and good for miles ahead. Here the trees drop away and the sky is:

Overhead the arch of heaven spread more ample than elsewhere, as over the open sea …
Charles Kingsley, *Hereward the Wake* (1866)

Your only landmarks now are the churches, which rise vertically like the skylarks — at right angles to the land. These churches, the Wiggenhalls — locally called Wiggenhall St Germans, Wiggenhall St Mary the Virgin and Wiggenhall St Mary Magdalen — are inches above sea level. They may not be used much now, they may smell of bat droppings and rising damp, but they are not empty. There are lots of people there. Plenty of stained-glass angels, carved pew-end figures, rood-screen saints — and the many lives of the families who have lived in those villages.

BOUNDARIES

Susan was my best friend at fourteen, and still is. Her family were more conventional than mine. I found it exciting to have boundaries; I still do. Susan's father had three beautiful girls with long flaxen hair who were not allowed to wear trousers on Sunday. Her father's mother had married into the Plymouth Brethren. Those outside the Brethren were not allowed to eat with those inside; Brethren were allowed to visit, but not attend the funerals of, non-Brethren. Her family were on the outside of the Brethren, but only just.

HEAVEN

I went to a Church of England secondary school because I failed my Eleven Plus. My sister did not. I also failed my twelve and thirteen plus, because I was 'slow'. I am not slow. I believed in heaven because that's what we were taught. My school spent their money on a chapel rather than a swimming pool. Heaven was somewhere you went to if you were good; at ten I felt good, it's the golden age. I wore corduroy shorts and not much else and can remember feeling it will never be so good again. I believed my lessons: I believed that I would receive a 'tap on the shoulder' from God and He would let me know He was there; but it was a bit slow coming, and other things took over. Susan's grandmother believed in Heaven — she had eight children. She had a small cottage and an apple tree as I have now. Heaven was a bright place, a nice place you were going to. It got you through.

A PLACE OF ABSTRACT THOUGHTS?

To the south it's wooded — there your ideas are furnished — but the Fens are a bare canvas. This particular day, when we were sixteen, we launched into this space, out over the Cut towards Tilney cum Islington, because Islington was to do with London, and that's where we were going. We seemed to be biking forever in a sea of fog. A village would loom up, a few houses straddling the street, then dwindle away again. There were right-angled turns, dead ends, straight roads with deep ditches either side that you could fall into, bungalows down tracks

with polytunnels and conifers, and me biking —
behind Susan. I had just left school; I was thinking,
'how can people live like that in this black land;
how can they live separated from others, isolated
and suppressed by this yellowing fog?'

Another evening we crossed those lines again,
the railway and the river. We swam in the New
Cut's glistening waters. The bank was bleak and
steep. Once they were lined with faggots of twigs
to stop them being washed away, nowadays they
are dredged. There was nothing to be seen below
the surface but I knew there were fish; I knew they
dragged for flatfish, mud-tasting dab and butt (as
Susan's father called them). There were boys away
on the bridge. Boys offered direction, too. After
swimming we had a half of cider, underaged, in
a room above The Cock.

Sitting next to the Great Ouse, nothing much
happening. It's August Bank Holiday. There is cow
parsley, some walkers with wagging labradors, cars
go noiselessly over the bridge, a St George's flag
flops about, the river's brown and slow. Then
there is a splosh, big, as if something's fallen in.
It's the other side of the bridge so I can't see what
it was, but I can see the effect it's had. Ripples of
waves come, keep coming, but nothing else. The
foam at the sides of the river circles in a different
direction. I think it was when the tide changed.

SKY, LAND
The sky is in the land. It's reflected in the ditches
that run either side of the road, which look like the
rills in formal gardens. The road runs straight out
into the Fen, which is golden cornfields at this time
of year. We are in a shiny black beetle car. Having
left the safe cover of the woods we are easy prey
from above. As we trundle out across the land
a beetle travels up inside my dress.

I got out. A great bird rose from the deep,
V-shaped ditch. It flapped around in circles,
cawing loudly. I was the only thing moving on
the open road. I put my bag over my head and
retreated back to the car.

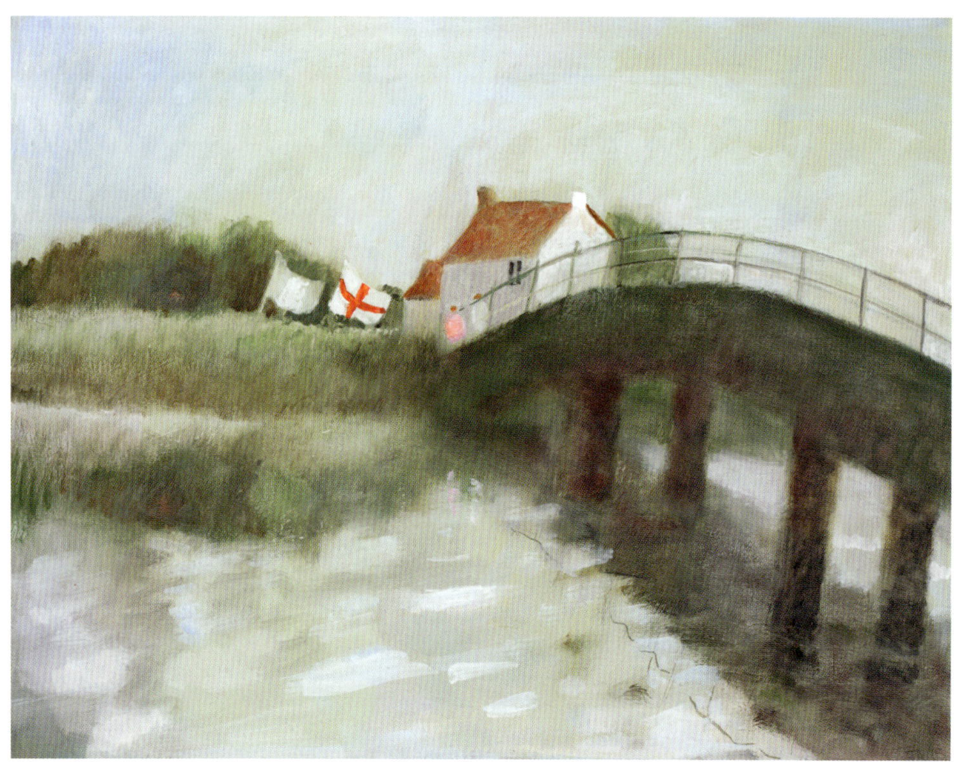

The Cock
2015 · oil on board · 31.5 x 40 cm / 12½ x 15¾ in

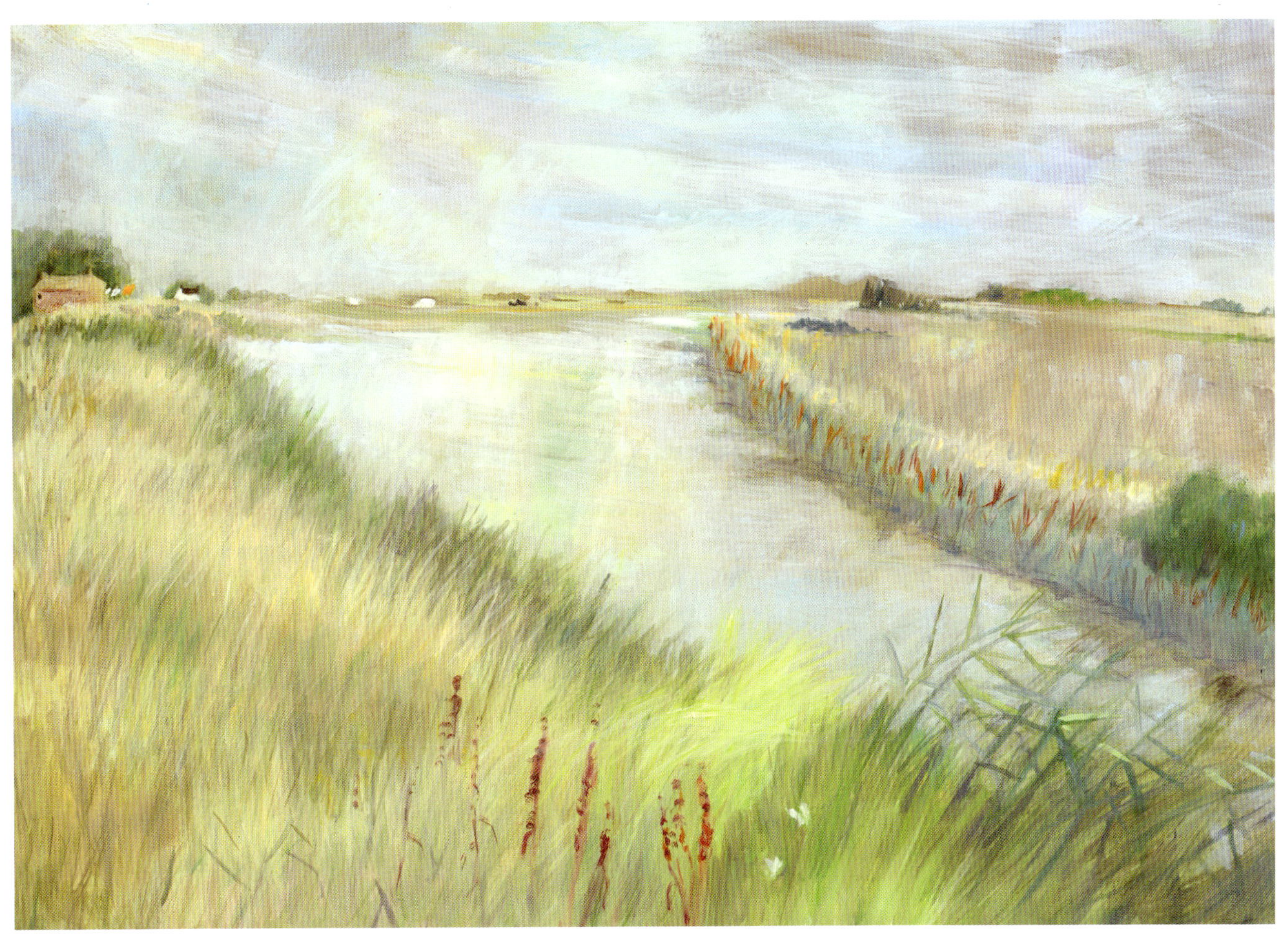

Relief Channel
2016 · oil on board · 46 x 62 cm / 18 x 24½ in

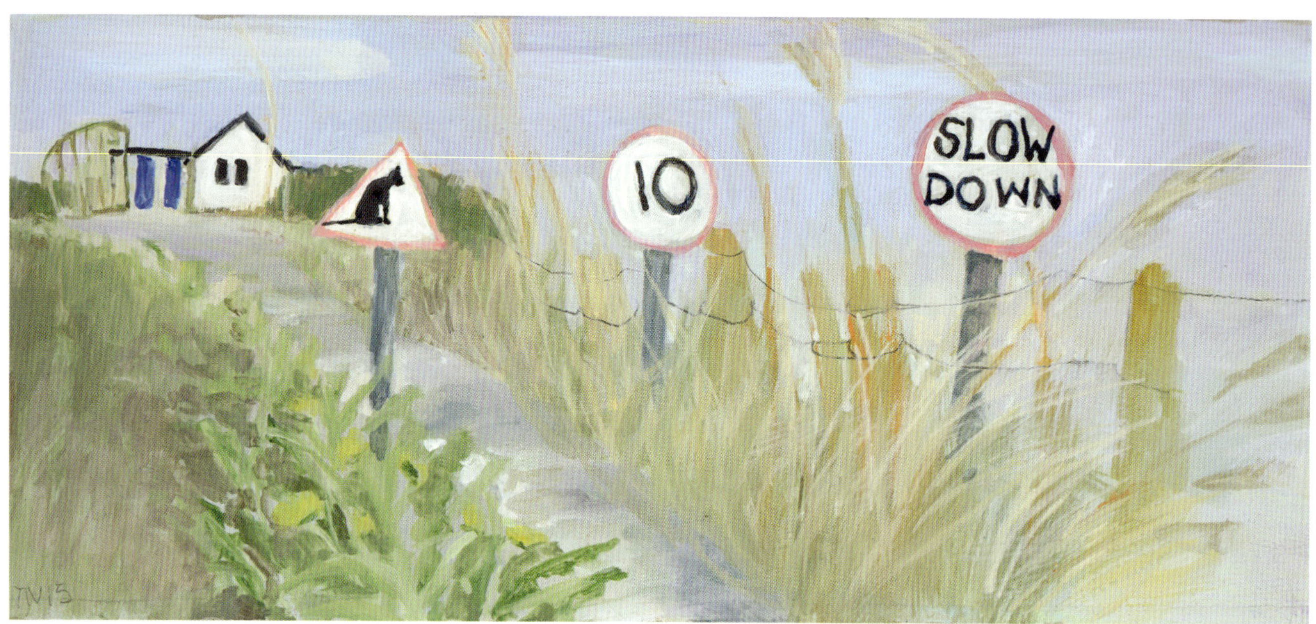

Dead End — Cat Sanctuary
2015 · oil on board · 12.5 x 28 cm / 5 x 11 in

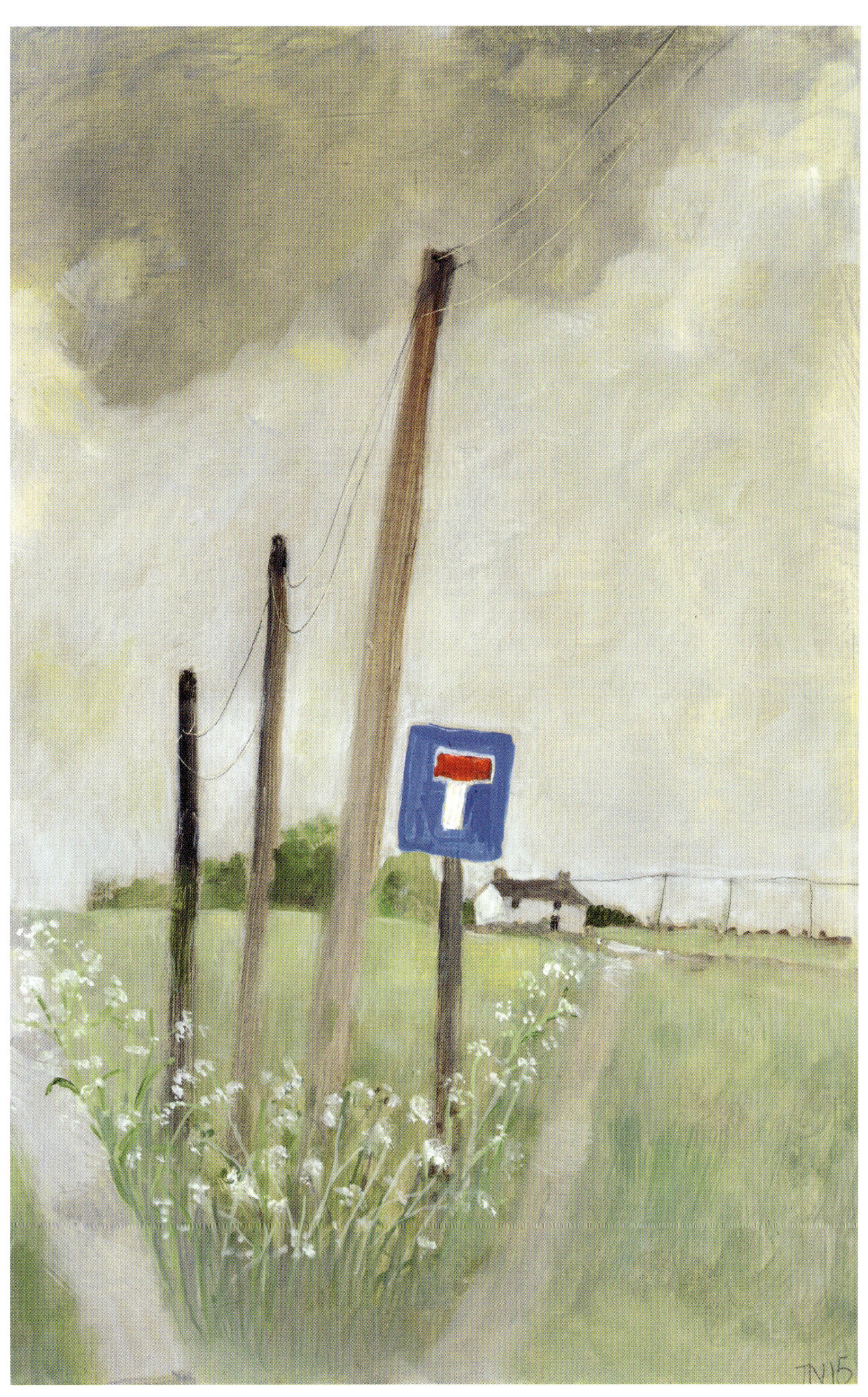

You Get a Lot of This
2015 · oil on card · 30.5 x 22.5 cm / 12 x 8¾ in

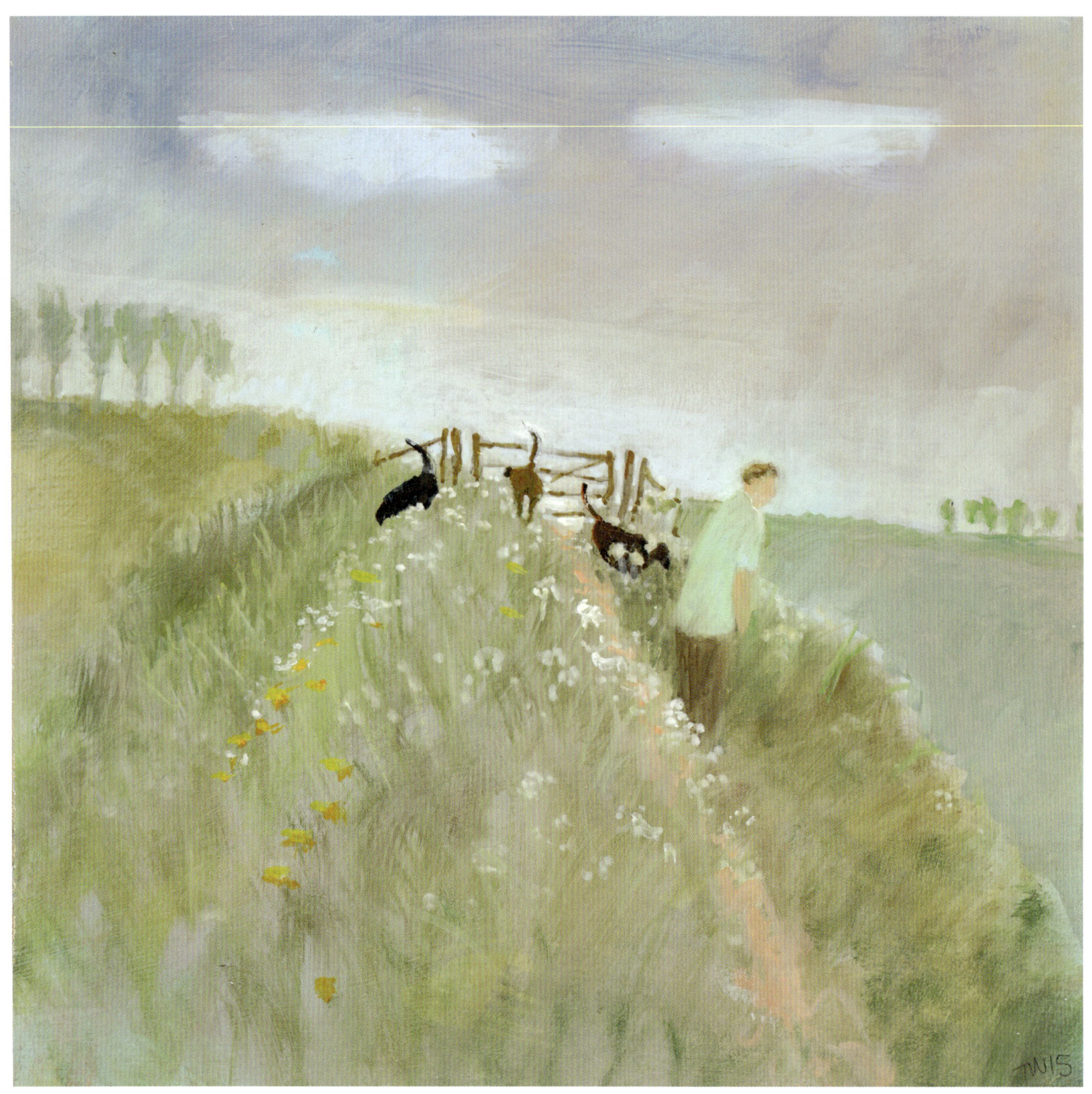

On a Bank on a Bank Holiday
2015 · oil on board · 21 x 21 / 8¼ x 8¼ in

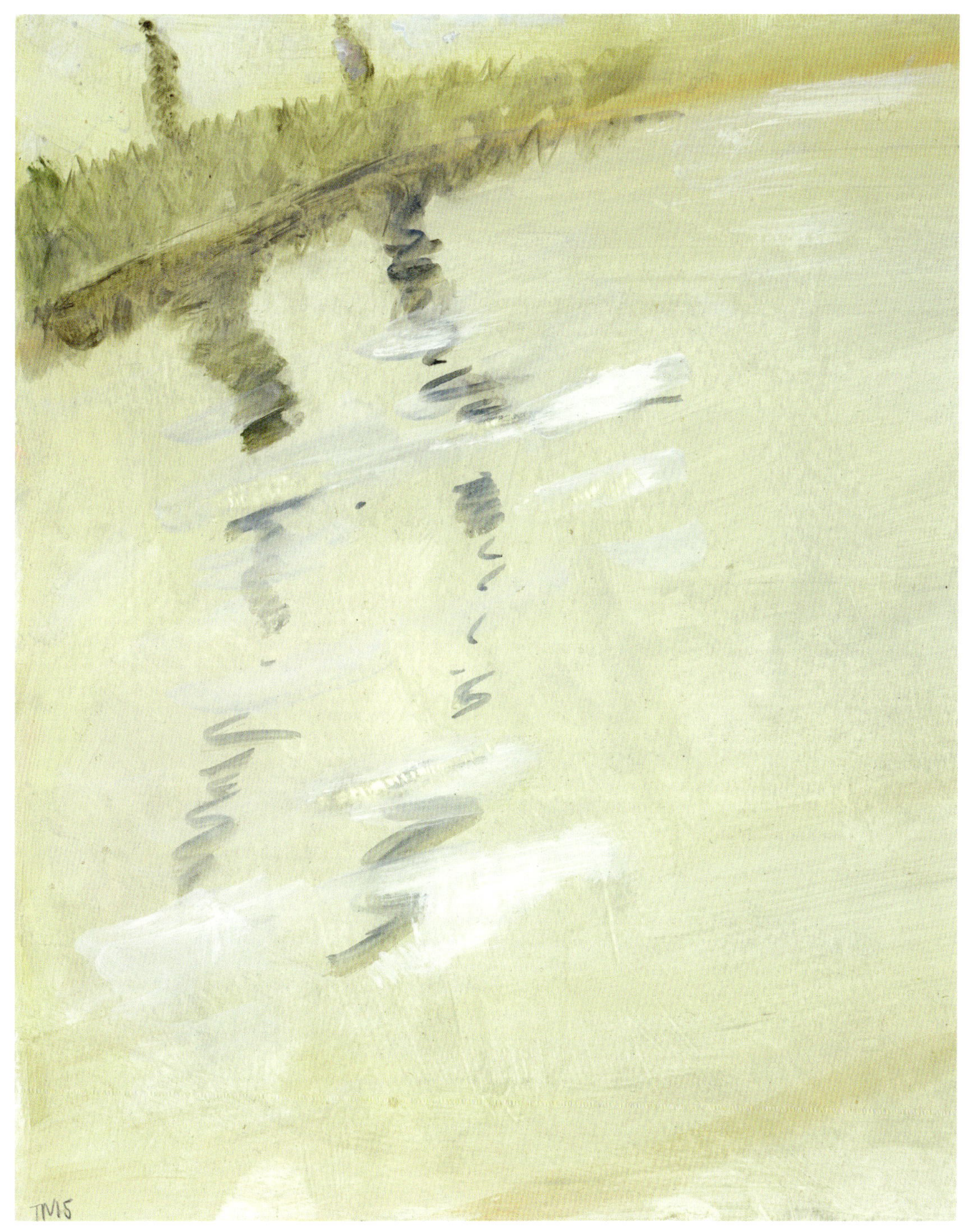

Wobbly People
2015 · oil on card · 23 x 18 / 9 x 7 in

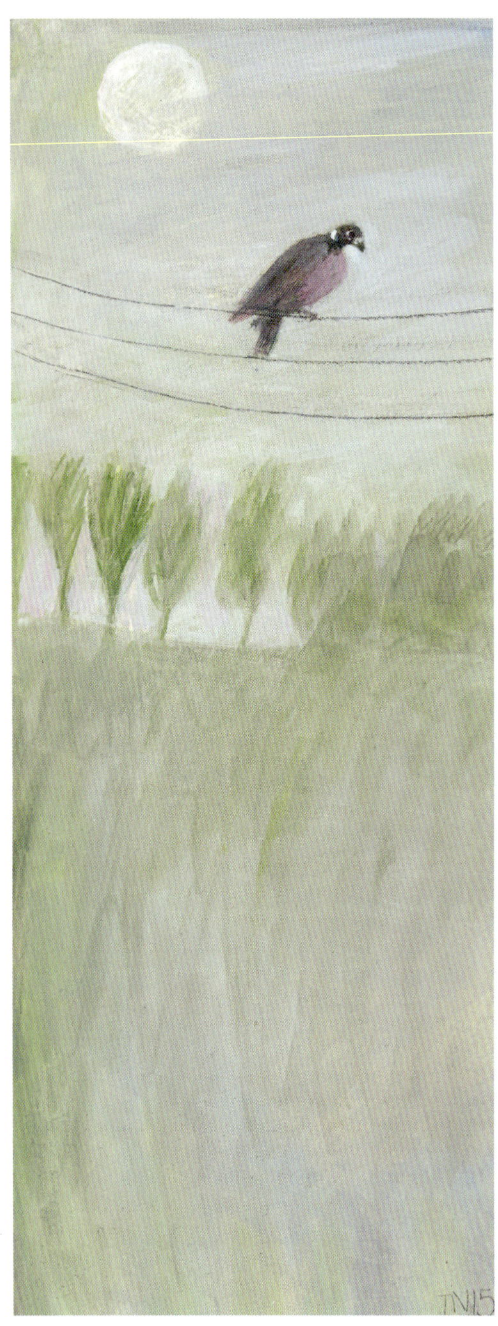

7.30 pm
2015 · oil on card
26.5 x 10 cm / 10½ x 4 in

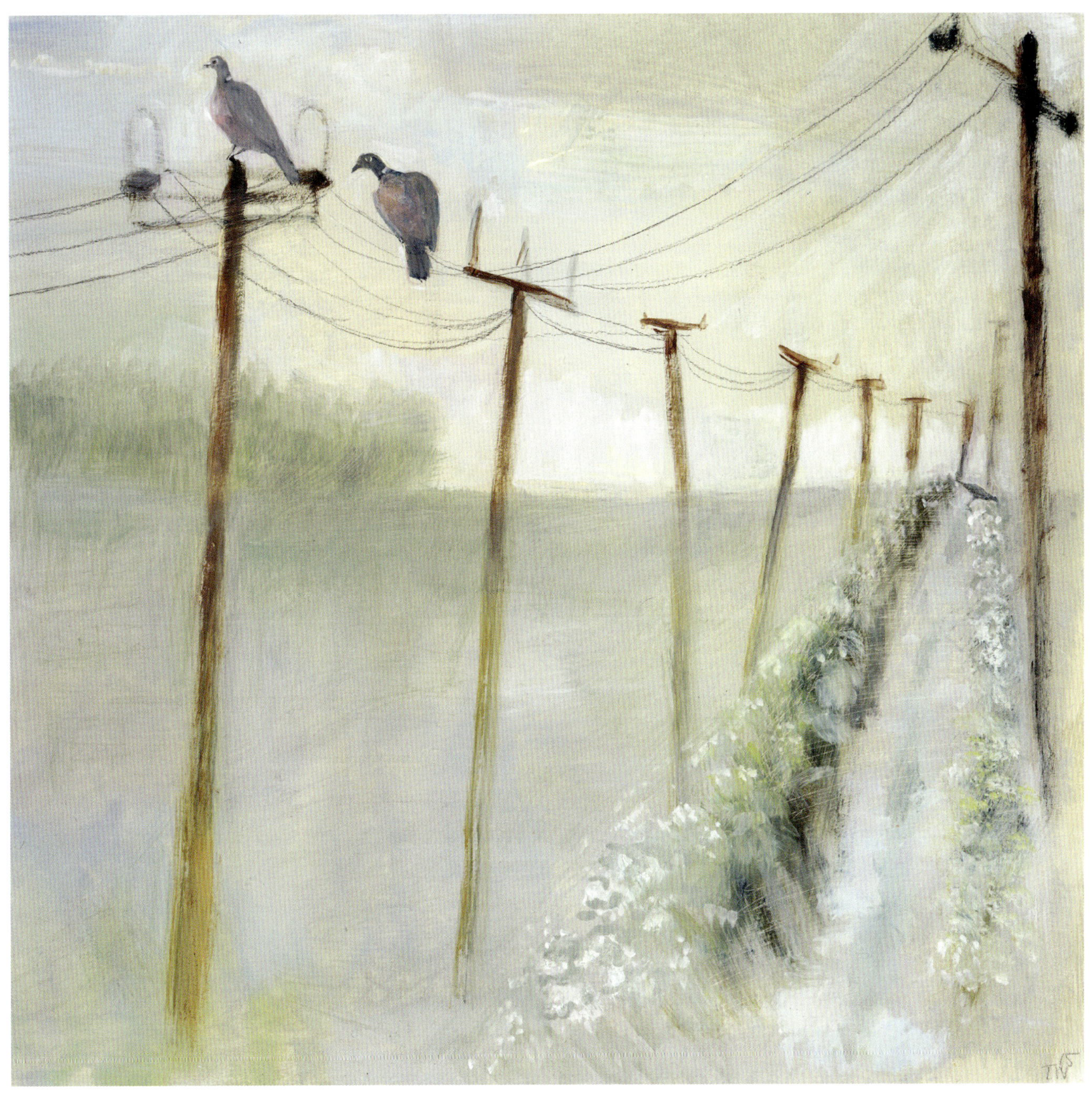

On Wires
2015 · oil on card · 31 x 31 cm / 12¼ x 12¼ in

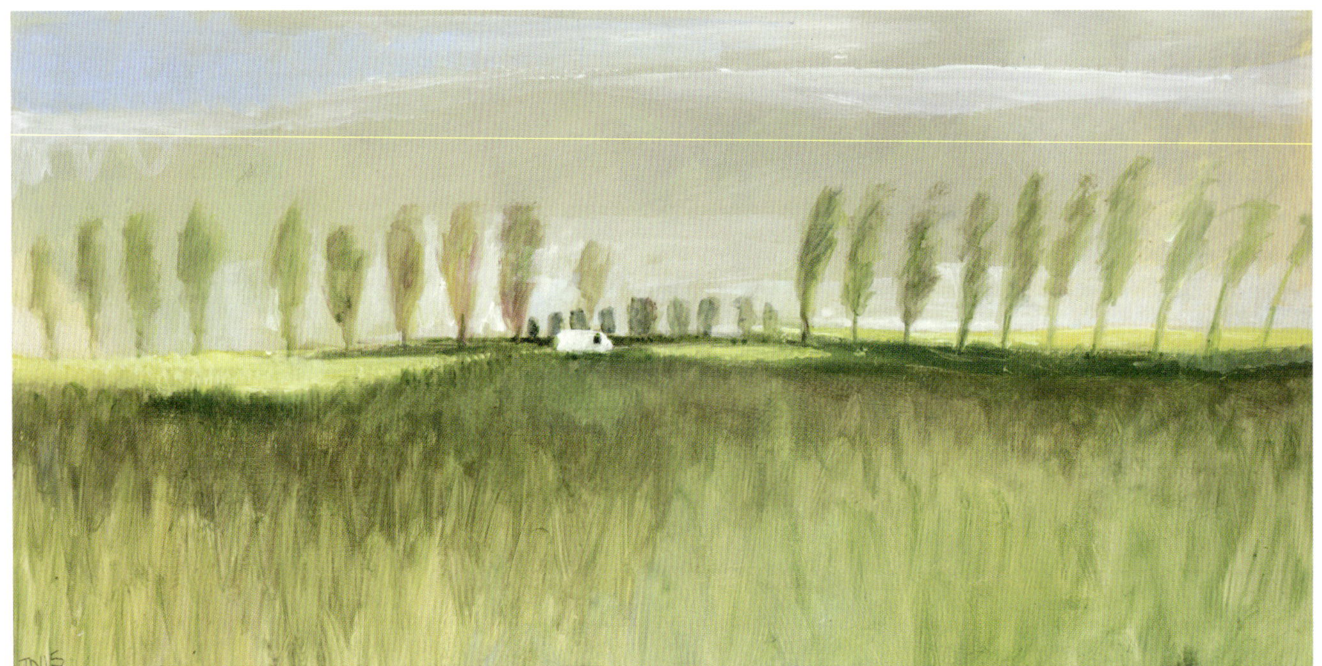

There Is Always a White Van
2015 · oil on card · 19.5 x 39 cm / 7¾ x 15¼ in

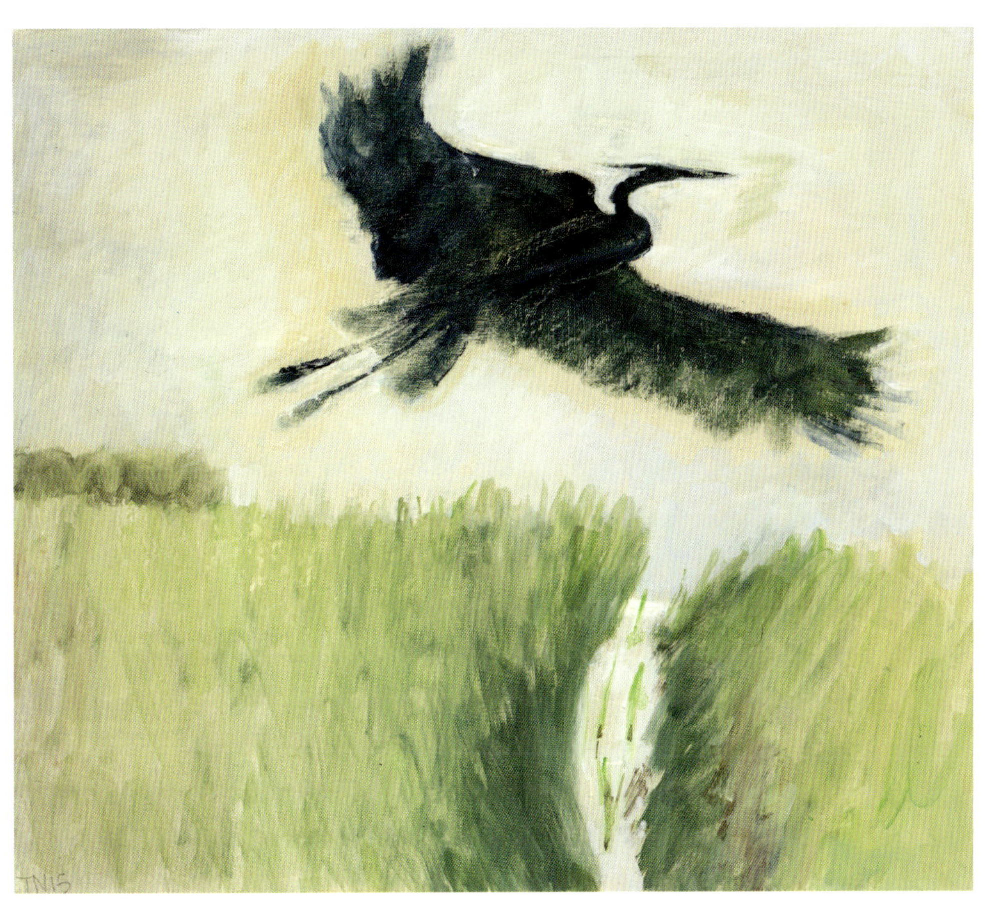

Heron Circling
2015 · oil on card · 23 x 25.5 cm / 9 x 10 in

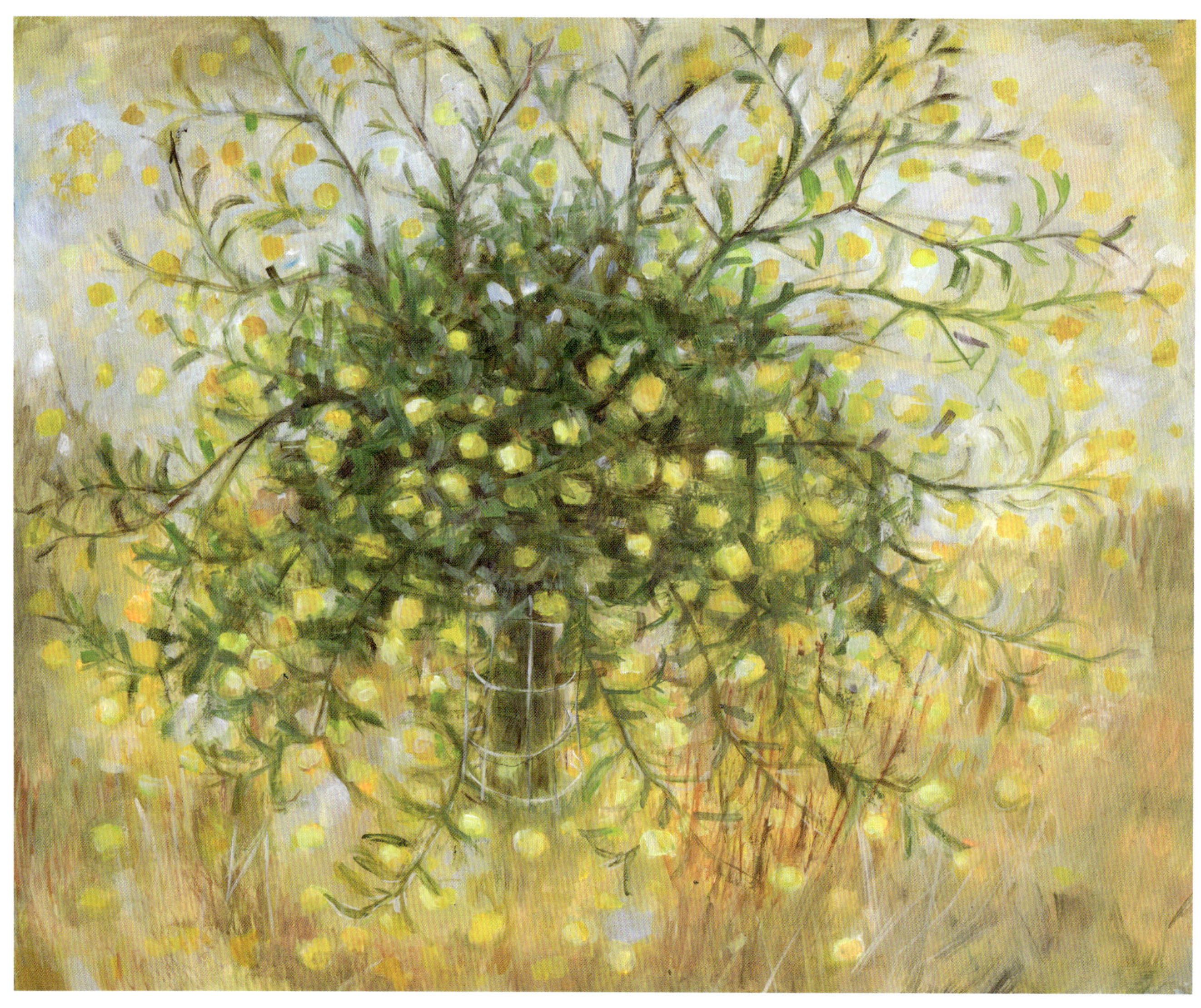

When Life Gives You Apples
2020 · oil on board · 51 x 61 cm / 20 x 24 in

3 · ST JAMES VILLAGE ORCHARD

This is a community orchard made out of a corner triangle of open agricultural land. It lies on the edge of the Suffolk village of St James South Elmham, where there was once a Pleasure Ground.

The land up there is the same as where we lived from when I was fifteen, on the high plateau of Suffolk. We lived one side of the disused aerodrome, and the orchard is on the other. Clay land — serious farming territory. Hedges were taken up in the '70s, creating bigger fields; easier for the machines but not so easy for the birds. The wind would whip off the topsoil and penetrate our timber-framed farm-house. This is a land I know, don't even like, longed to get away from, yet keep returning to. I feel as my mother felt as I walk the straight roads up there, staring into the verges. It's the known vegetation, the known land.

The orchard's home is called the Greshaw Green Enclosure, and it's the last bit of the village's common land. The Enclosure Act of 1845 meant that large areas of common land were hedged into small pieces and then owned by landowners, becoming private land. John Clare, the poet, felt himself going mad because his land, his places he could go to, were being enclosed; he was being shut out of the places he felt safe in. The Pleasure Ground, as the Greshaw land was once called, was saved, given to

… the Churchwardens and Overseers of the Poor … to be held by them and their successors in trust, as a place for exercise and recreation for the inhabitants of the said Parish and Neighbourhood.

Trust Deed, 6 September 1855, County Records Office, Ipswich

The orchard started with a vision. Christine and Rob like the paintings of Evelyn Dunbar. In the Second World War, she was employed by the War Artists Advisory Committee to record the work of the Women's Land Army. There is a painting, *A 1944 Pastoral: Land Girls Pruning at East Malling* — all women, ladders and headscarves — which is bordered with twelve images that show apples and hands holding pruning equipment. Christine wanted more damsons for her jams, wildlife needs places to live, the village needed a Pleasure Place for activities, and that piece of land needed to be saved from becoming just a corner of a field. This vision came together with the intent of four others — Chris, Lynda, Jeremy and Mary — plus village volunteers. And so the one acre was rented and sponsored and planted. There is now a destination along from St James South Elmham village that you walk to or from.

This one acre is a triangle. The gate's at one point and two straight roads run along two sides, but they are quiet roads — it's not a populated part. Two houses can be seen over the hedges; their steep, pitched roofs are triangles pointing into the vast sky.

The planting is in straight lines. Nearly a hundred trees were planted, grouped in a rather nice way. If you are picking stone fruit, then you want them all together, so your Marjorie's Seedling plum is a neighbour of the Merryweather damson. With the apples, your eaters are together, like D'Arcy Spice and Kidd's Orange Red, cookers such as Lord Stradbroke and Doctor Harvey are near neighbours, and so are the cider-makers — Dabinett and Dunkerton Late Sweet.

Apples: my parents used to make slipware dishes, my father throwing them and my mother decorating them with slip — rich creams, honeys, burnt umbers, and black. Around the edges of them ran some words from the Song of Solomon (2:5) that are expressed in many variations:

Comfort me with apples: for I am sick of love
Refresh me with apples, because I am lovesick
Refresh me with apples; for I am faint with love
Let me be comforted with apples — I am overcome with love

They used the first line for their 'comfort me' bowls.

The orchard's trees are all so different: differences in the varieties of fruit and in the shapes of the leaves and the branch formations — and so in the overall shapes of the trees. Great differences, too, in the crops — the Greensleeves trees recently produced hundreds of apples, whereas Lord Lambourne only managed a few. There are also some unusual ones: sorbus, medlar and quince. There is a group of cobnuts, and the hedges are very good for blackberries and dog roses.

There has also been an almond tree — with a tale attached. A couple of years ago, it was looking really bonny and had a good crop. But the almonds proved to be very bitter, and potentially poisonous. So, unfortunately, the tree had to come down — to be replaced by two Howgate Wonder apple trees.

The orchard is again used as a Pleasure Ground: they have had a rather splendid strawberry tea, with lots of bunting, union jacks and summer frocks amongst the ox-eye daisies. There has also been a celebration tea with music and cakes, visits from schools, and an art group who put on a little exhibition in the shepherd's hut.

The hut comes from the village; it once stood under an apple tree, covered in brambles. It's been a gathering place for the village children, farm workers have eaten their lunch there, and it has been the bus stop. It needed quite a lot of rebuilding, but it must still hold a bit of experience. Now it's down the road in the centre of the orchard. It has an Indian red roof of corrugated iron, matt black walls, and a window that reflects a square of sky. You can go inside and shut the door; it's like a cool sauna — your world in the middle of nowhere.

The birds have come back: a family of grey partridges get out of my way, skylarks rise from the arable; there are linnets, chiffchaffs, snipe and wrens. They have constructed an owl box, which is rather high and forbidding, but for three years the kestrel has shared it with the stock dove.

Now the orchard's a living space. Somewhere that was not there before. It is binding together the topsoil, the flowers and grasses, the animals, insects and birds, and the people of the parish.

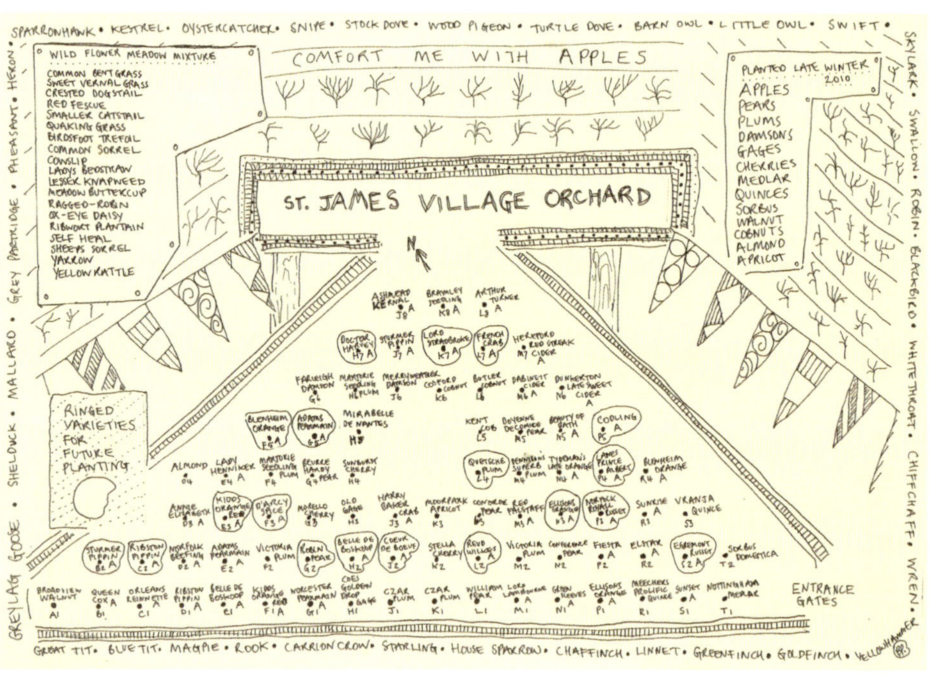

Rob Parfitt · *St James Village Orchard*

2010 · ink on paper

from a plan to commemorate the planting of the orchard · courtesy Rob Parfitt

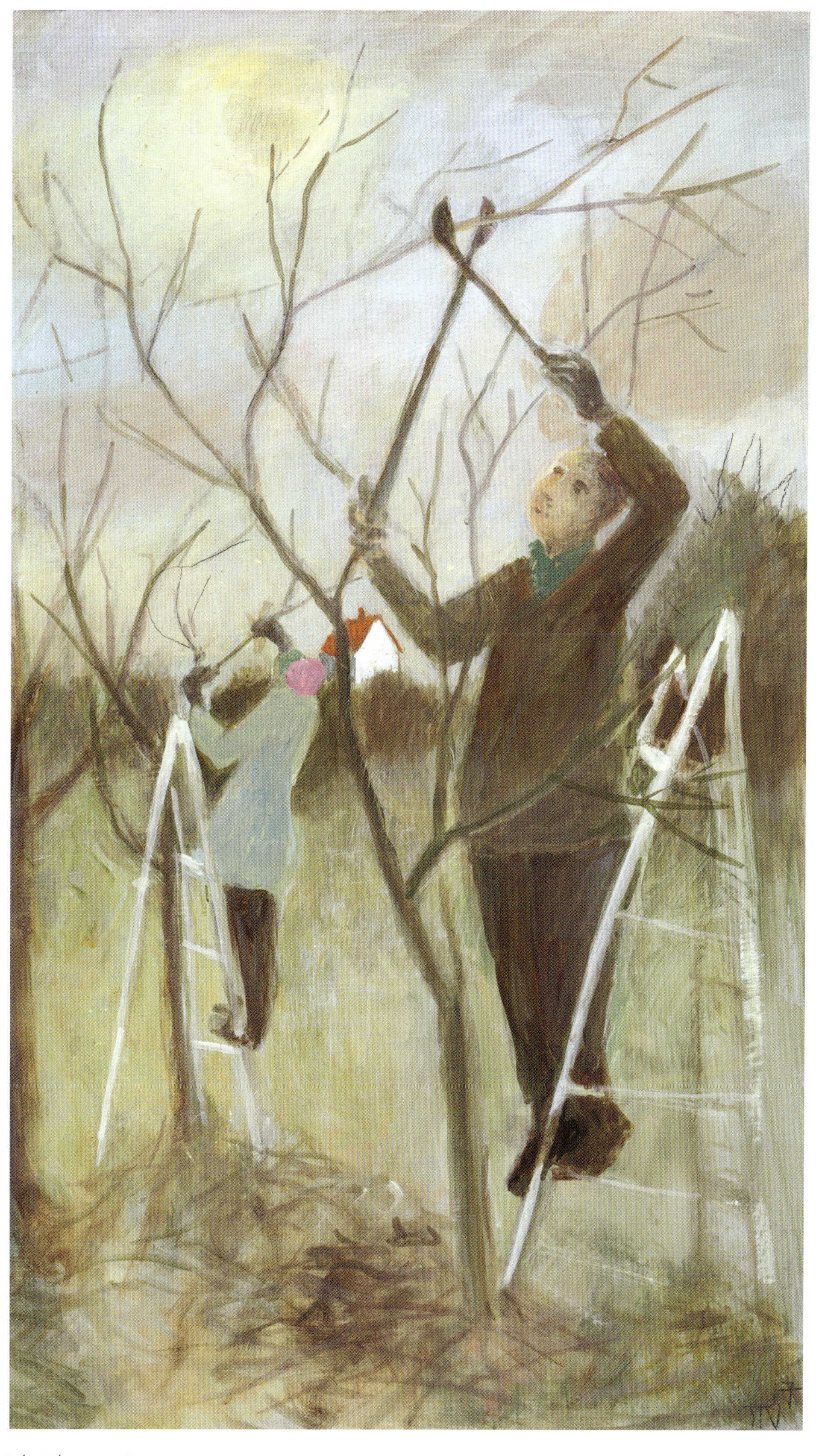

The Thinning Party
2017 · oil on board · 28 x 16 cm / 11 x 6¼ in

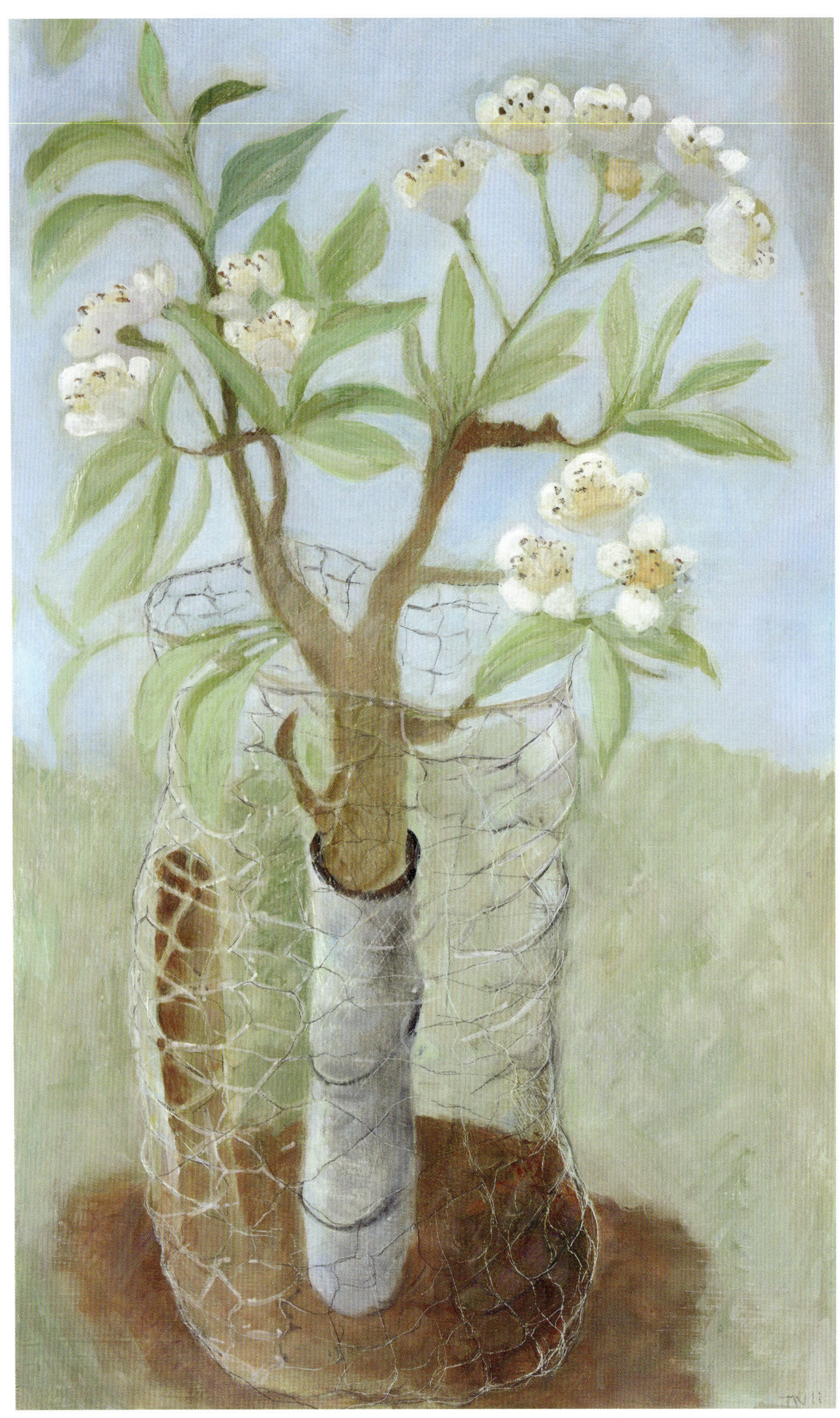

Young Tree
2011 · oil on board · 51 x 30.5 cm / 20 x 12 in

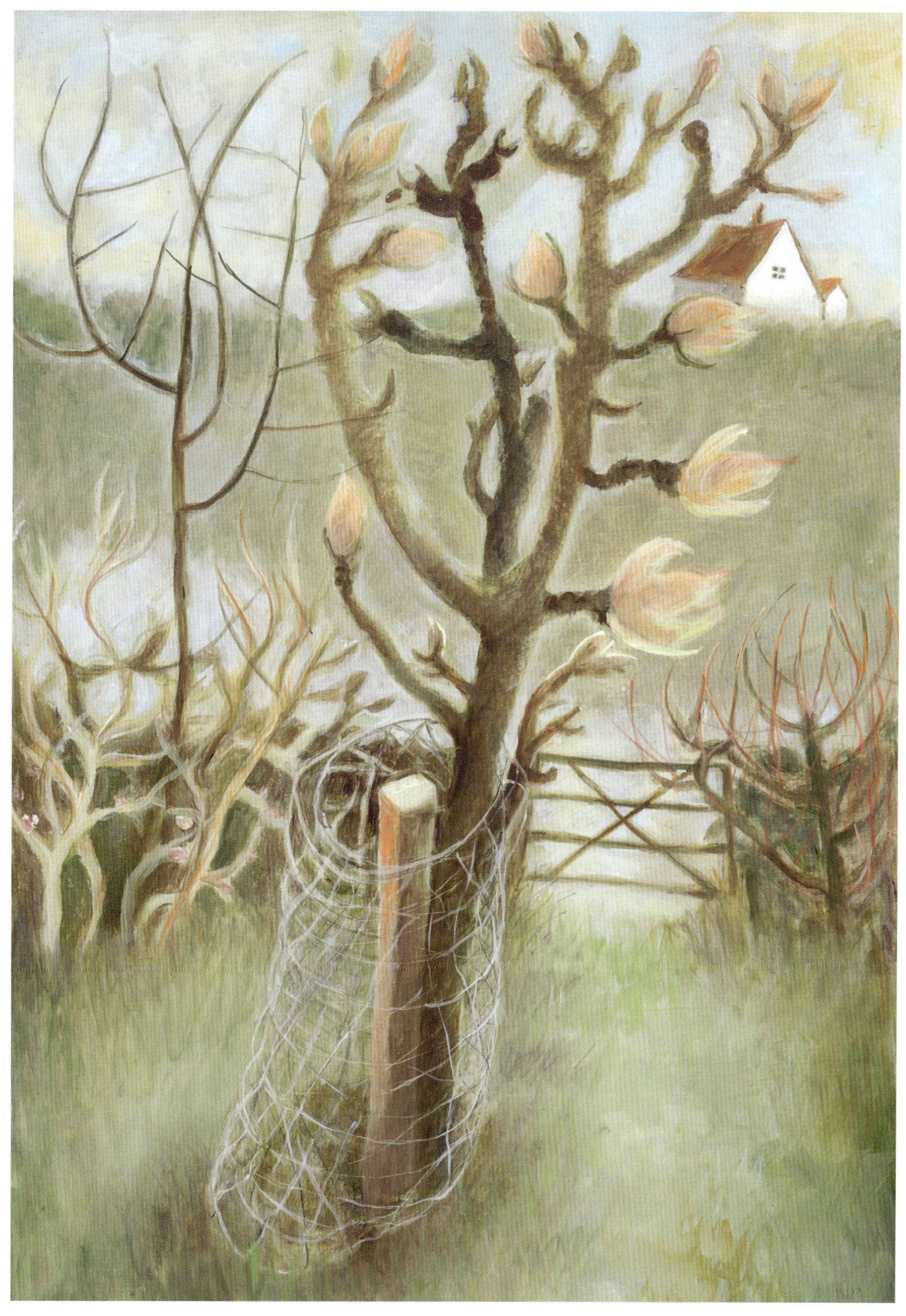

Young Pear Tree
2019 · oil on board · 55 x 38 cm / 21¾ x 15 in

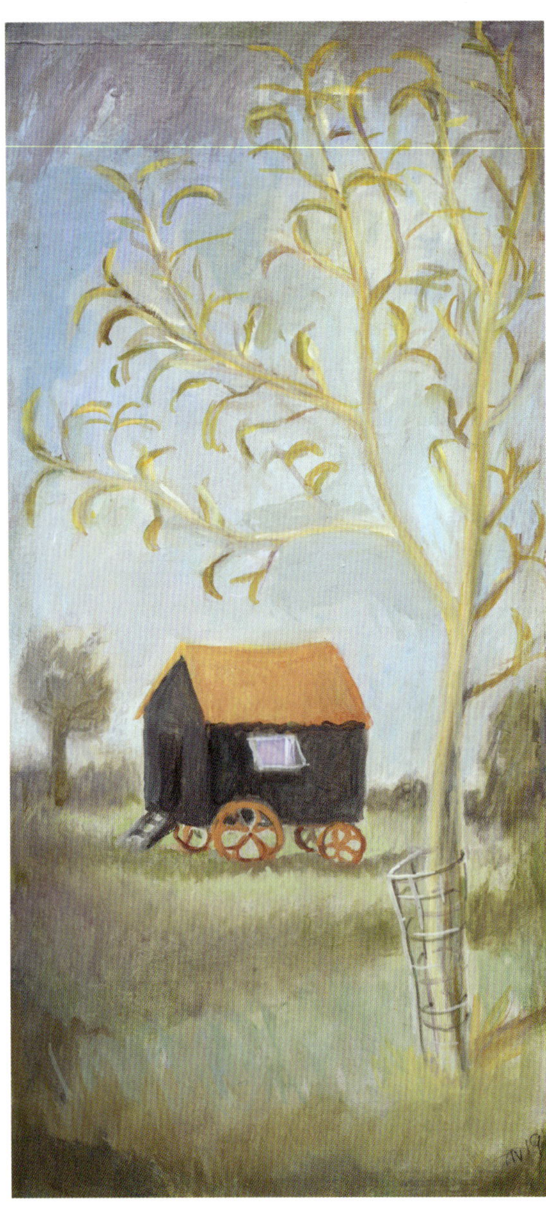

The Shepherd's Hut
2019 · oil on board · 28 x 13 cm / 11 x 5 in

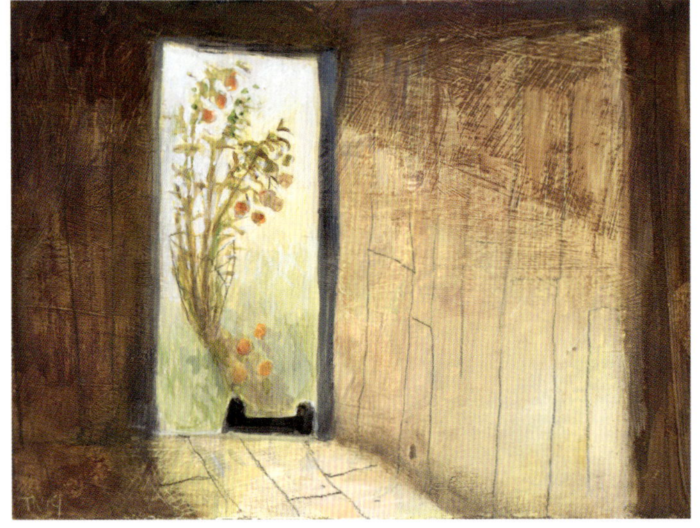

Inside the Shepherd's Hut
2019 · oil on board · 12.5 x 16 cm / 5 x 6¼ in

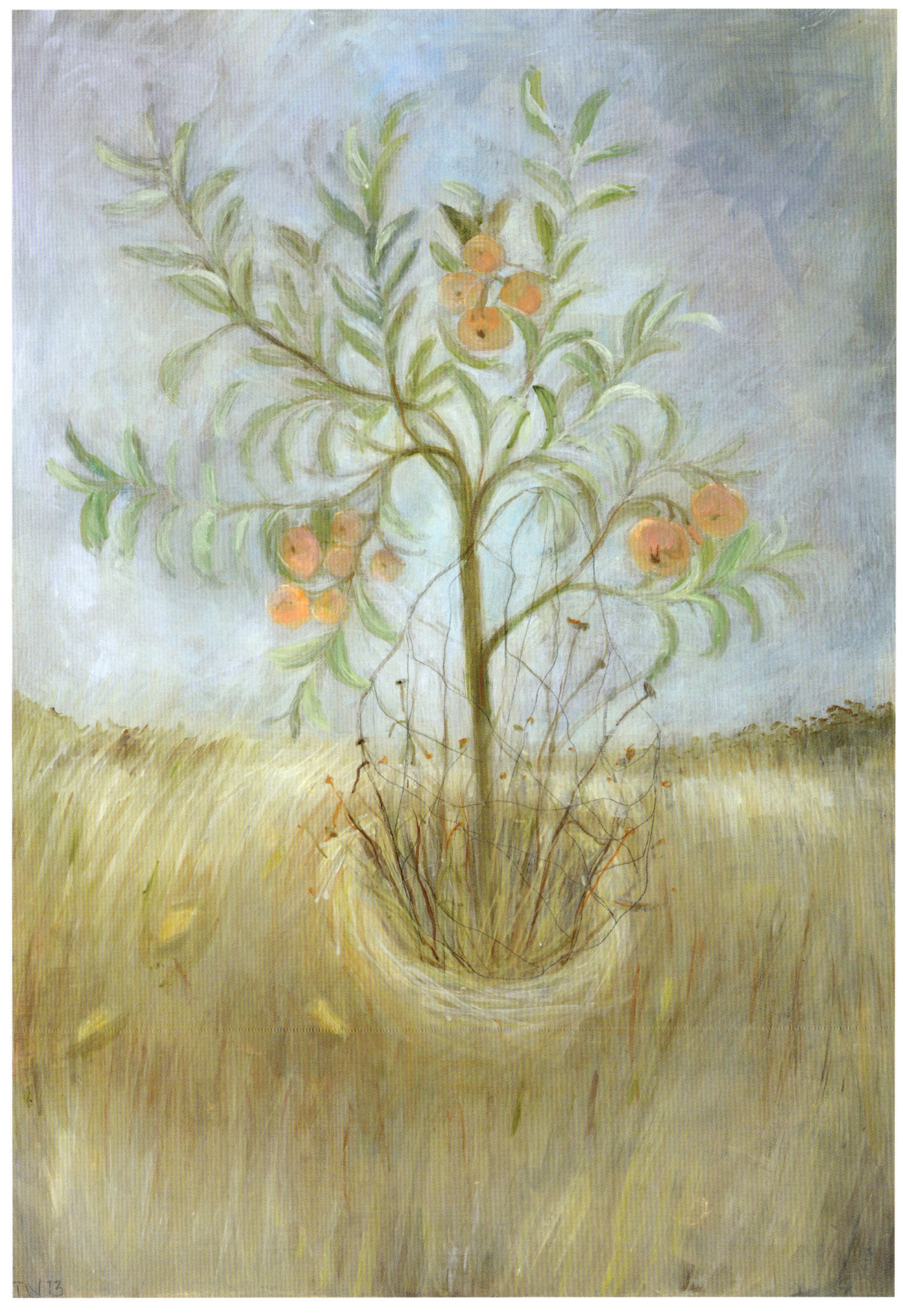

Ellison's Orange Apple
2013 · oil on board · 38 x 26.5 cm / 15 x 10½ in

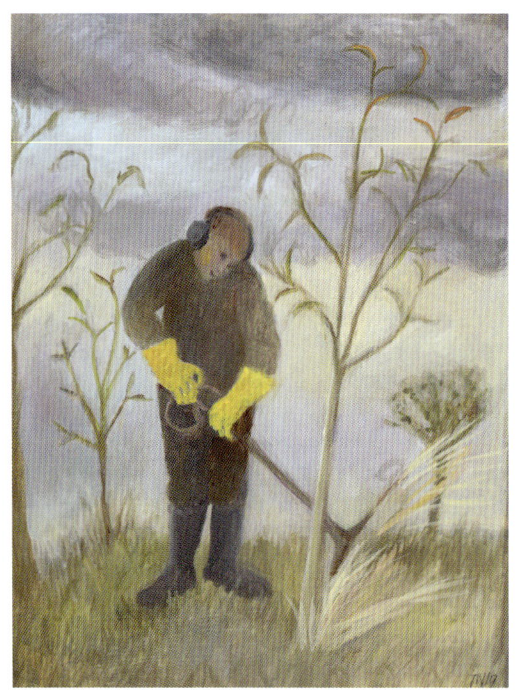

The Gentle Strimmer
2019 · oil on board
21.5 x 16.5 cm / 8½ x 6½ in

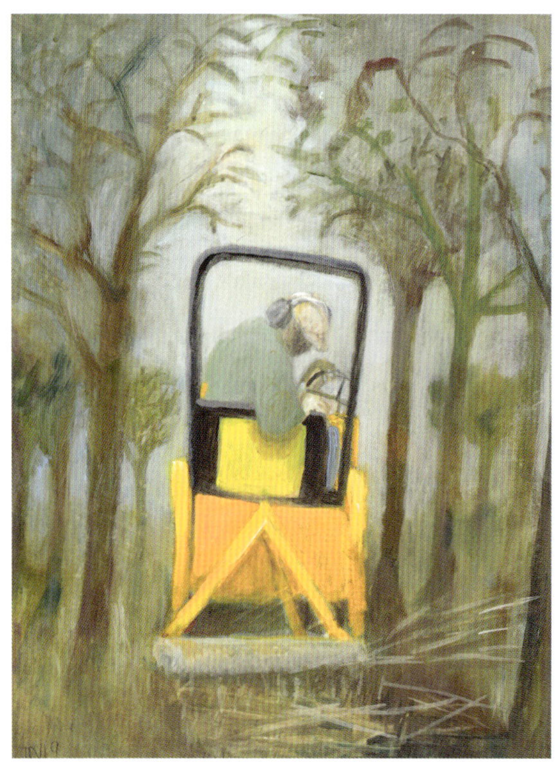

The Orange Machine
2019 · oil on board
26 x 19 cm / 10¼ x 7½ in

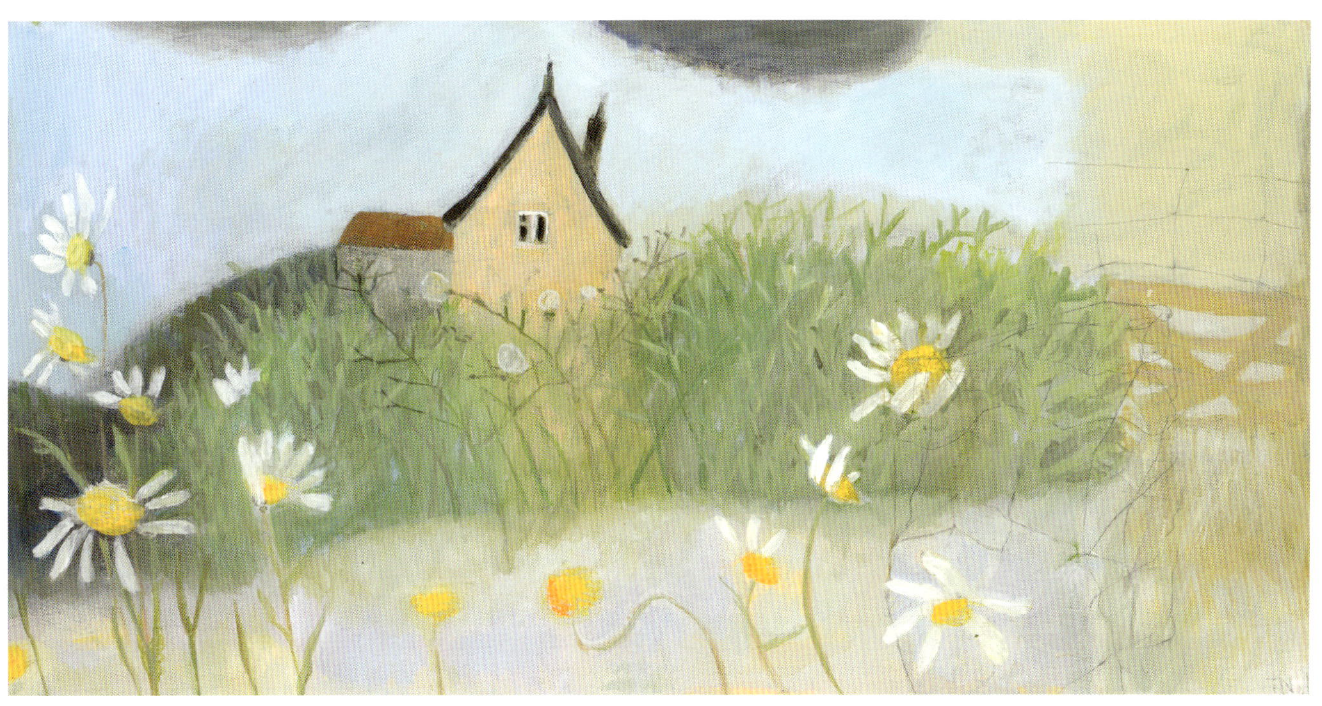

The Hedge
2013 · oil on board · 24 x 46 cm / 9½ x 18 in

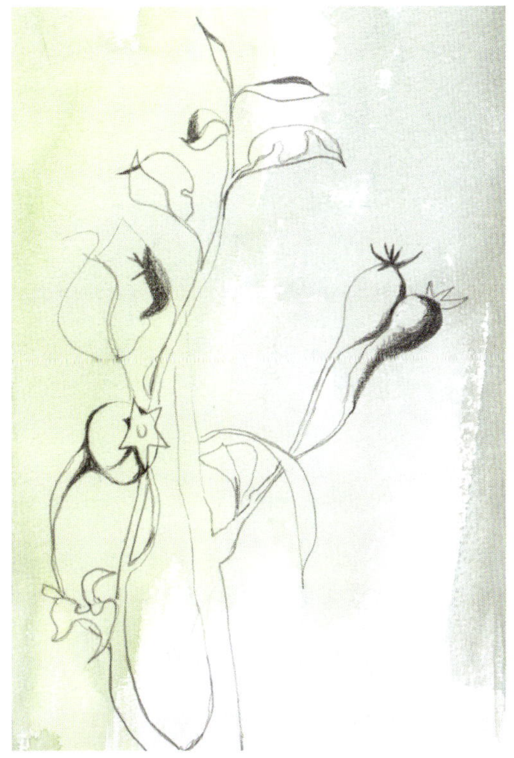

Concorde Pear
2011 · watercolour and pencil
26 x 18 cm / 10¼ x 7 in

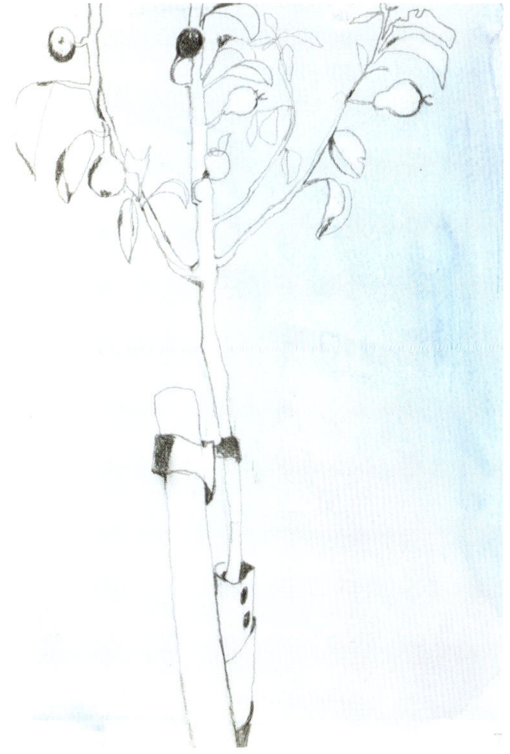

Williams Pear
2011 · watercolour and pencil
25.5 x 18 cm / 10 x 7 in

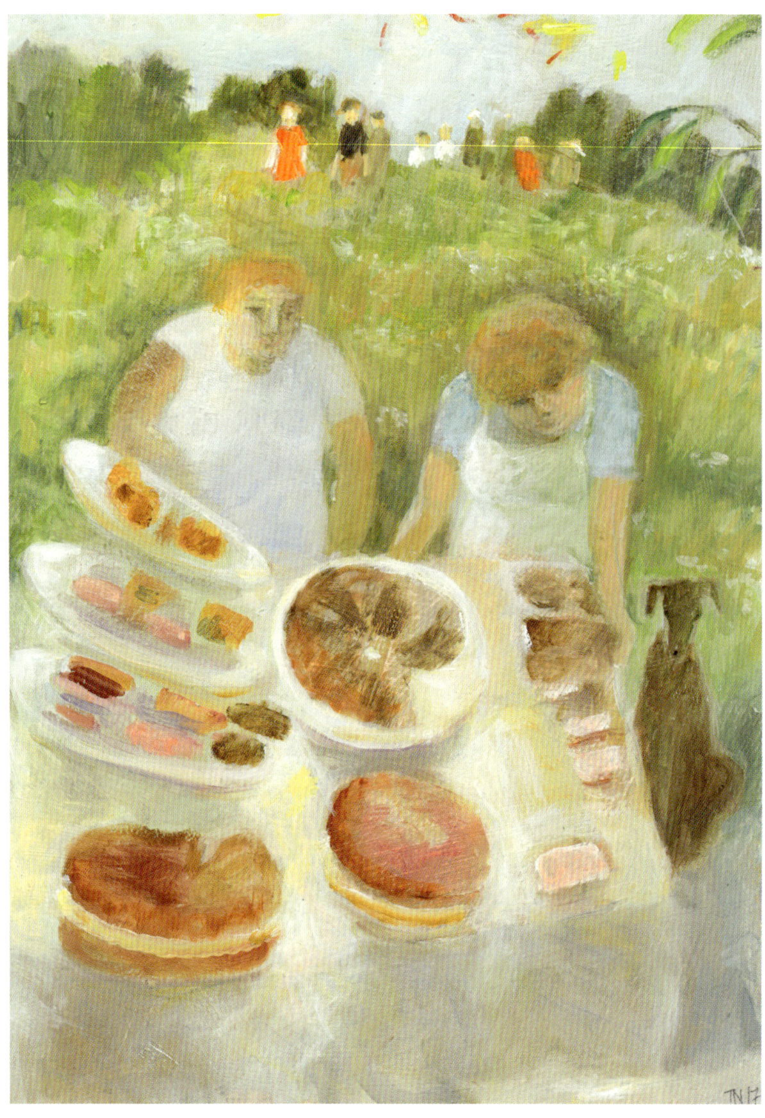

They Come for the Tea
2017 · oil on board · 26.5 x 19 cm / 10½ x 7½ in

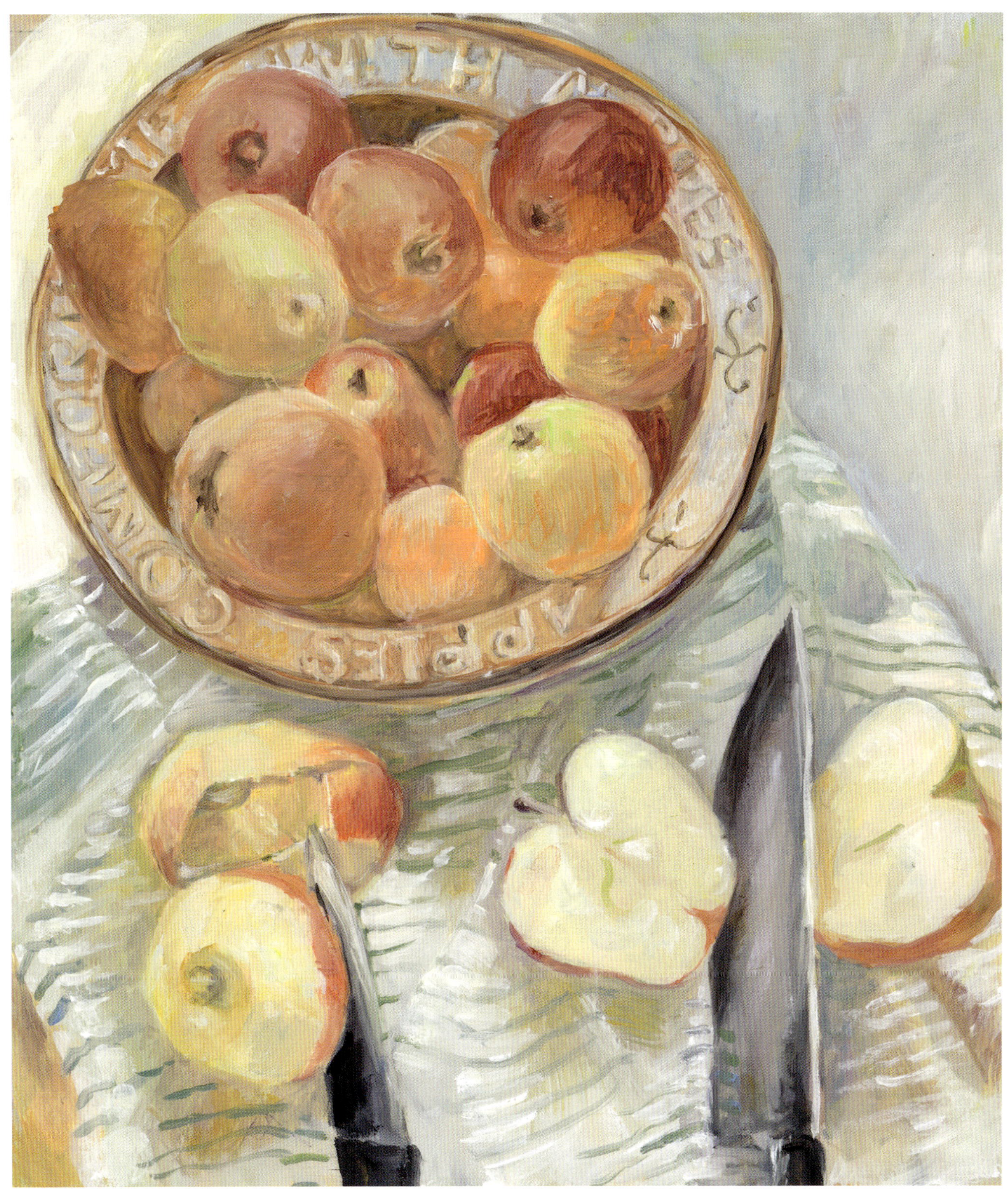

Comfort Me with Apples
2020 · oil on board · 35.5 x 30.5 cm / 14 x 12 in

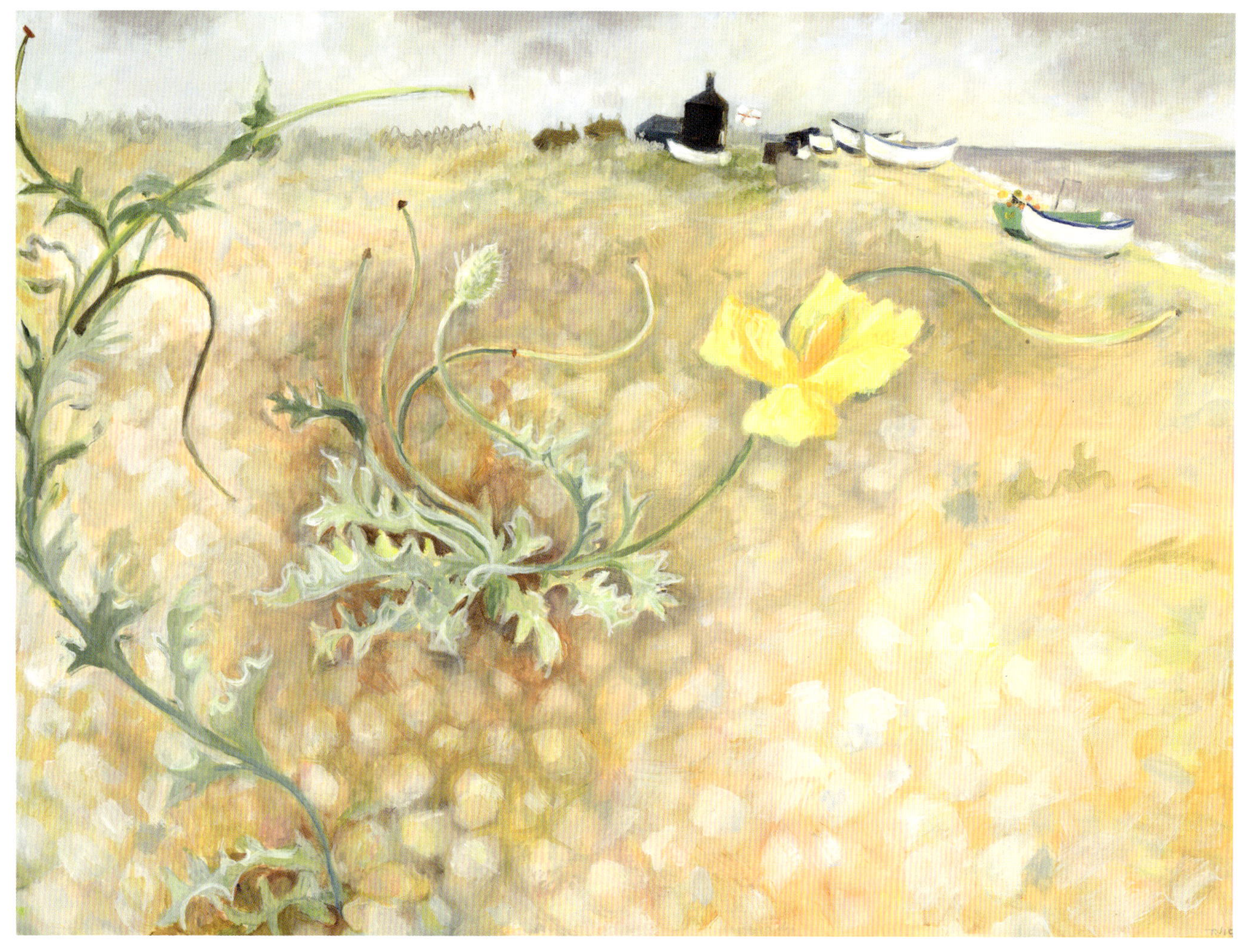

Yellow Horned Poppies
2019 · oil on board · 39.5 x 63.5 cm / 15½ x 25 in

4 · YELLOW HORNED POPPIES

Yellow horned poppies are courageous plants. They live on land that's subject to shifting. They manage to live in a salty environment, having hairy lower leaves to retain any fresh water. Through summer they give us yellow flowers whose petals have to hang on for dear life in those prevailing winds. Just as the ancient wind tears constantly at the torn flags on the fishermen's boats, it also rips at the scraps of yellow crepe of the petals, which seem to have been there all season, at home in this land of wide skies. I thought all skies were like this because it was what I knew. I liked Dorset but driving back into Suffolk it felt like the curtains had been opened.

The shingle coastline of East Anglia is an unstable place, subject to the power of the sea. The sea can chew and deposit the land and break through the shingle banks, creating new inland waters overnight. Aldeburgh has Crag Path, which is the promenade that runs parallel to the sea and beach, separated by the sea wall. On the inland side of Crag Path are large houses and on the other there is the land, which has its own agenda. Salt travels under the sea wall and then emerges as unsightly patches that blow out of the plaster in people's sitting rooms.

Thorpeness, a bit further north, has beach houses built on this inbetween land. I have heard it said that in the flimsily built prefabs pebbles wedged in the cracks would move with the coast on a windswept night as if they were still part of the shore. Like the coast yellow horned poppies have a tenuous existence. In some places they can be found in larger clumps where one imagines they have sent a strong taproot down and found some good soil to get a hold on, but for others it's hard to imagine what they are holding on to. In the winter they are barely there, reduced to just a rosette of deeply lobed bluey leaves. As things warm up the plants return, the upper leaves greener and clutching the stems, and then the buds form, then the flowers, then the flies arrive and then the horns. The splendid horns are the seedpods, which arch up to thirty centimetres long. They are lime green before turning blacky brown.

These poppies grow on disturbed ground. A colony appeared where the bulldozers had been. They live for five years at the most: the flowers have their day, and the seeds — do they lie dormant, wedged deep between pebbles? Yellow horned poppies survive harsh conditions; they also have power. Break the stem and out will ooze a foul-smelling orange sap; it's toxic — all parts of the plant are toxic. It can affect the brain. This plant was once called squatmore (a squat being a bruise) and is still called bruisewort, because it was once thought to heal bruising. It contains glaucine, which is an anti-inflammatory.

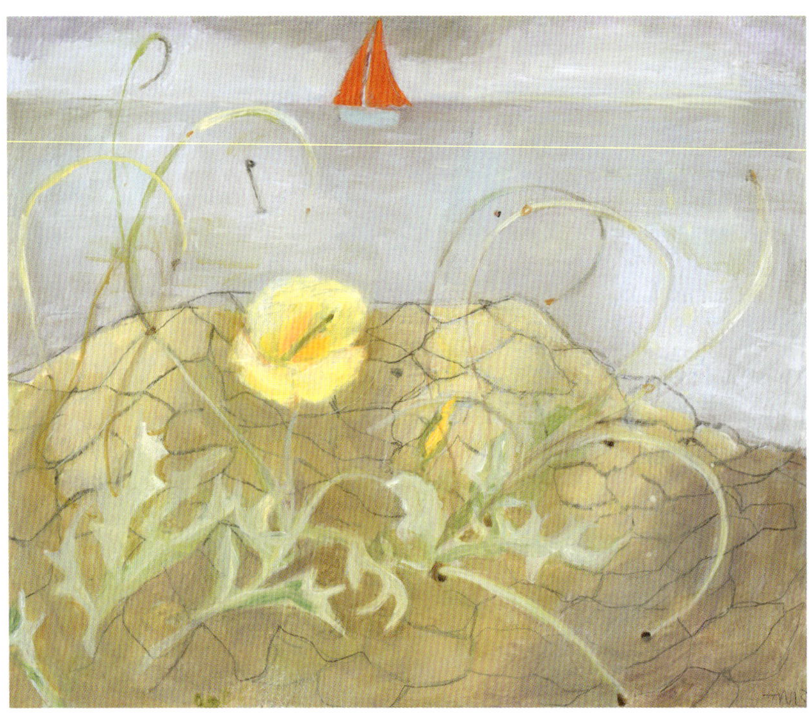

A Boat Was There
2013 · oil on board · 20.5 x 23 cm / 8 x 9 in

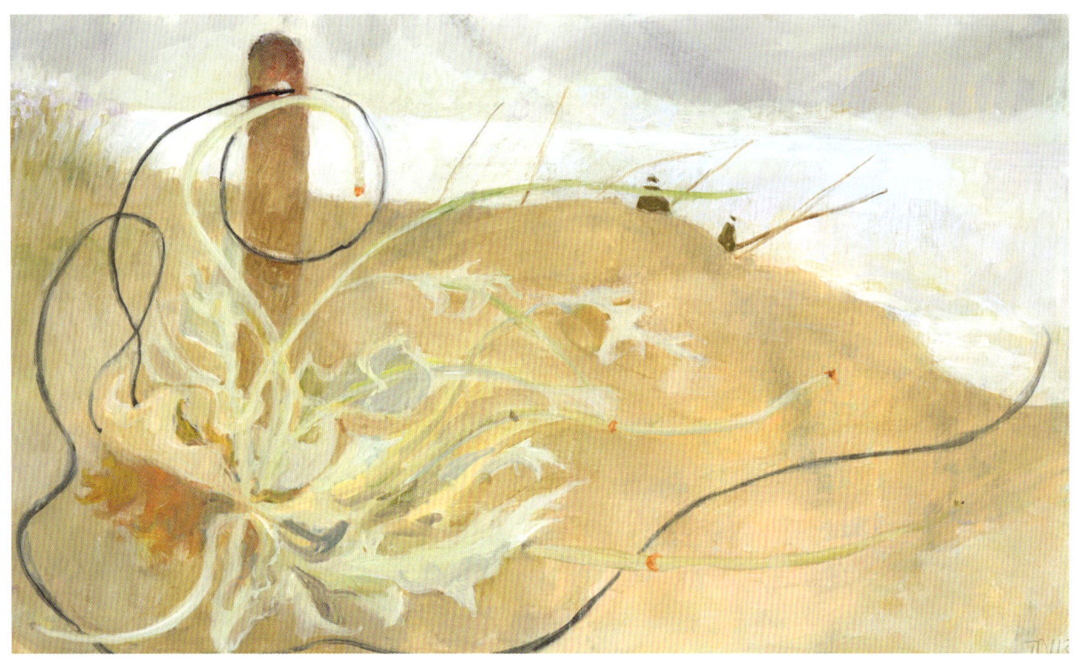

Unravelling
2013 · oil on board · 18.5 x 30.5 cm / 7¼ x 12 in

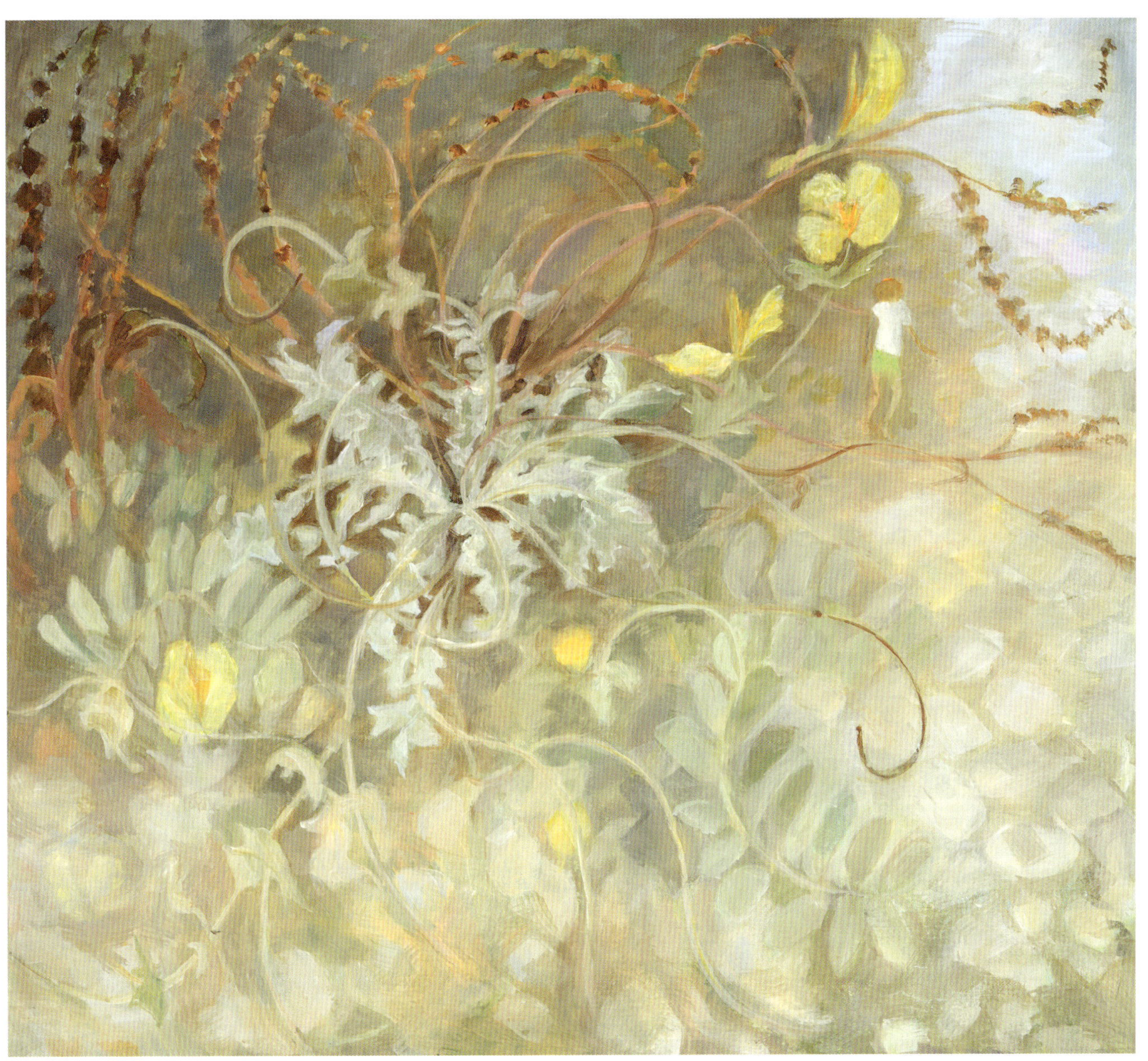

Last Legs of Summer
2013 · oil on board · 55 x 61 cm / 22 x 24 in

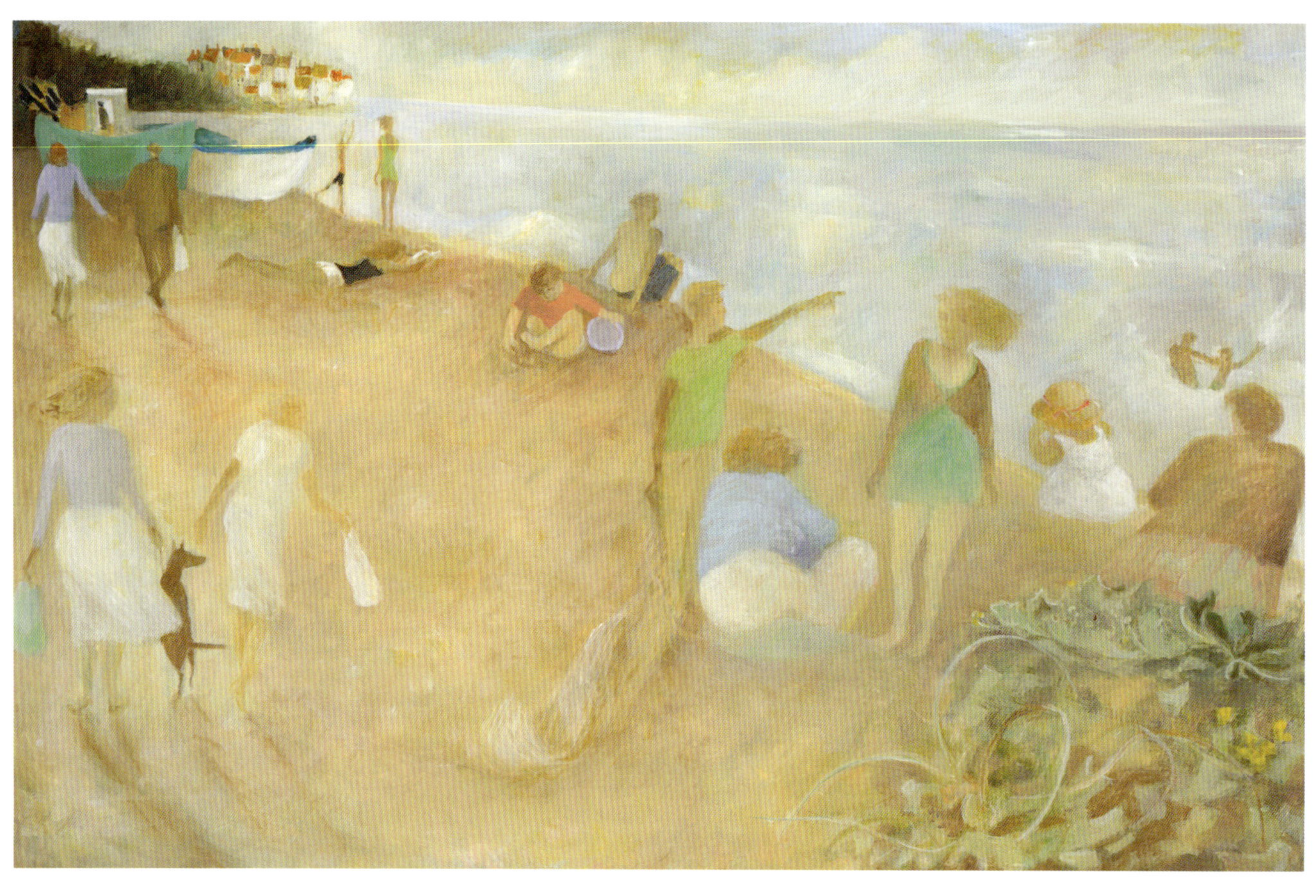

After Exams
2014 · oil on canvas · 58.5 x 87.5 cm / 23 x 34½ in

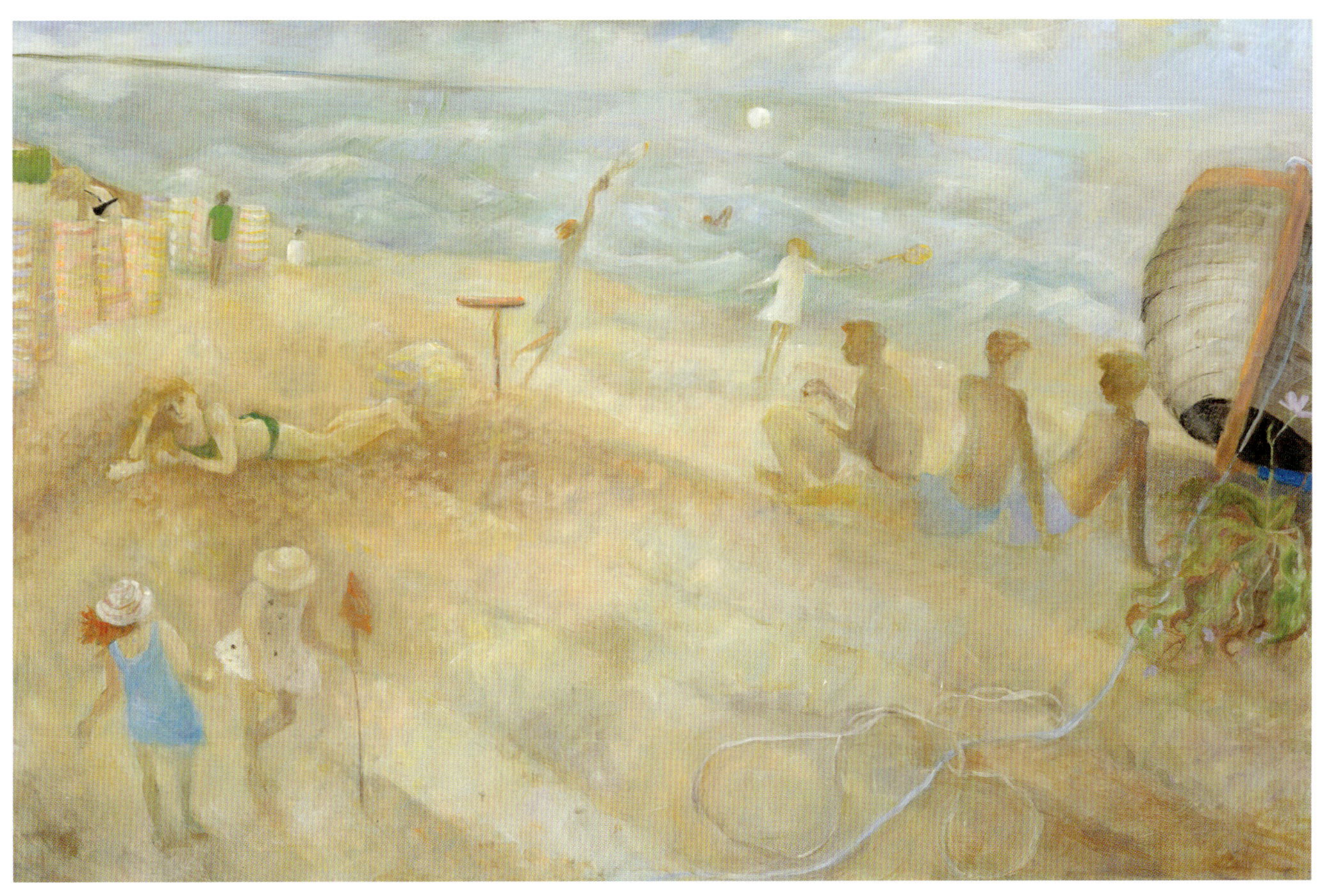

August
2014 · oil on canvas · 61 x 91.5 cm / 24 x 36 in

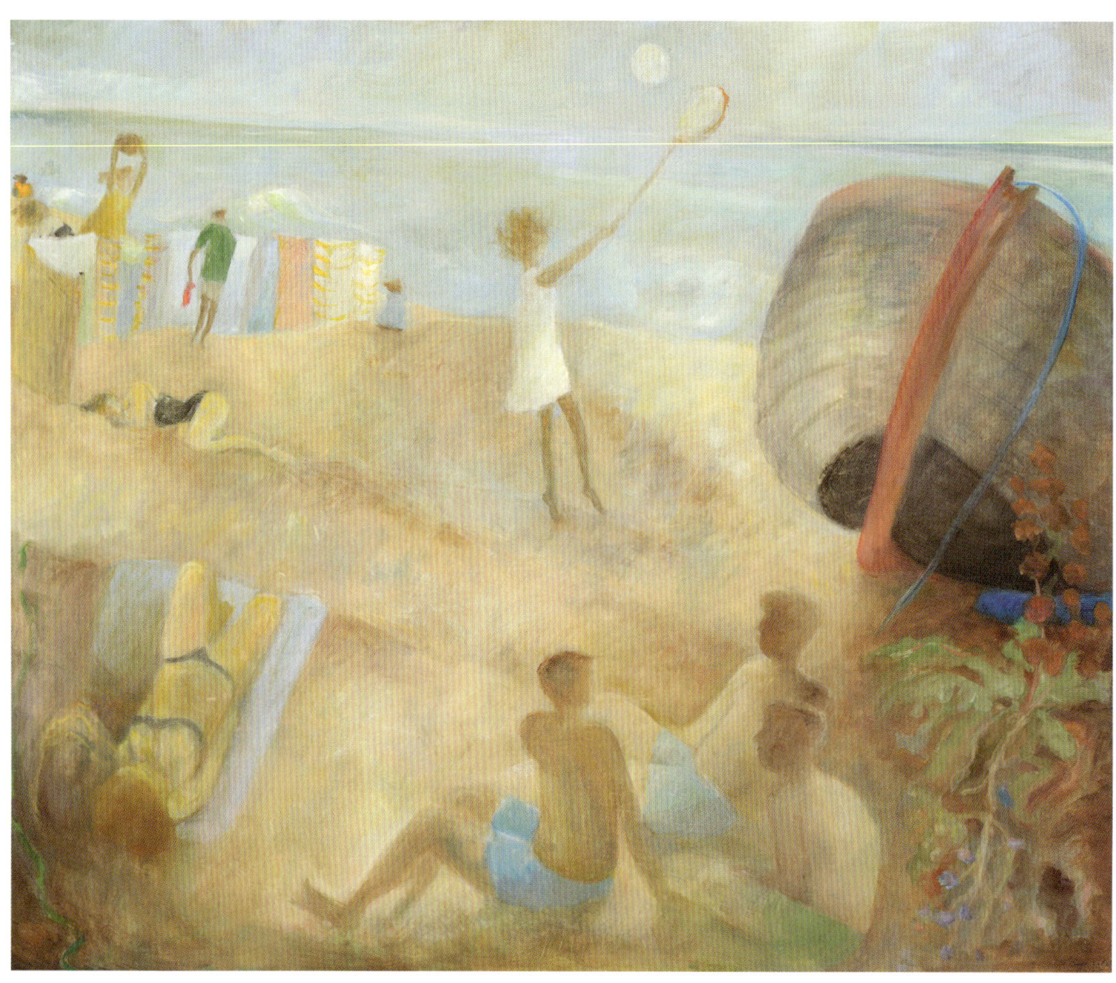

Games
2014 · oil on board · 54.5 x 62 cm / 21½ x 24½ in

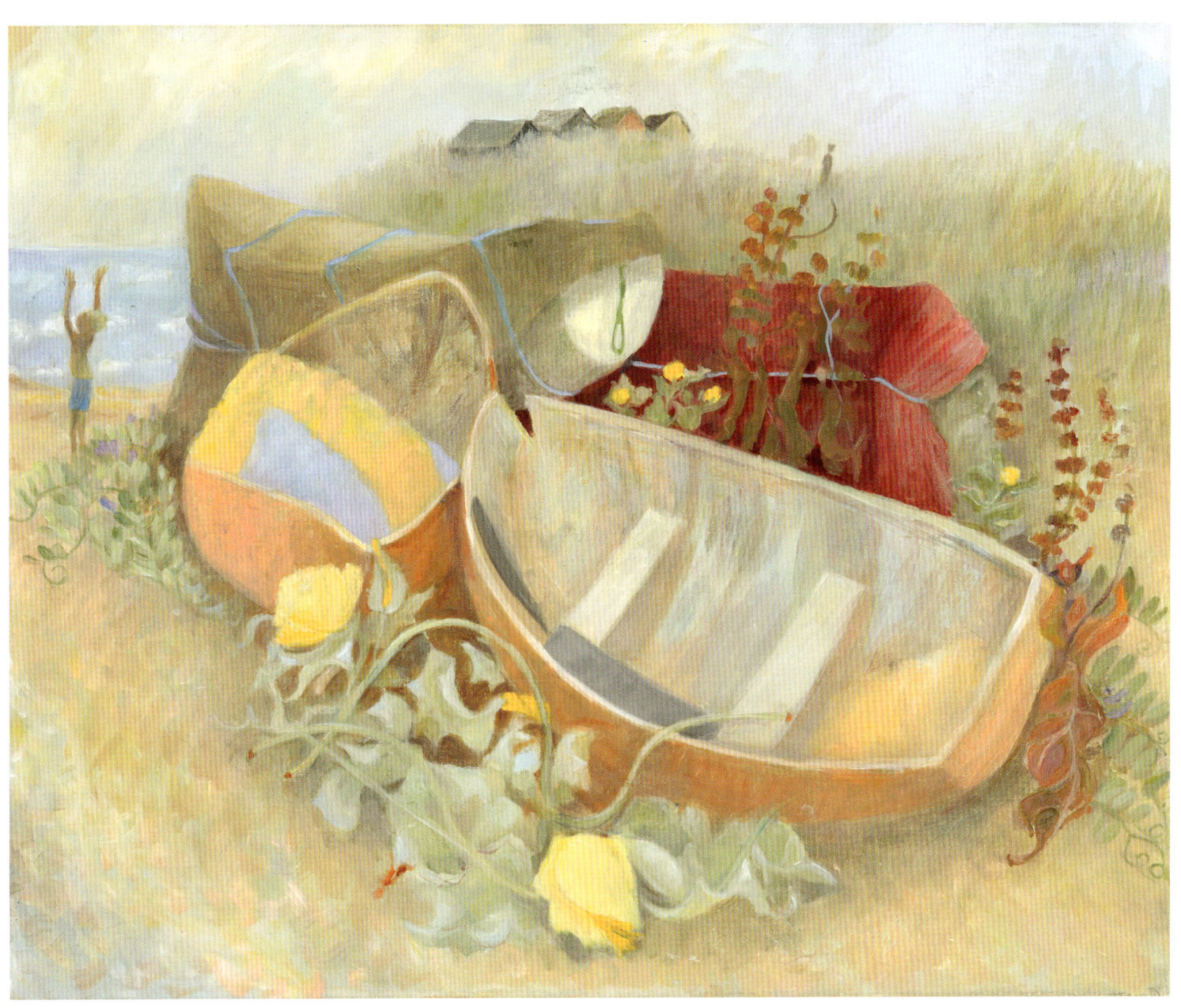

Still Life on the Beach
2013 · oil on canvas · 63.5 x 76 cm / 25 x 30 in

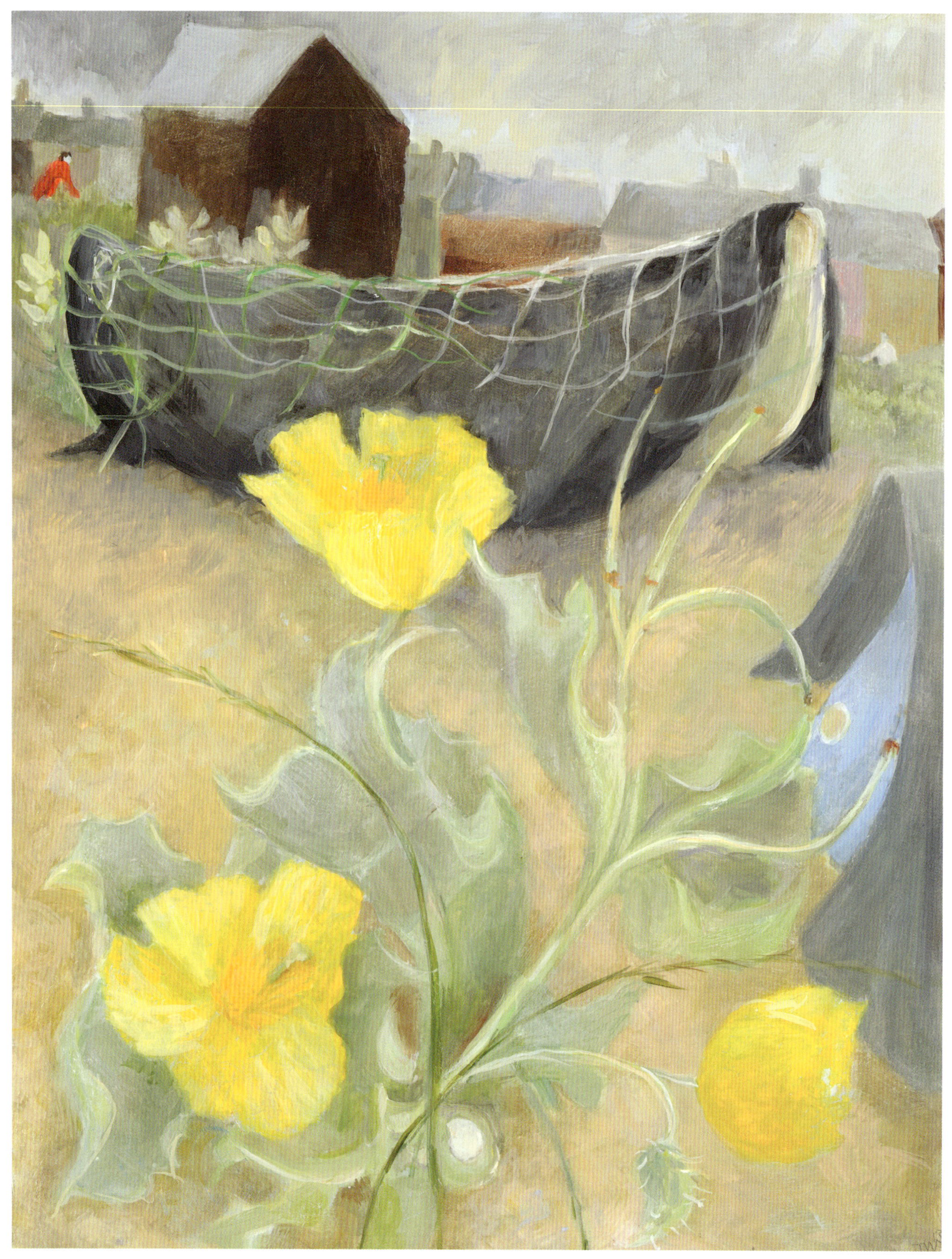

Strong Plants
2013 · oil on board · 39.5 x 30.5 cm / 15½ x 12 in

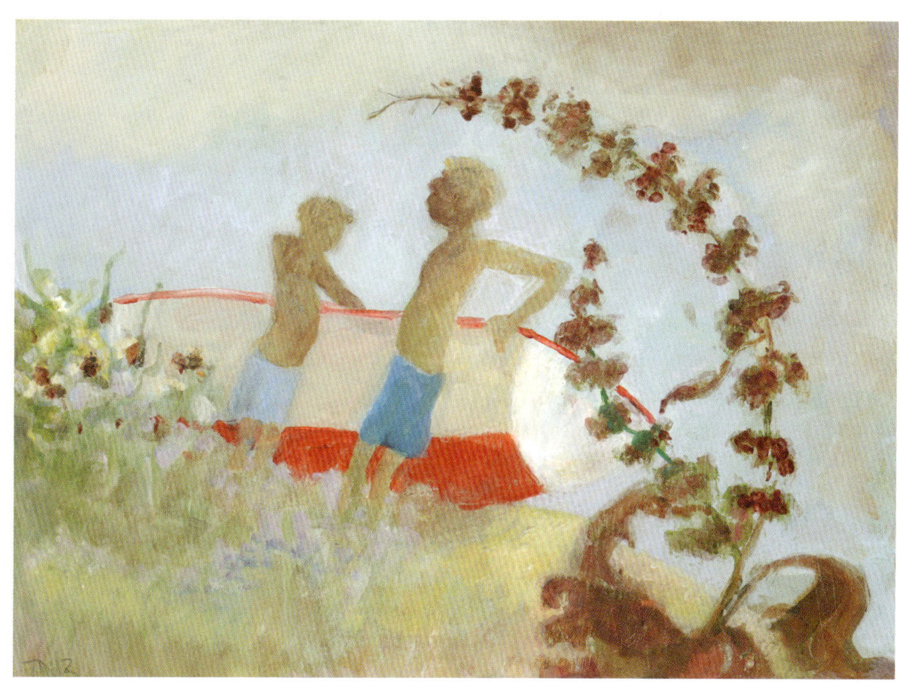

Young Men
2013 · oil on board · 16.5 x 22 cm / 6½ x 8¾ in

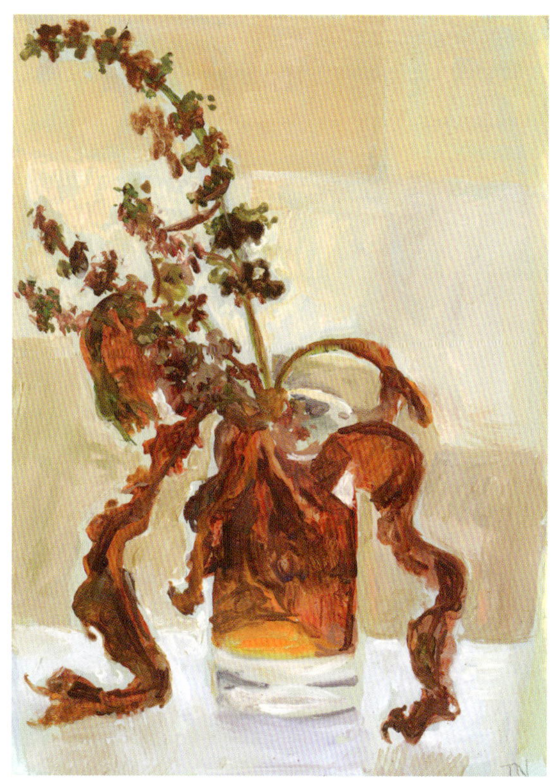

Ragged Robin
2013 · oil on board · 18 x 12.5 cm / 7 x 5 in

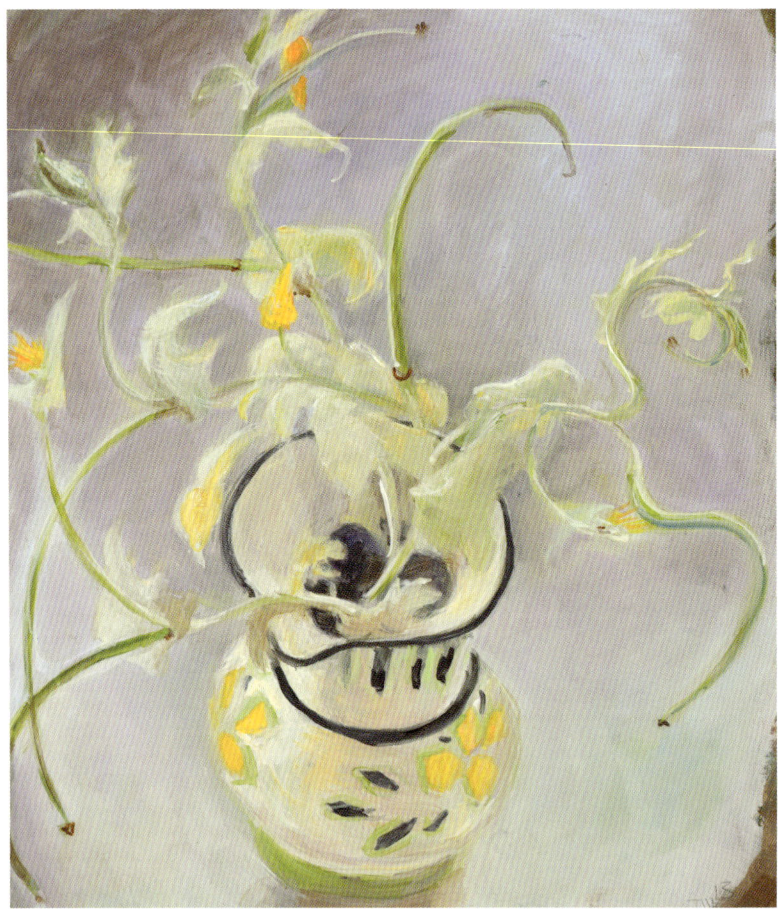

Painting Dead Sea Plants While Everyone Else Is on the Beach
2013 · oil on board · 30 x 25.5 cm / 11¾ x 10 in

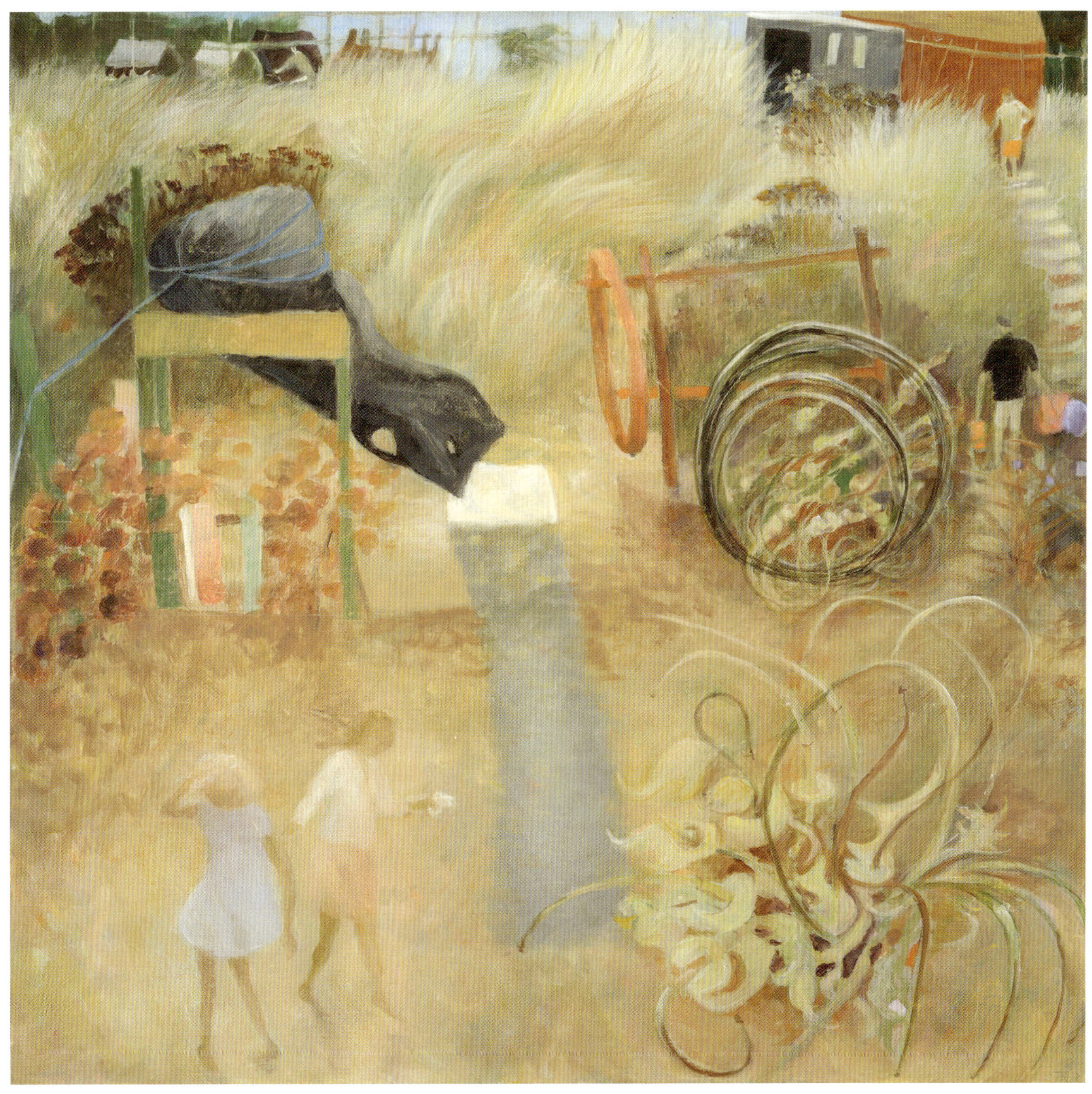

Uneasy Beach
2013 · oil on canvas · 61 x 61 cm / 24 x 24 in

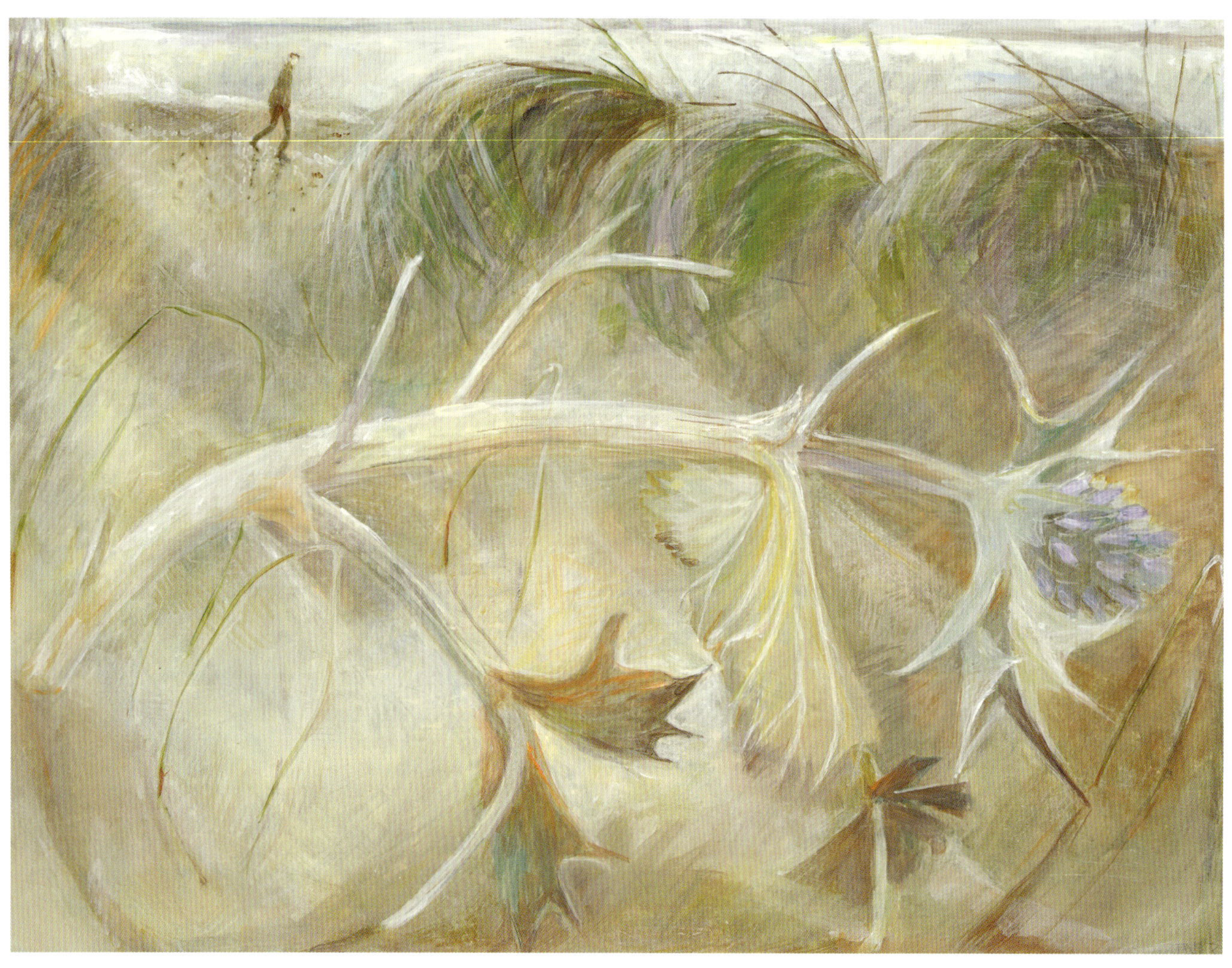

Sea Holly Drying on the Beach
2013 · oil on board · 42 x 53.5 cm / 16½ x 21 in

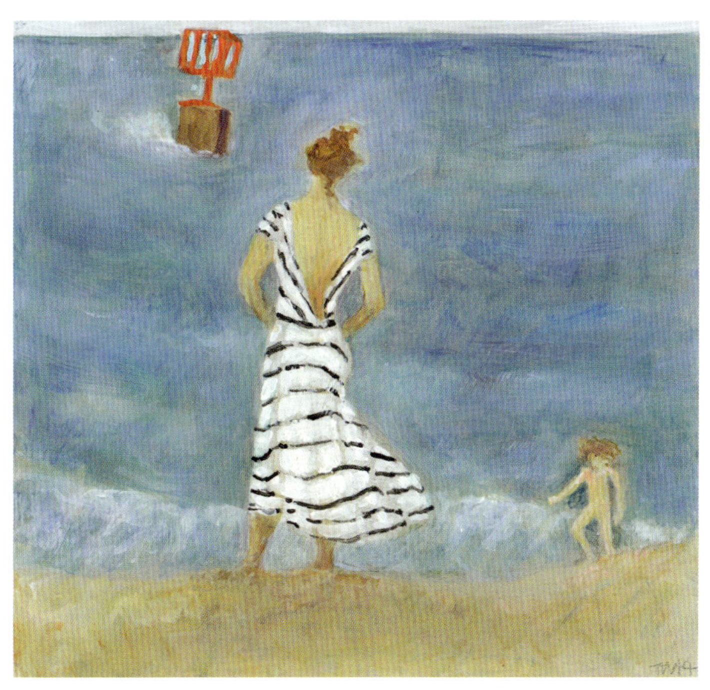

A Young Mother Looks Out to Sea
2014 · oil on board · 17 x 18 cm / 6¾ x 7 in

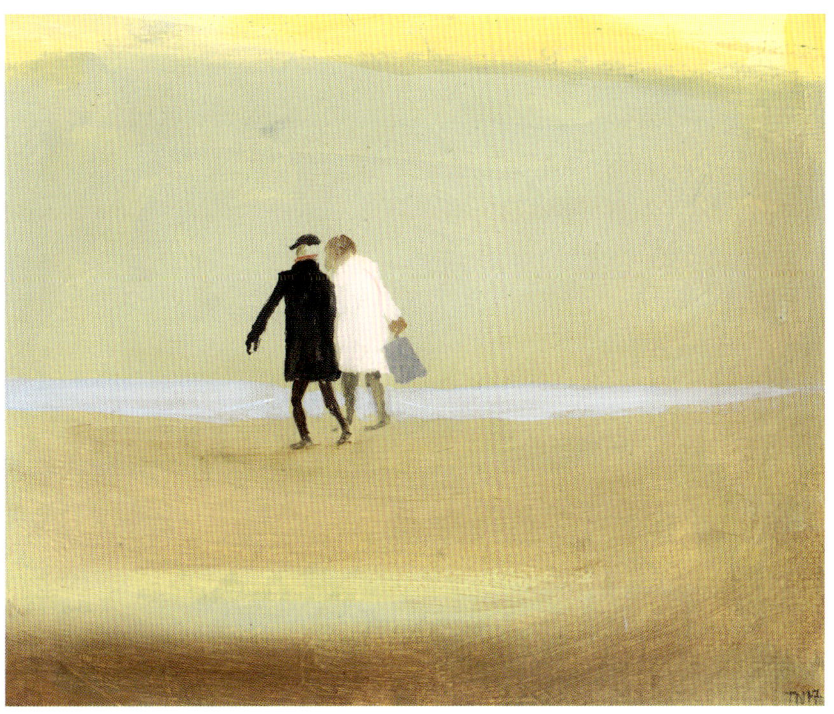

Ping
2017 · oil on card · 18 x 21.5 cm / 7 x 8½ in

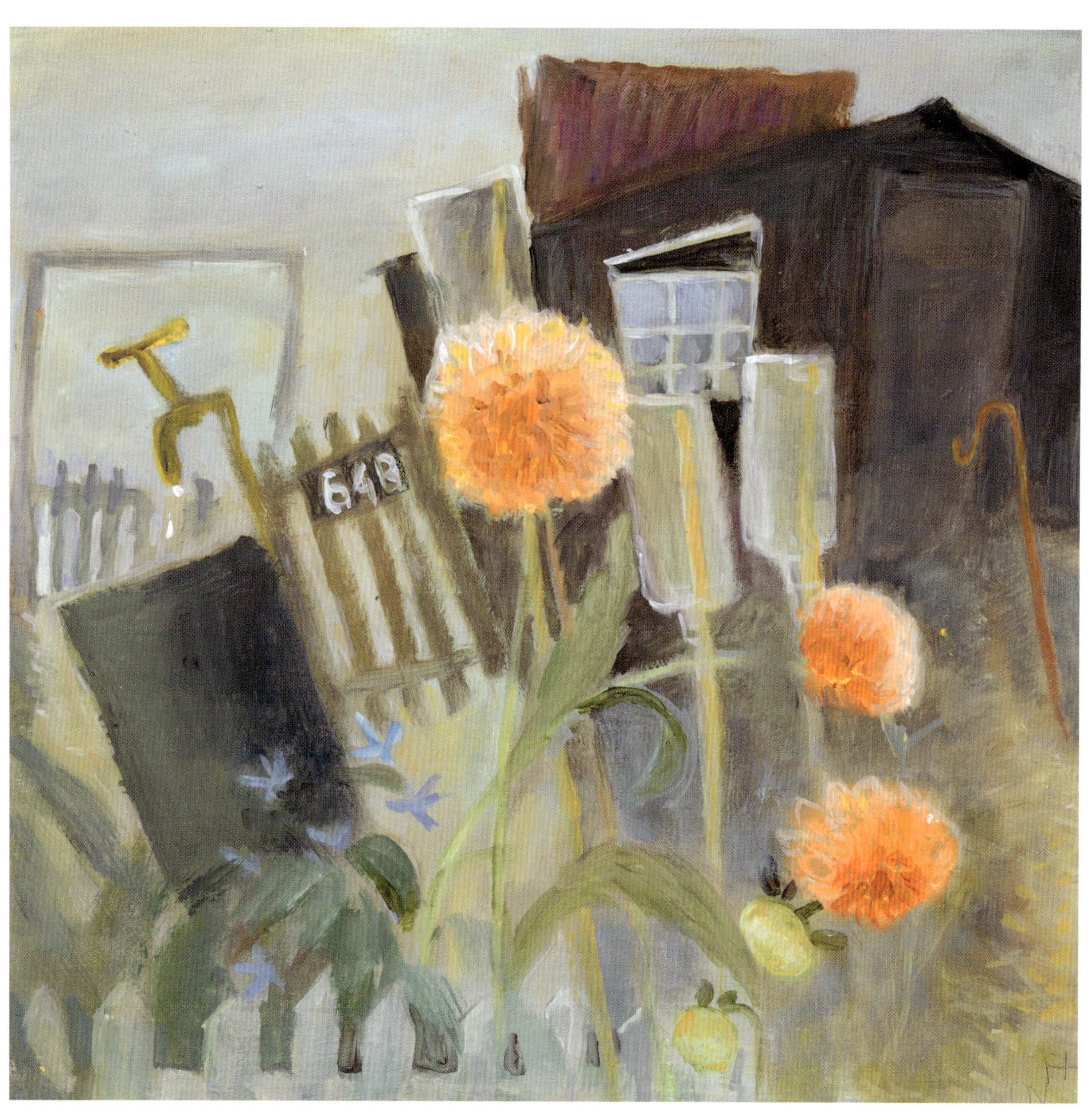

Plot 64B
2017 · oil on board · 18 x 18 cm / 7 x 7 in

5 · PLOT 64

for & by Telfer Stokes*

The man who had an allotment opposite me died on the way to getting his Sunday paper. The man who has his allotment on the other side died after being ill for some time. Neither of these people did I meet in any other circumstance other than on the allotment. For that reason we had an uncluttered relationship. Of course within a few weeks their respective allotments had gone to pigs and whistles. I met another man on his allotment planting his potatoes on a Sunday morning near Easter. He said it was a bit like going to church. The bells were ringing; there was a sense of order, of tradition. He said even the smell was the same.*

PASSING ON THE TOIL

If you have been away, thinking about the allotment is not good because predominantly you feel a sense of guilt. It has 'gone back'. Tidying up and digging over the beds renews the tentative relationship but you are never in complete control of the situation. You are tending it for your time. By working a plot it becomes yours. That plot goes back and back to previous owners who, if you are lucky with your plot, have fed it with muck and turned the soil, left benefits that you can reap. Toil is passed on.

You seem to spend the growing months just trying to catch up with what you have planted and what you have not, because the growing is in charge. It's in the autumn and winter months when the land is back to its bare bones that you can become conscious of the people who have inhabited the plot before you.*

ORDERING THE SEEDS

This is evening gardening, after changing the clocks. On many allotments people have formed a syndicate for buying seeds. Bulk-buying is best. The catalogue is on the kitchen table. Very nice – particularly those new things to try. Restrain yourself. New folks always order too much, thinking that what you see on the packets is what you will see in the allotment. Older folks save seeds and beans.*

A FIGHT WITH MICE

You can plant your beans early in autumn instead of the spring so you get a head start, but the problem can be mice. They smell the beans. They make a little hole in the earth, then dig down. Your beans can disappear. Once they have sprouted they are usually safe, except in a bad winter. The other way round is to get rid of the mice.*

CHARD AND CHICKENS

My friend Marion has grown vegetables for more than thirty years. She introduced us to chard and squash. Now she does not need so many vegetables for herself but still needs to grow them – gifts for her friends, neighbours and family.

A new couple are wanting chickens on that plot again, broody and hopeful. An old man pauses, watching them, thinking 'there have been chickens there before'. Some plots are passed on to family members, some to unknown strangers.

THE OUTSIDER'S VIEW

You see them through the train window, you see them on the outskirts of towns – somewhere between waste land, light industry and the gas works. A scattering of old untidy sheds. Abandonment, an absence of people.

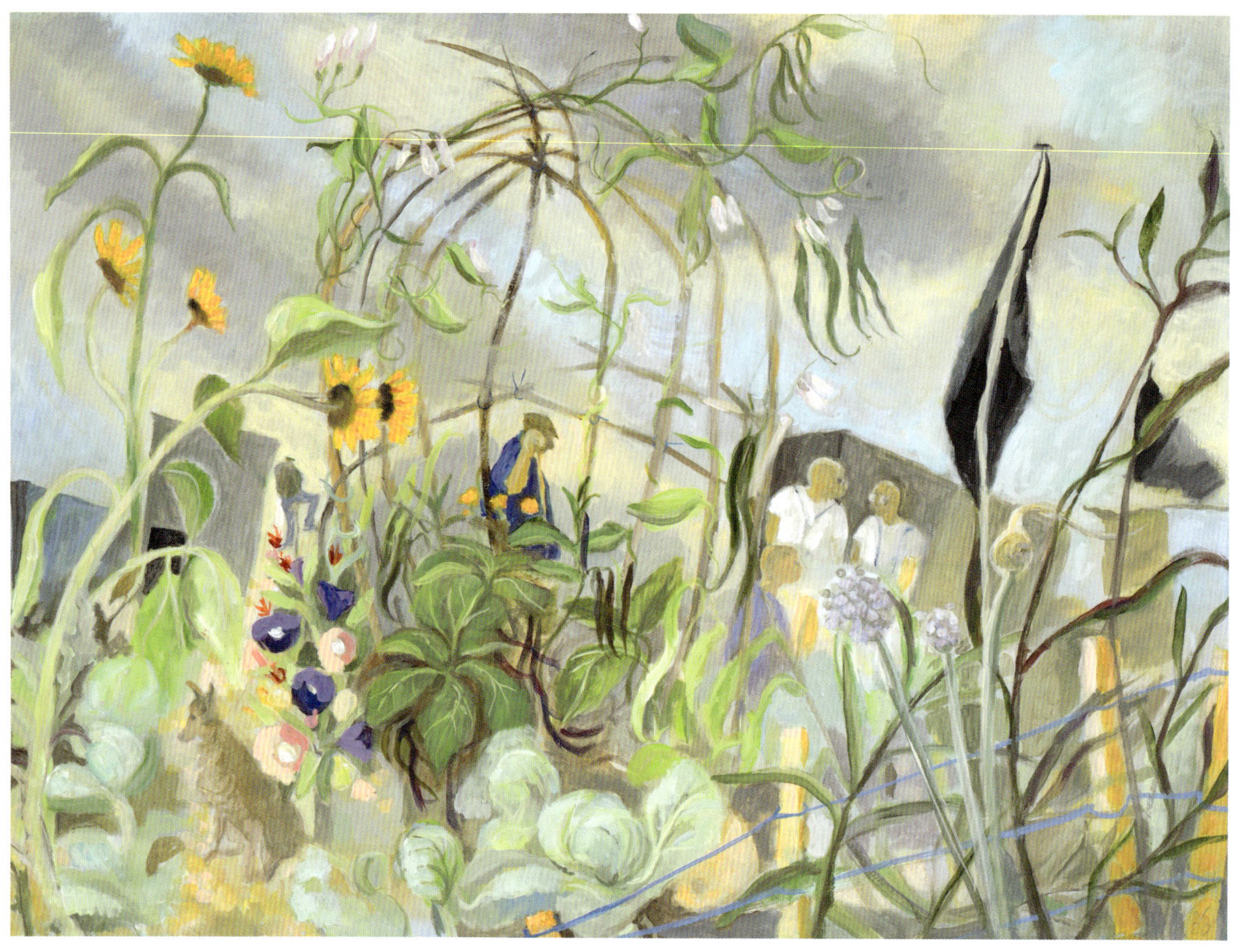

On a Good Day
2020 · oil on board · 46 x 61 cm / 18 x 24 in

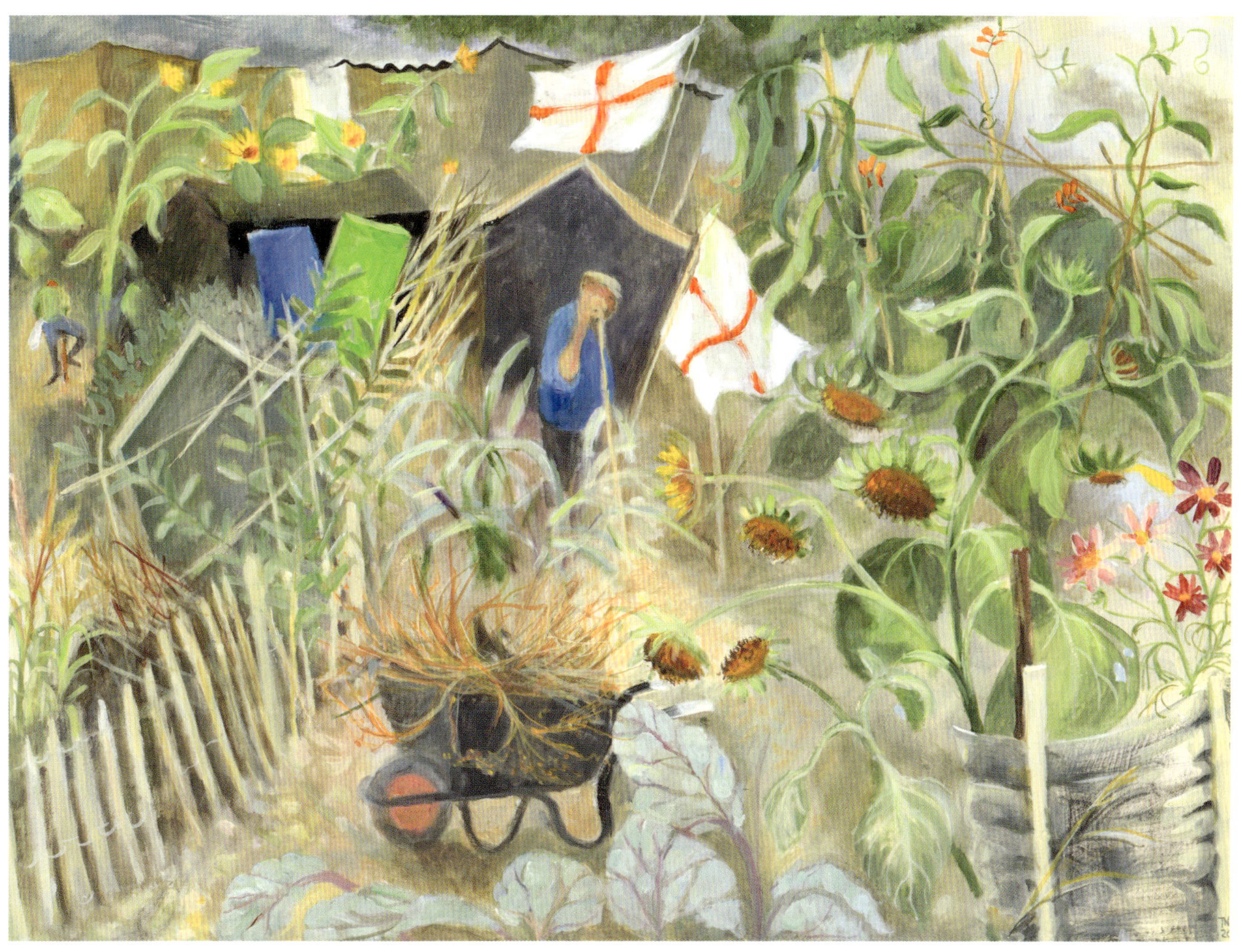

Making Sense of It All
2020 · oil on board · 46 x 61 cm / 18 x 24 in

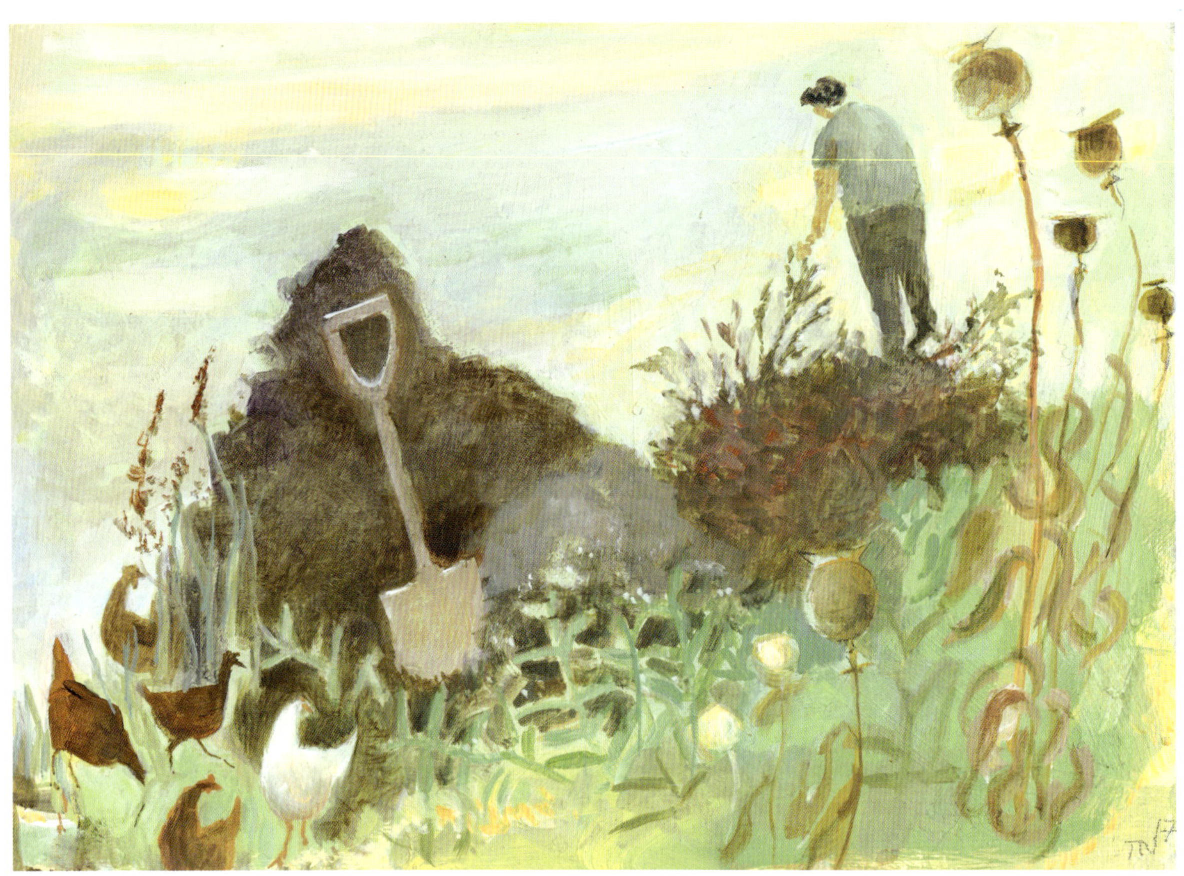

Accumulated
2017 · oil on board · 17 x 21.5 cm / 6¾ x 8½ in

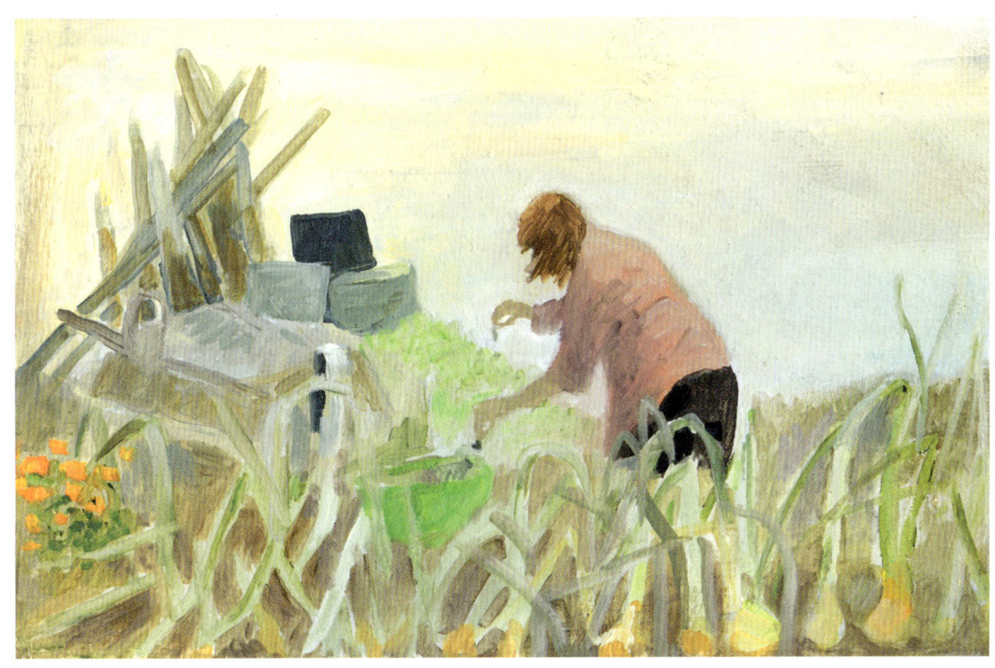

Picking
2017 · oil on board · 11.5 x 17 cm / 4½ x 6¾ in

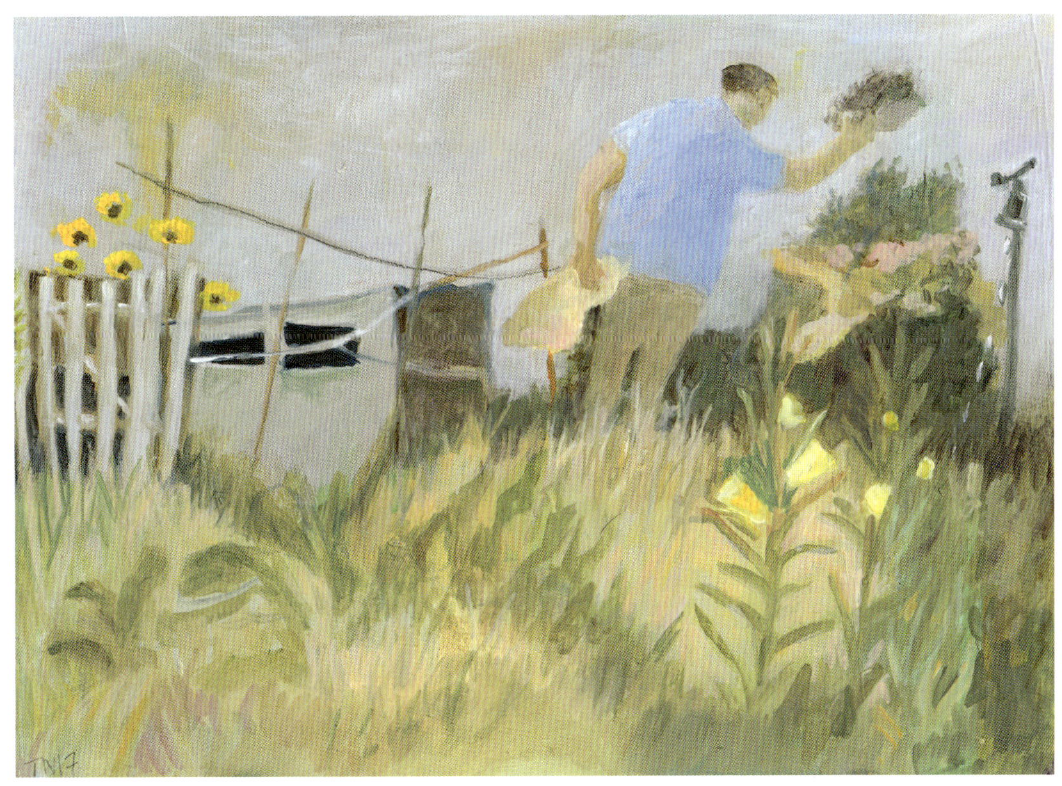

Goodbye to All That
2017 · oil on board · 14 x 19 cm / 5½ x 7½ in

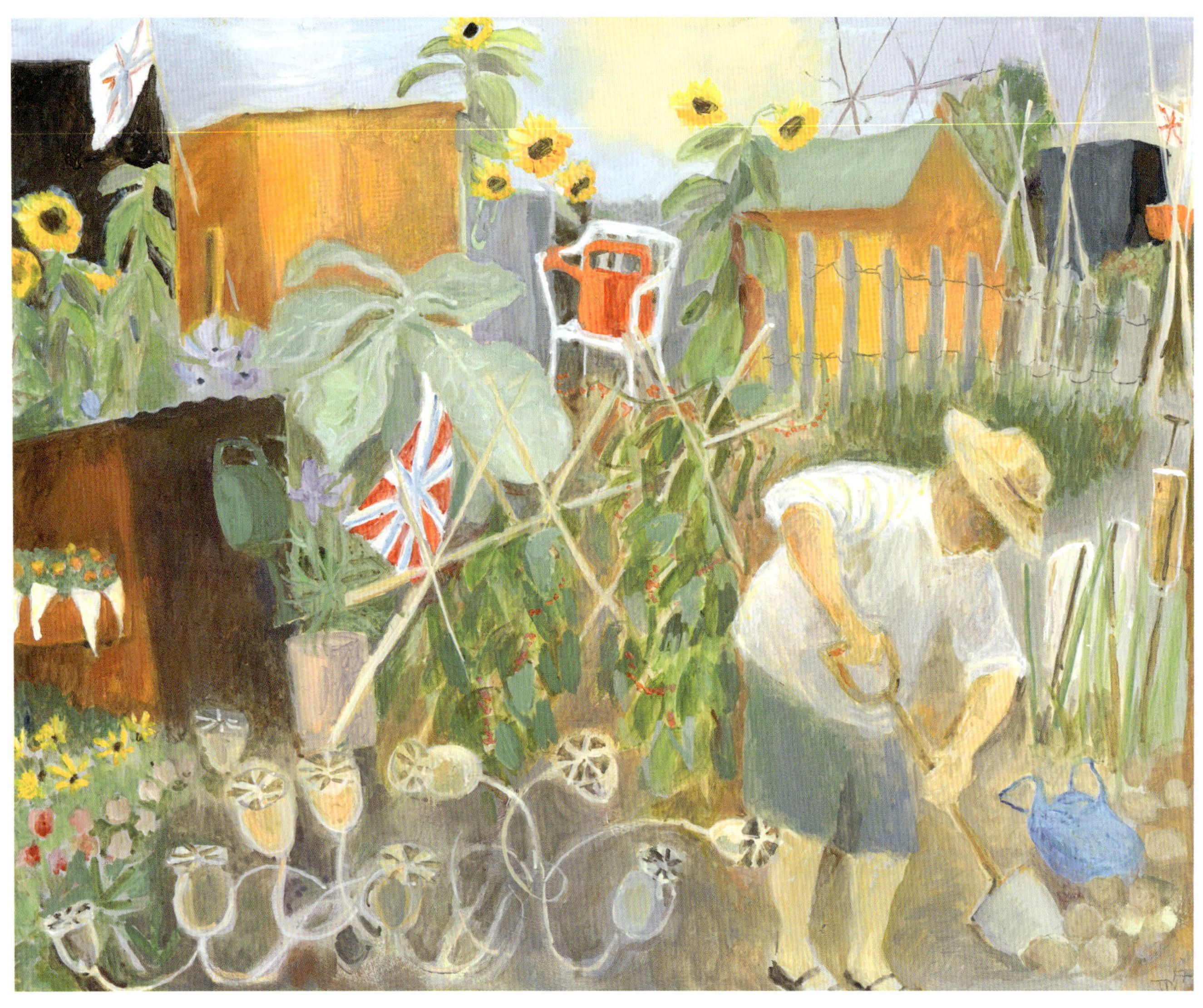

Toil
2017 · oil on board · 27.5 x 33 cm / 10¾ x 13 in

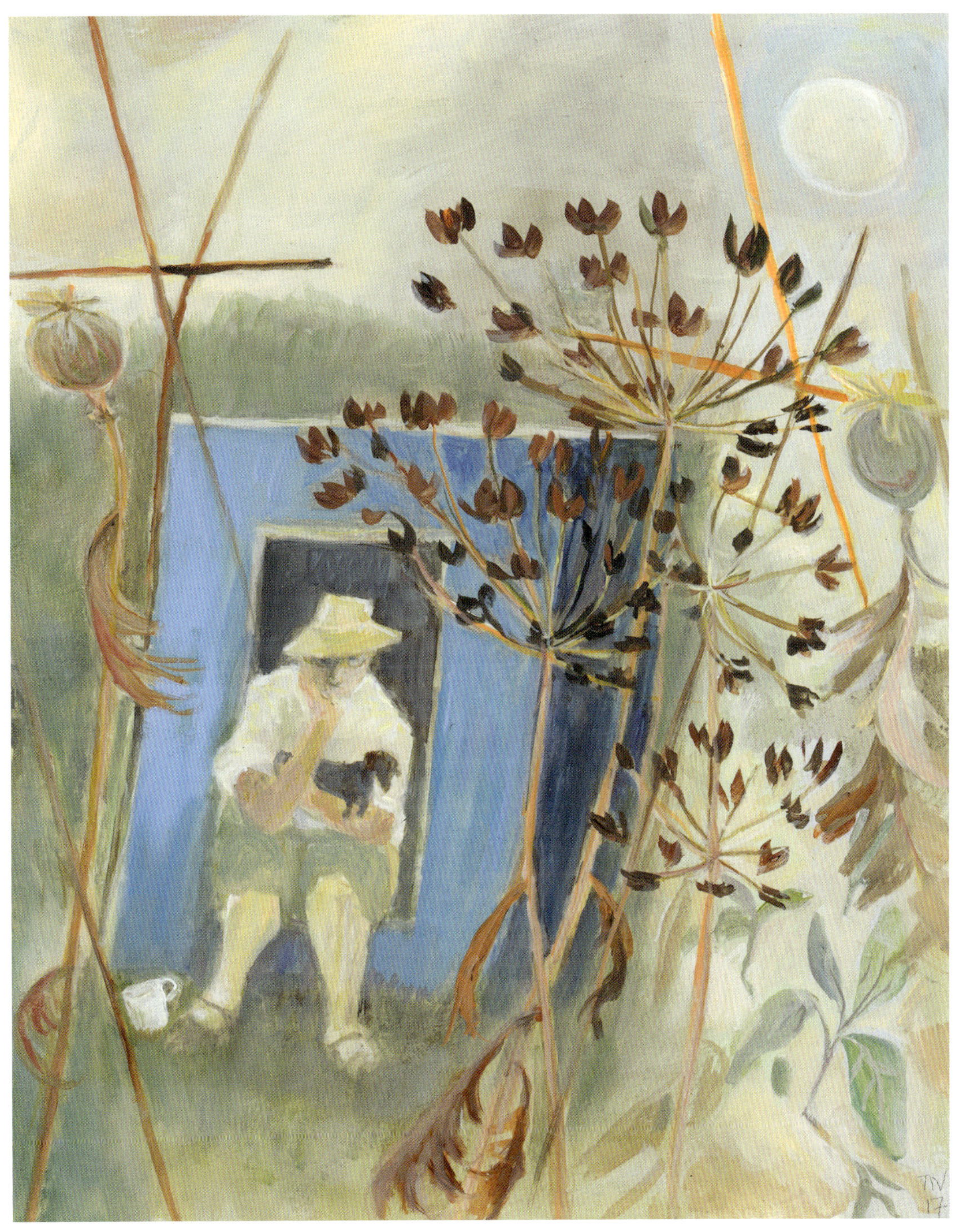

Thoughts on the Plot
2017 · oil on board · 32.5 x 25.5 cm / 12¾ x 10 in

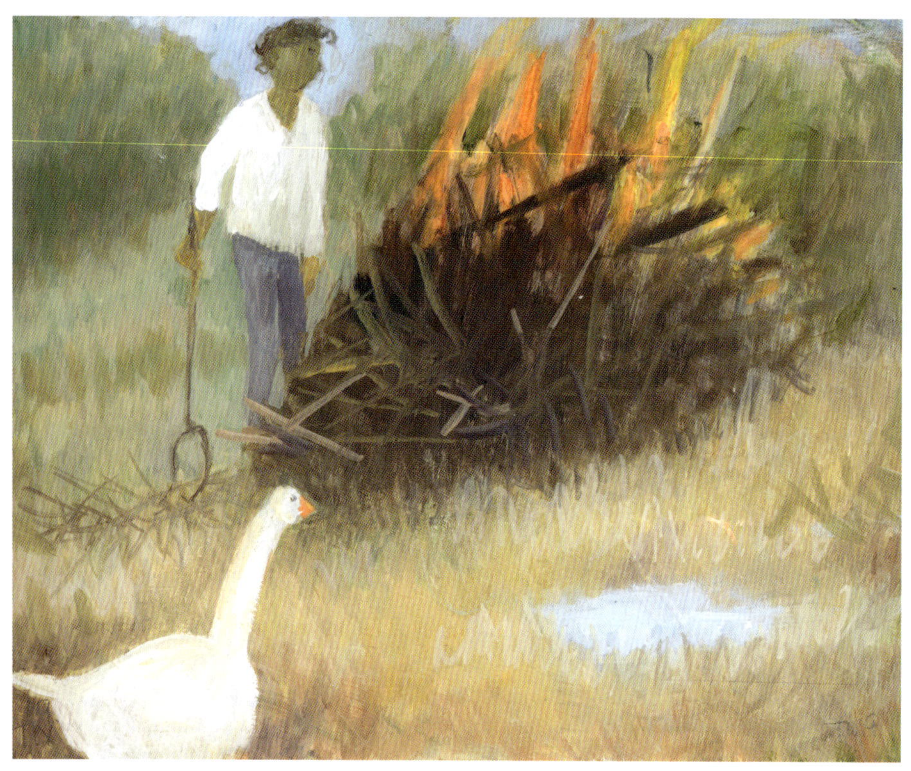

An Event in January
2019 · oil on board · 14 x 17 cm / 5½ x 6¾ in

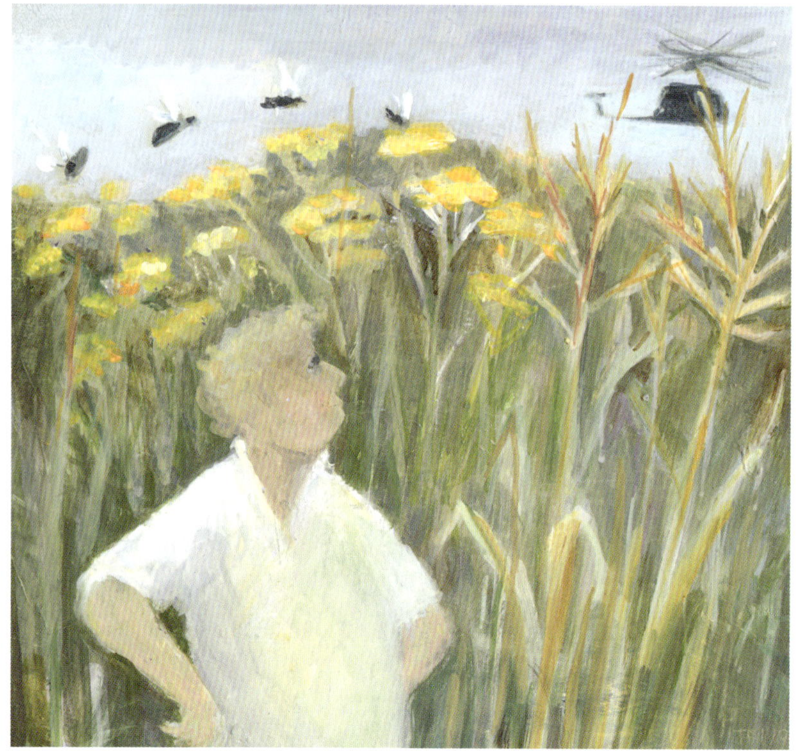

Bees
2019 · oil on board · 14 x 15 cm / 5½ x 6 in

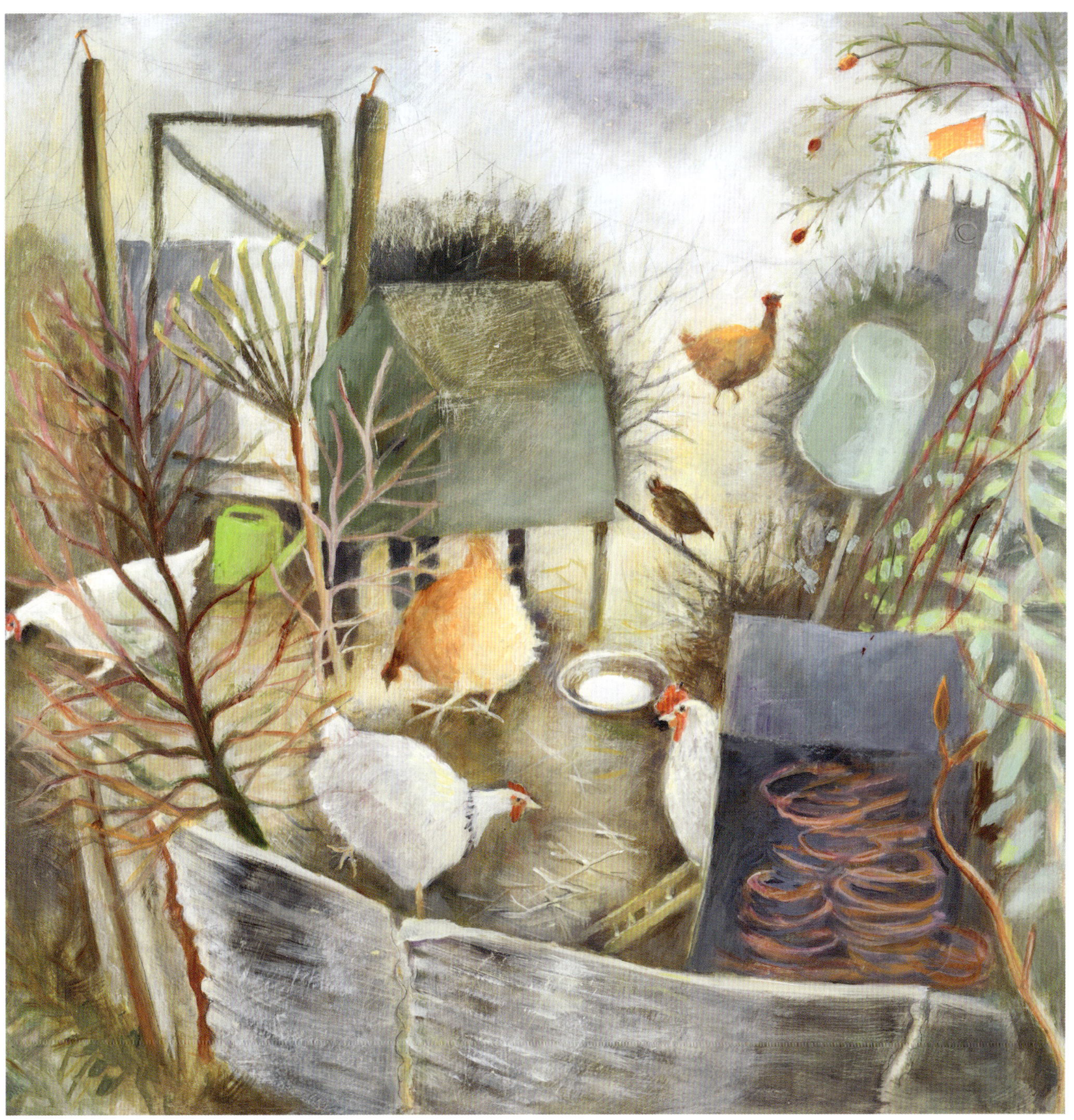

End of December
2018 · oil on board · 46 x 44 cm / 18 x 17¼ in

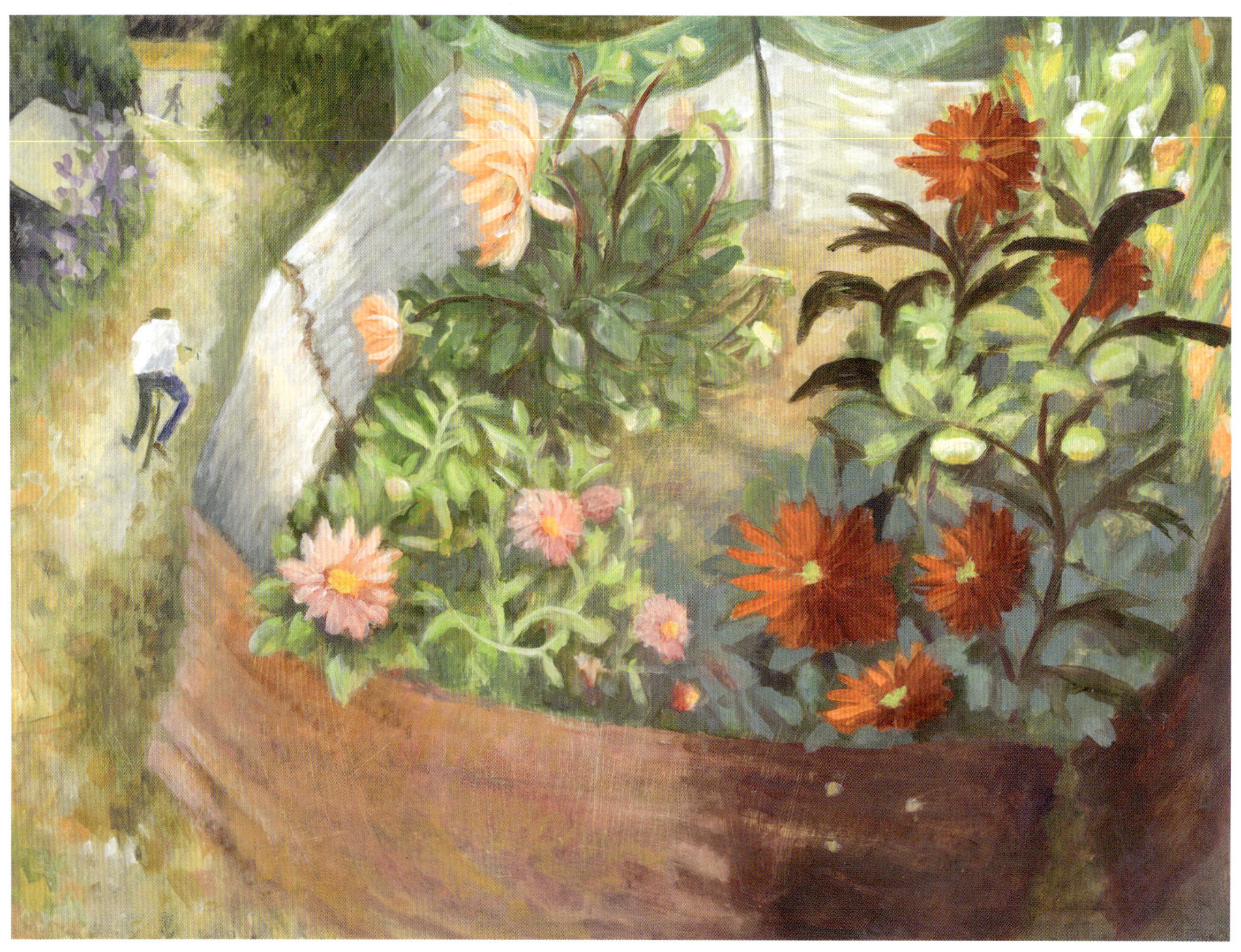

They Didn't Notice Us
2020 · oil on board · 46 x 61 cm / 18 x 24 in

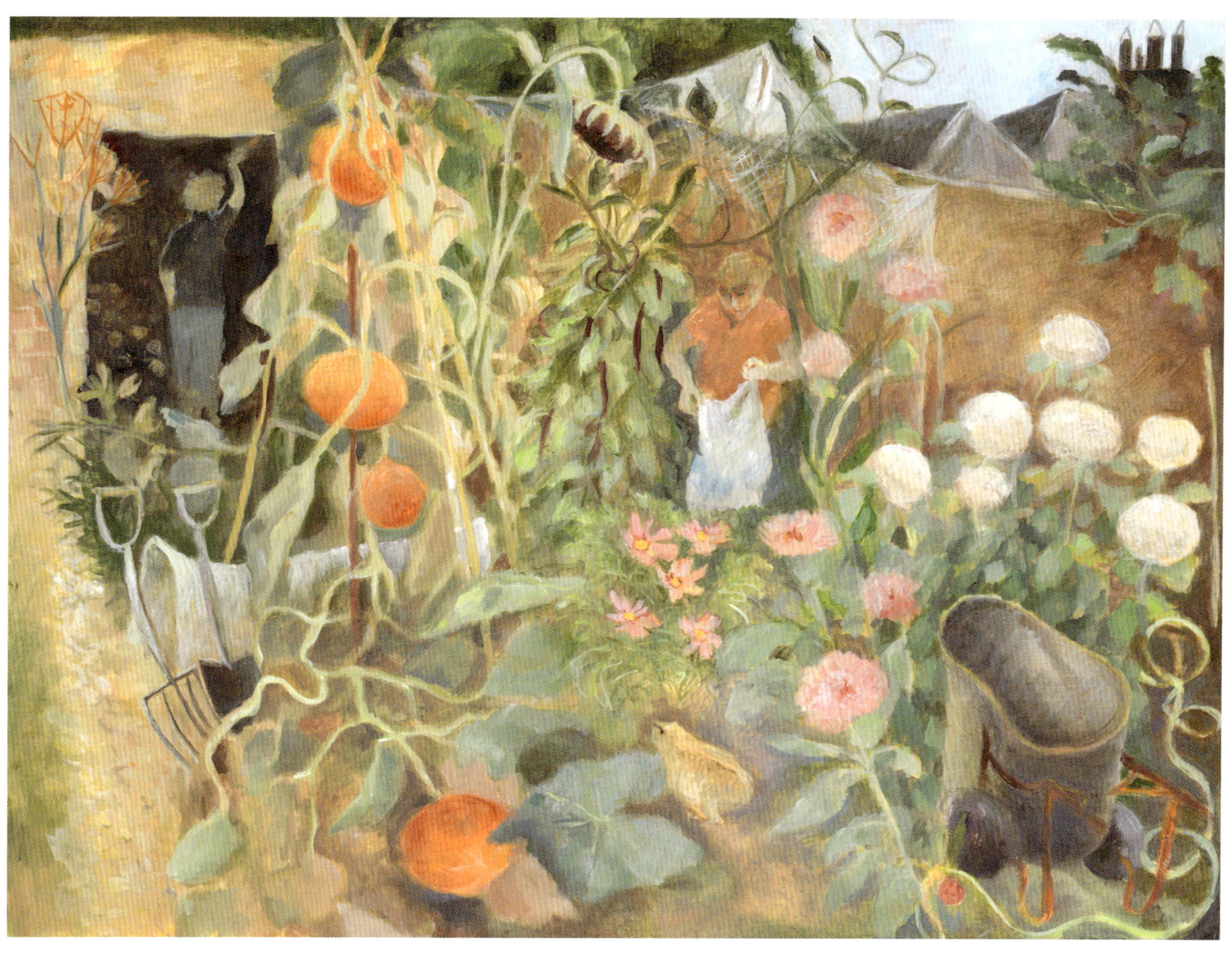

Pumpkin Pyramid
2020 · oil on board · 46 x 61 cm / 18 x 24 in

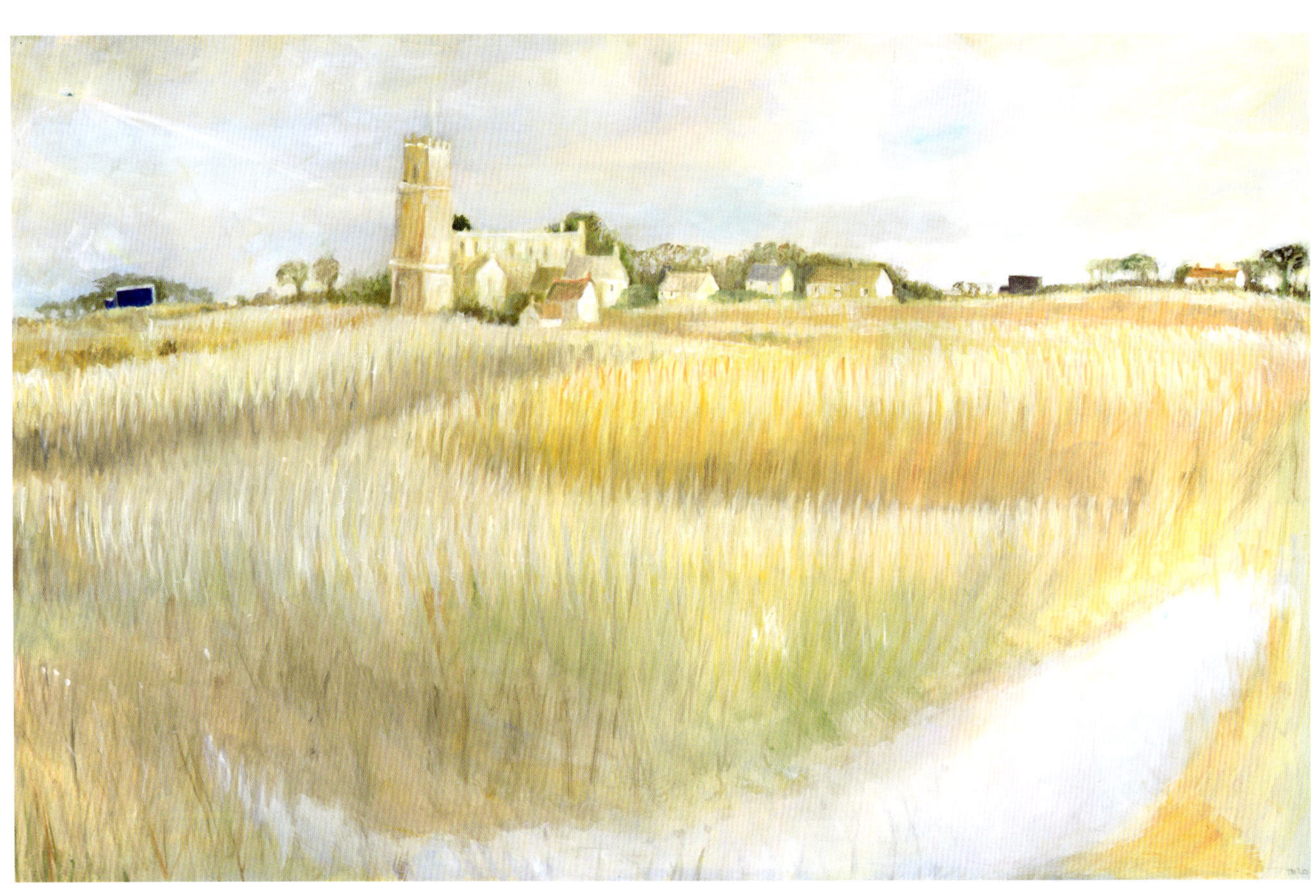

The A12
2020 · oil on board · 58.5 x 89 cm / 23 x 35 in

6 · THE CATHEDRAL OF THE MARSHES

You can cut the holiness with a knife. That's the best way I have come across to describe what it feels like when entering this church — Holy Trinity Church, Blythburgh. As if holiness is softish pink jelly that fills this vast space.

I struggled for some time with how I could describe my feelings on entering this church, expecting to come to a neat conclusion, but I have not. When a priest said I might never be able to say what it is I am wanting to I stopped trying and felt better.

One summer's day both large doors, north and south, were open, and the church space filled with the marsh air. Sometimes the church is filled with sound. I have heard Olivier Messiaen's ethereal music fill it to the high angels and come back to me. The acoustics are superb.

WHAT DO YOU FEEL?

Just as the marsh air can fill the church, being on the marshes can bring the same feelings as being in the church. It can feel right when I feel part of nature, not a separate element. It felt like that swimming in the river there from what is known as the beach below the church toilets. Joined up with the landscape, nothing more or less. Or as Richard Jefferies talks of becoming transparent. In *The Story of My Heart* (1883), he climbs a hill, entirely forgetting 'the petty circumstances and the annoyances of existence'. As he says, becoming lighter and lighter. Sometimes, when you walk far enough along the beach, you can forget your thoughts.

I asked myself what I feel when entering the church. I feel OK. Then I asked other people what they felt:

'Cold. Marsh air trapped. Conscious of the cold ground.' / *'Light, white, a birdcage of stone.'* / *'Height, great height with high windows bringing the light down to the floor.'* / *'The past, can we feel the past? It's an ancient place, far older than the church.'* / *'One woman told me that when her husband was dying, she cut a hole in the hedge, and then could see the church and felt better.'* / *'Safe, I feel safe in there, looked after.'*

I like R.S. Thomas's feelings. The Welsh poet has talked of experiencing something that has gone, is now absent, when finding a hare's 'form' and putting his hand in it. It was still warm. We never actually come across the hare or God but we know they are there. The presence remains but the life has moved on.

BIRDS

I was trudging along the bank on a brown day. It had rained all morning. The ochre-coloured clouds hung over the ochre church, the marshes were brown but studded with pink-red sorrels, the banks a very dark chocolate and the low river ginger. Then a pure white egret rose like an angel.

Once, driving along the main road, cars were slowing down. They were watching crows baiting a marsh harrier, whose impressive wings are said to have inspired the wings of the angels beating their way across the wooden sky of the church roof — to borrow a poetic idea from Ronald Blythe's *The Time by the Sea*.

THE CHURCH AT NIGHT

It's a November evening but it seems like night as it has been dark since 4 pm. The church is spot-lit. Some people feel that churches should not be lit, that we should be allowed our darkness. It's

impressive, though. It acts as a beacon across the
marshes, shining all the way up the valley from its
elevated position. Close up, the flints and tracery
are highlighted and, even when the church is shut,
by reaching up to look through the window you
can see the shadow patterns played out on the
walls inside.

The dead seem more present at night. The
tombstones appear to be standing up a little more.
Someone's busy on the path below the graveyard.
It's a badger on his night ramblings. Often we see
just signs of badgers, but now we are actually seeing
one. I imagine him curling up in his set amongst
the bones.

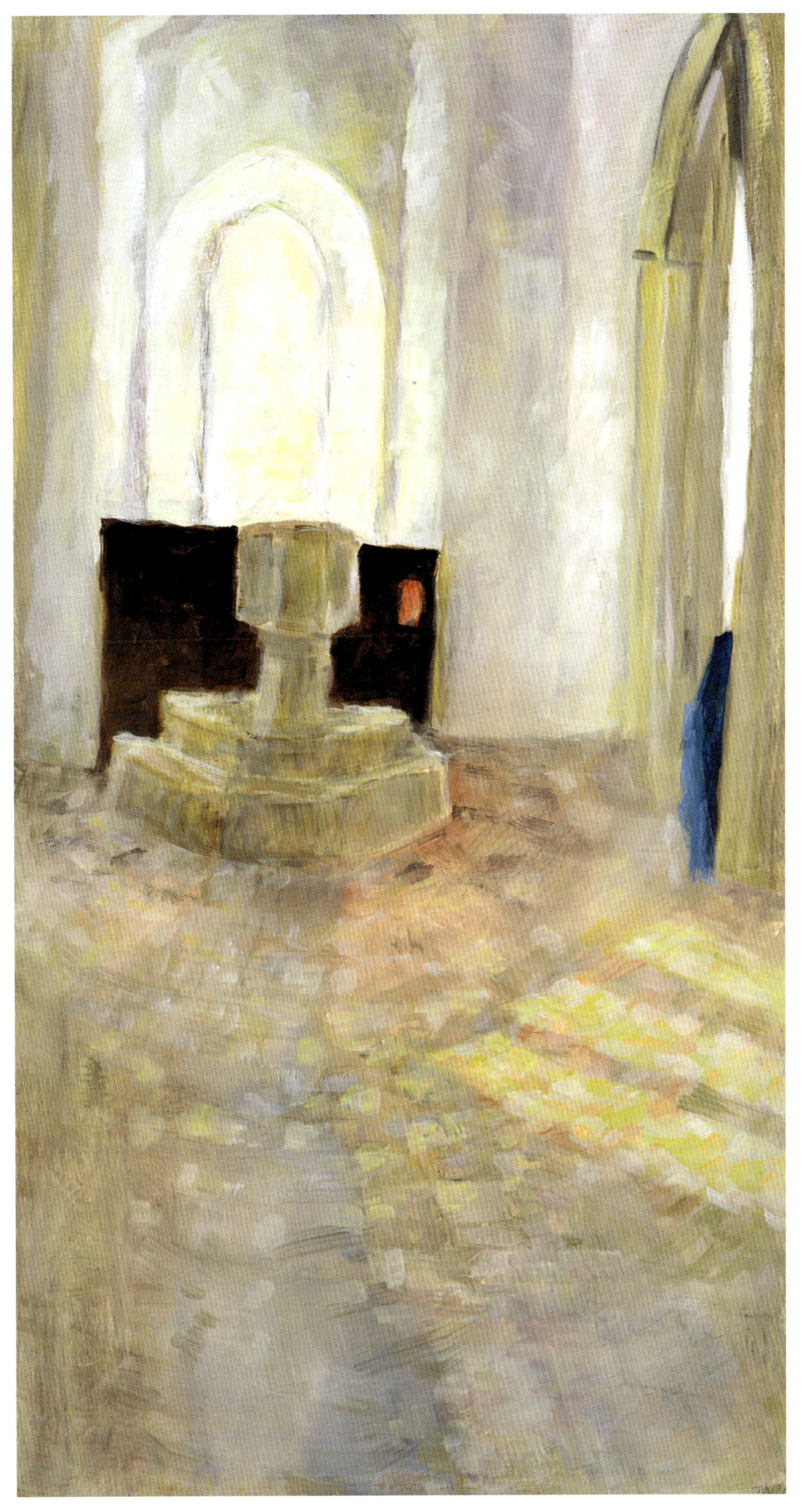

The Light
2020 · oil on board
43 x 23 cm / 17 x 9 in

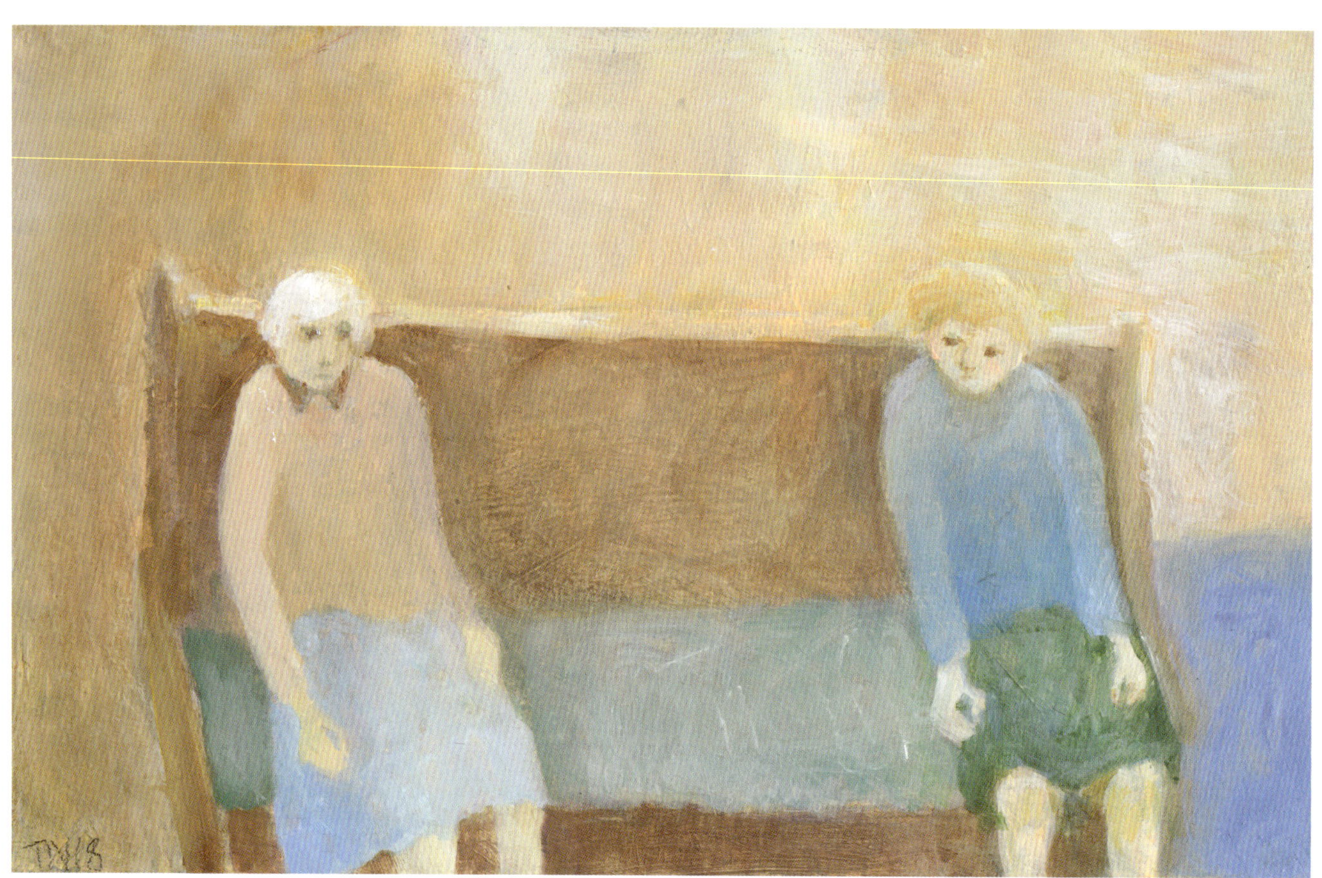

With Her Mother
2018 · oil on board · 15 x 23.5 cm / 6 x 9¼ in

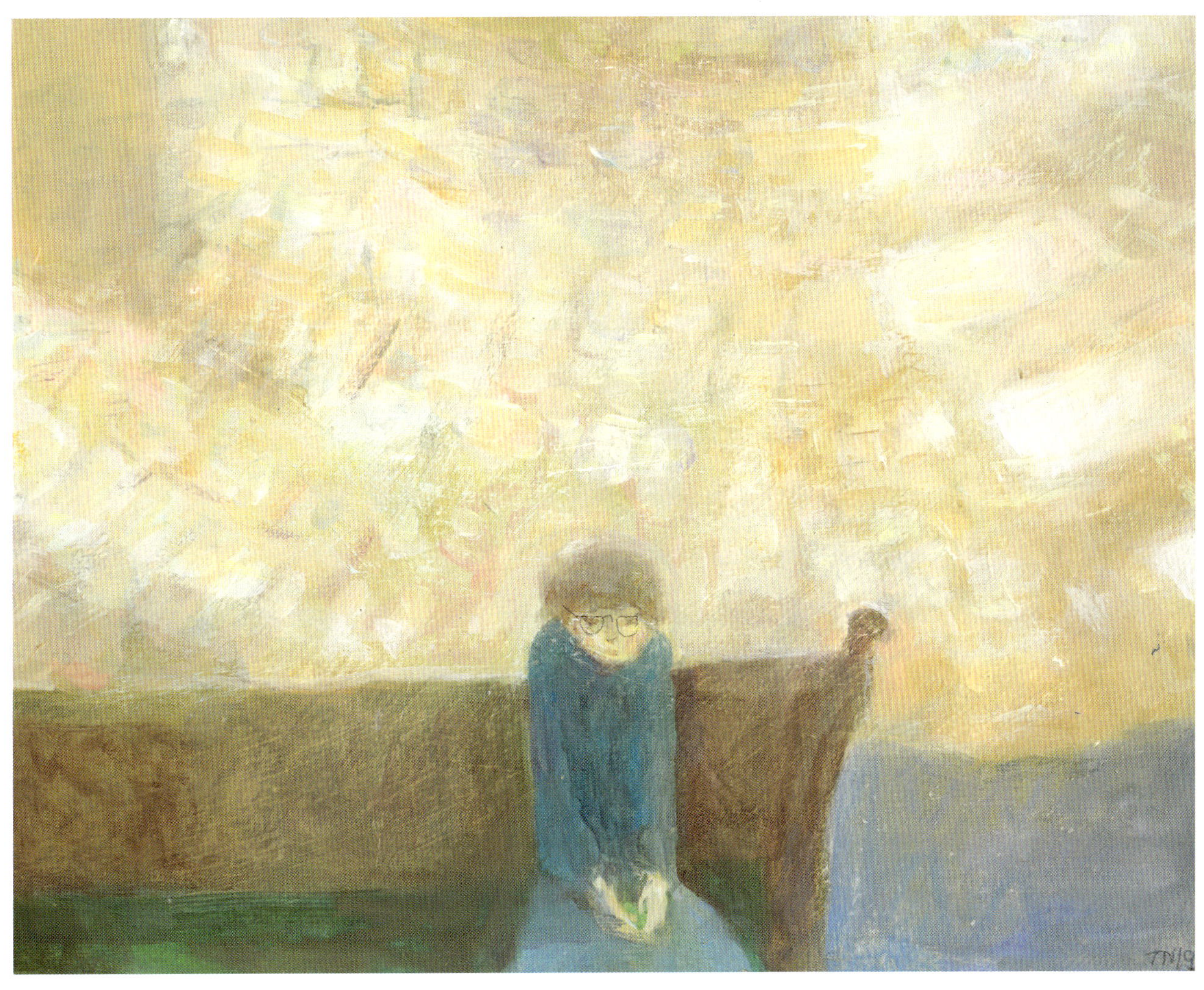

Having a Sit
2019 · oil on board · 18 x 22 cm / 7 x 8¾ in

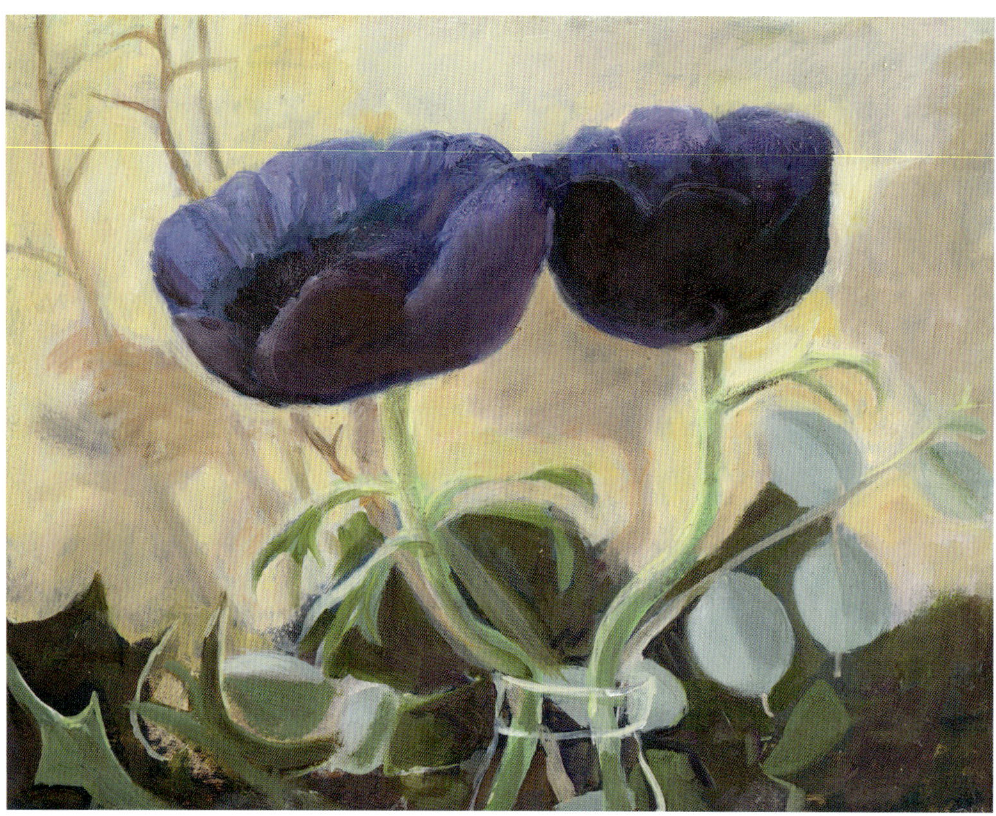

Church Porch Flowers
2018 · oil on board · 20.5 x 25 cm / 8 x 9¾ in

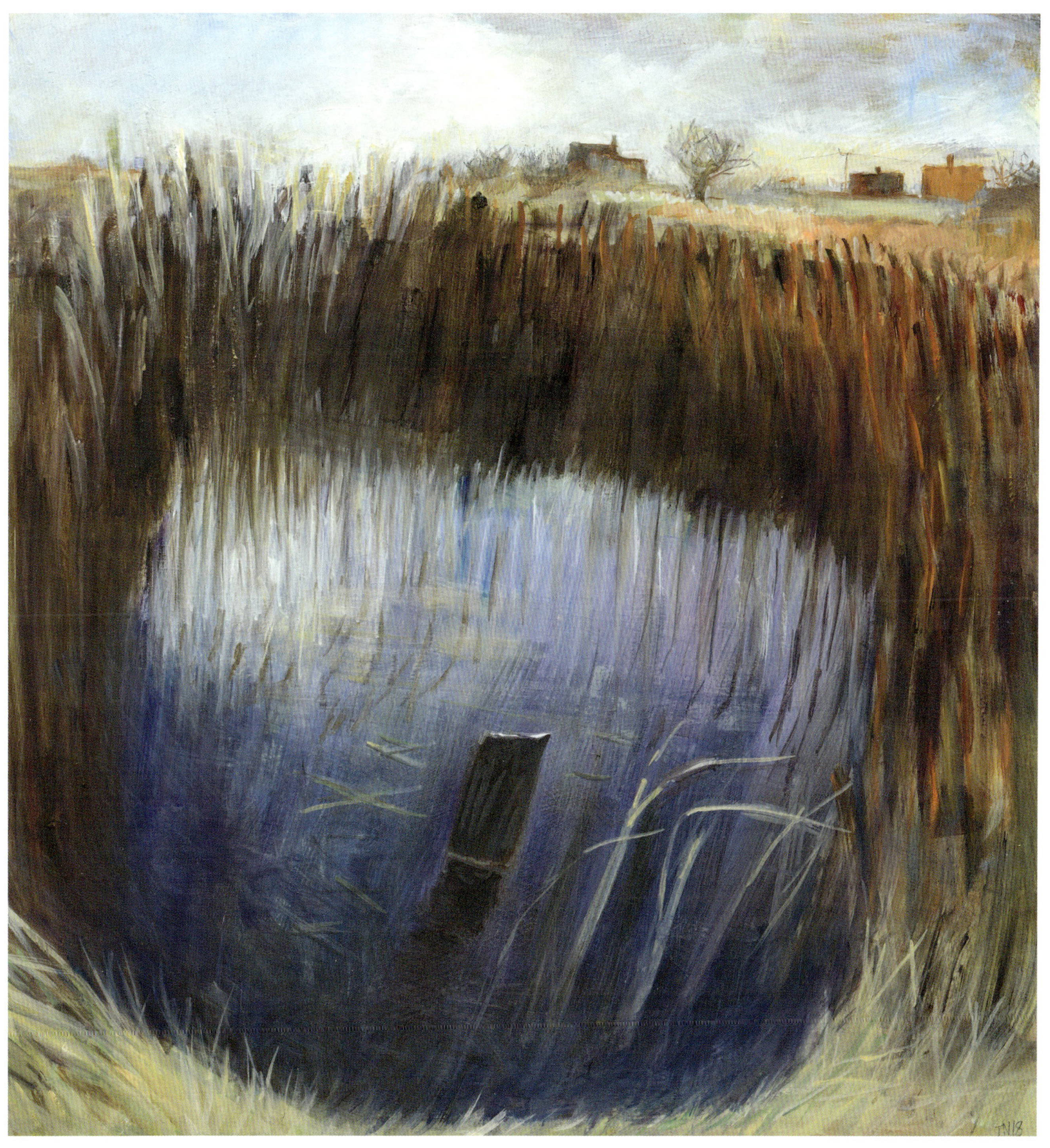

Cold Marsh Pond
2018 · oil on board · 47.5 x 43 cm / 18¾ x 17 in

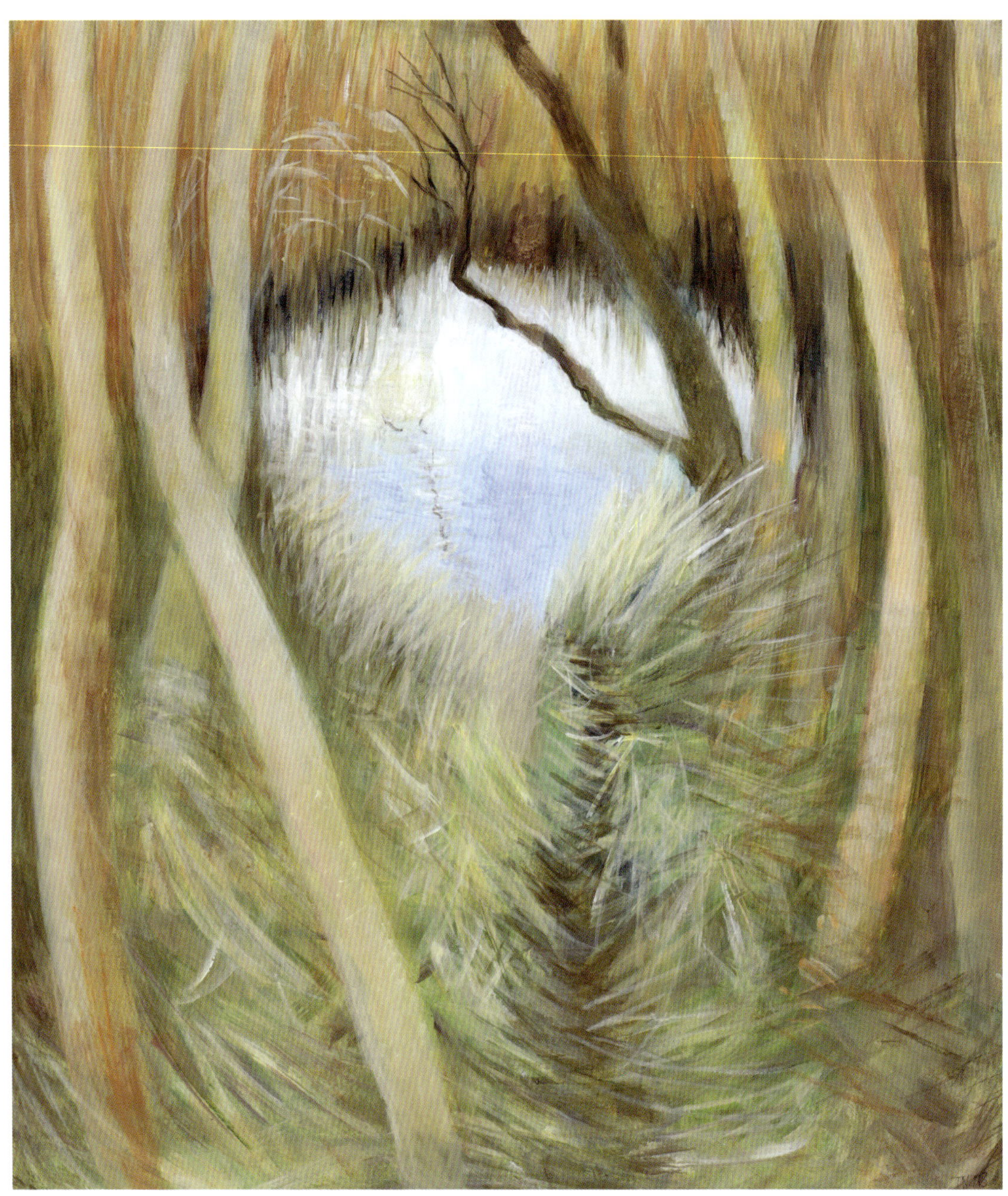

An Animal Path to a Pond
2020 · oil on board · 39.5 x 33 cm / 15½ x 13 in

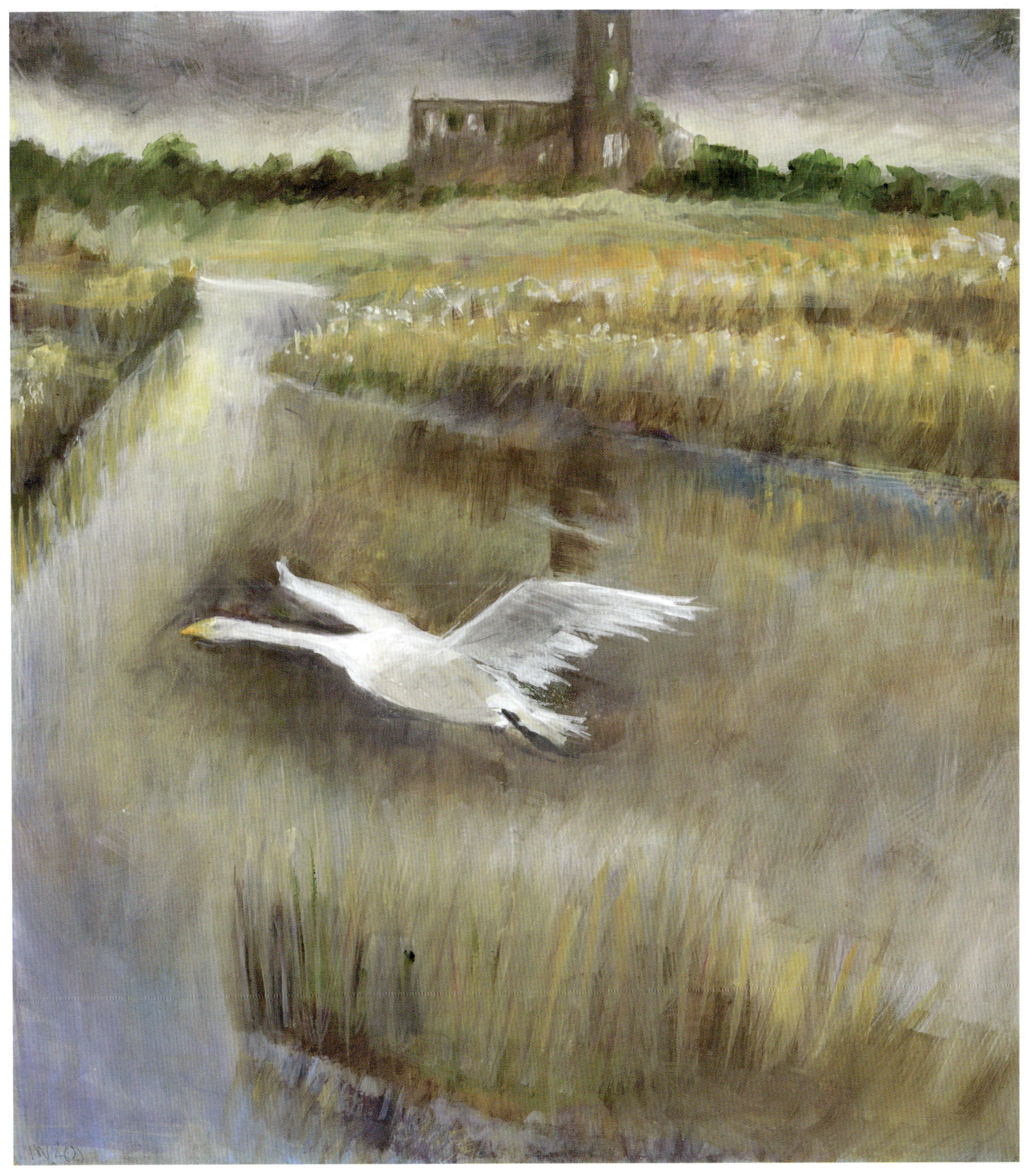

Brown Day
2020 · oil on board · 46 x 40 cm / 18 x 15¾ in

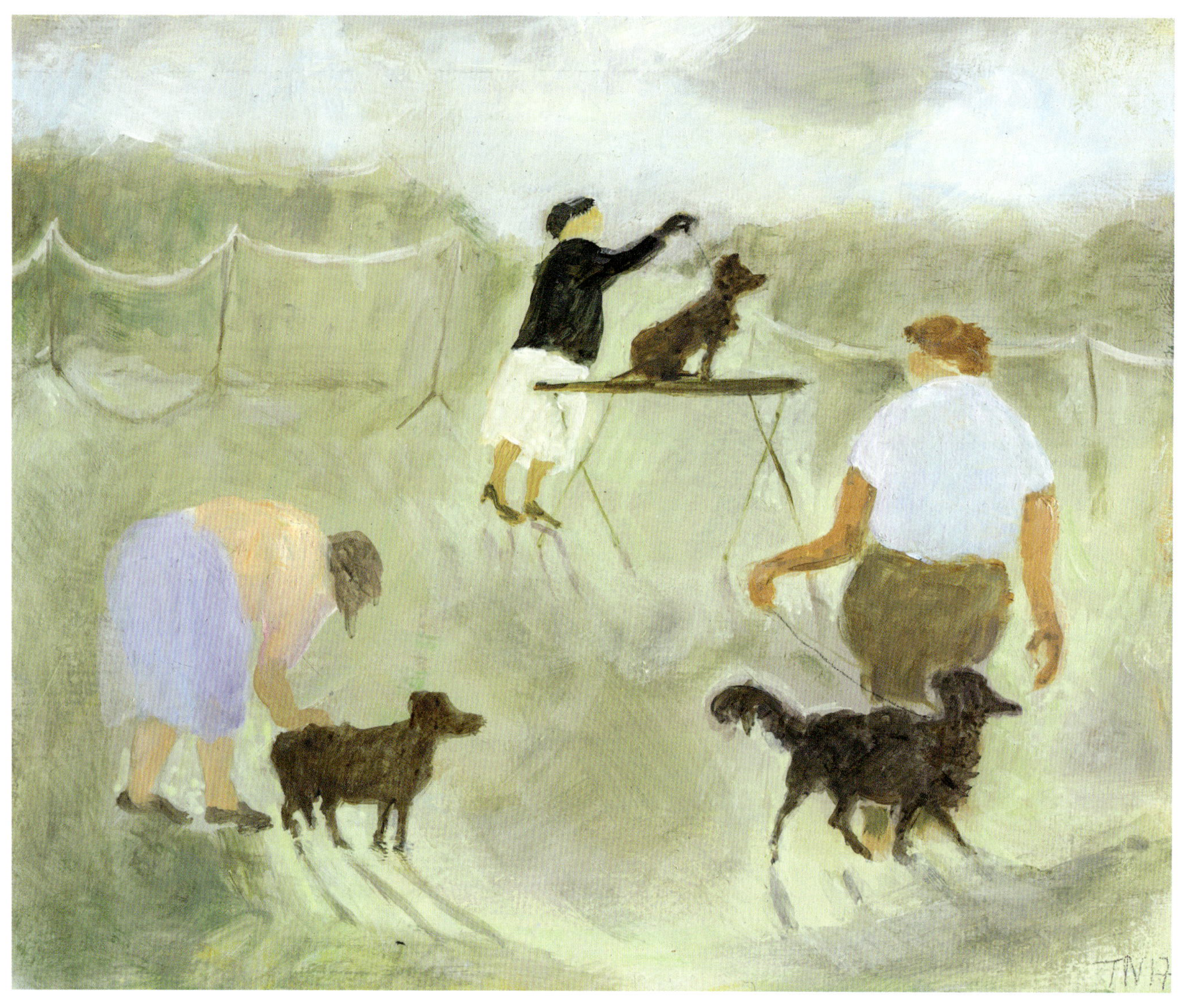

Looking Their Best
2017 · oil on board · 15 x 18 cm / 6 x 7 in

7 · DOG SHOWS

I go to the dog show as an outsider. It makes it easier to be an observer. I have not taken my dog (a miniature dachshund) again, because when I did she was so terrified it was cruel. I go to dog shows without a dog.

A dog show is an event that people turn out for. There are many spectacles, many people, and then there are the dogs. It's so noisy, even a little show has a loud tannoy. The thing is they are often a sub-event to a main show, so you might get a County Show or a Tractor Plough Day with the Dog Show in the corner. You can tell as you arrive because owners are mingling with their exotic-looking dogs amongst the tractors and birds of prey.

SHOWS LARGE AND SMALL

There are the professional dog shows, which are out of my league, and there are the smaller ones. The second sort tend to start around 11 o'clock with the serious classes: Best Dog Under One Year, Best Small Dog, Best Pedigree and Best Bitch — which are important to the owners and for getting your dog seen if you are a breeder. Families are often known for one breed, so you see family groups of people and family groups of dogs.

After the lunch break we have the fun classes, or sometimes you just get a Fun Dog Show — questionable whether the dog finds it fun, particularly if they have to be dressed up. Young Handlers' classes are nice as often the children are impressive with their understanding of an animal. Then: Golden Oldies; Dog Most Like Its Owner; Happiest Dog (this was a lovely event, with all the terms of endearment usually only heard at home. One elderly man stood with his greyhound for ages in the hot sun. He did not need to say anything to his dog; you could see the bond between them.); Waggiest Tail; Dog the Judge Would Most Like to Take Home with Him. Often the same dog appears in many classes while the family sit on the bales behind the ropes, silently cheering them on.

In a small show the classes cost £1 to enter. You put your name on as many as you want. It all takes ages. The dogs go round, then the judges go round. The dogs are individually presented in the way that best shows off their breed and there is a bit of banter between the owner and the judge that one can only imagine because of the loud tannoy from other events. And then they return, and then the dogs go round again, and then they are pulled out to the centre in reverse order. Finally the rosettes and the free packets of dog biscuits are given out and the contestants go round again before they leave the ring.

FANCY DRESS

Usually a nice kerfuffle of dogs and children. But one man new to the event, and rather keen on military outfits, got himself all done up in uniform, complete with jackboots, whereas the dog only had a studded collar. It did not go down well with the judge. You dress the dog, not yourself. The prize went to a small girl with an angel on a lead.

TERRIER RACES

Terrier Races, often a separate event in the main ring, are very exciting. The super-excited terriers are released from a van and then charge, hell-for-leather, through hoops and over hurdles after whatever the quarry is. It is a short event and much fun, because everyone likes a happy dog.

DOG RACES

There is another show that has The Dog Race
as the finale after the children's races, after all
the coconuts have been knocked off their perches
and won, after the fruit and vegetables have been
collected from the marquee. The giant pumpkins,
as if they had been pumped-up for the judges' eyes,
now begin to collapse, a trickle of liquid from their
bases staining the table. They are so big they will
have to be dealt with later.

For The Dog Race, we all gather on the bales
lining the racetrack. Small dogs first at one end
with their handlers and an up-ended bicycle
contraption at the other, which is hand-pedalled
as fast as possible to tow the lure just faster than
the yapping pack. Then the middle-sized dogs,
which goes off quite well. Then the large dogs.
But — there is a problem with the bicycle contraption and a delay and fiddling with the wire.
Tension mounts. At the far end the handlers
crouch beside their hounds, which are straining
at their leashes and looking very big. Finally the
wire is untangled. Then Off! — they hurl themselves towards us but don't stop. Now it's like a
medieval hunting scene. They pass the bait, leap
the bales, and career onto the field, very pleased
with themselves, and have to be captured by their
owners before anything worse happens.

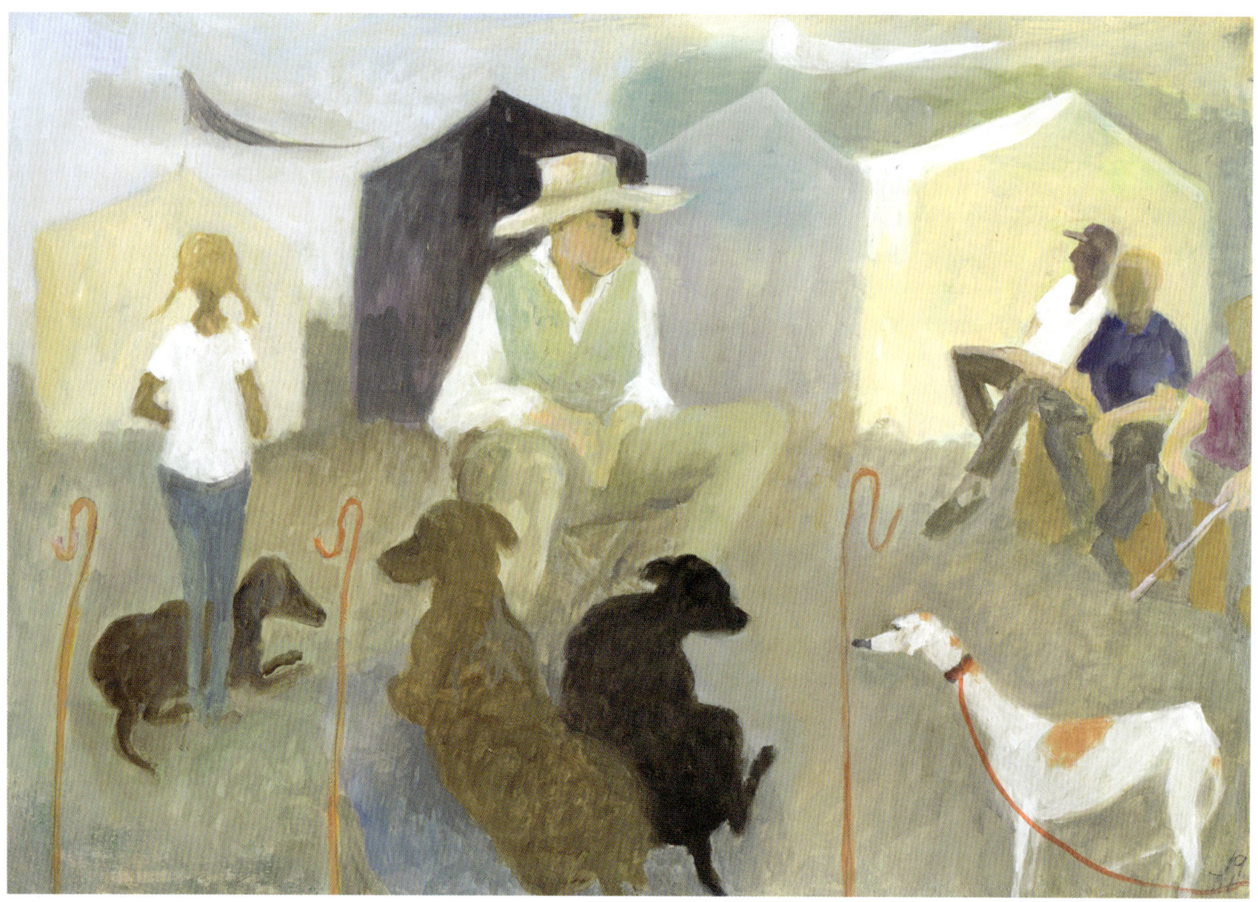

We Watch Different Things
2019 · oil on board · 20.5 x 27.5 cm / 8 x 10¾ in

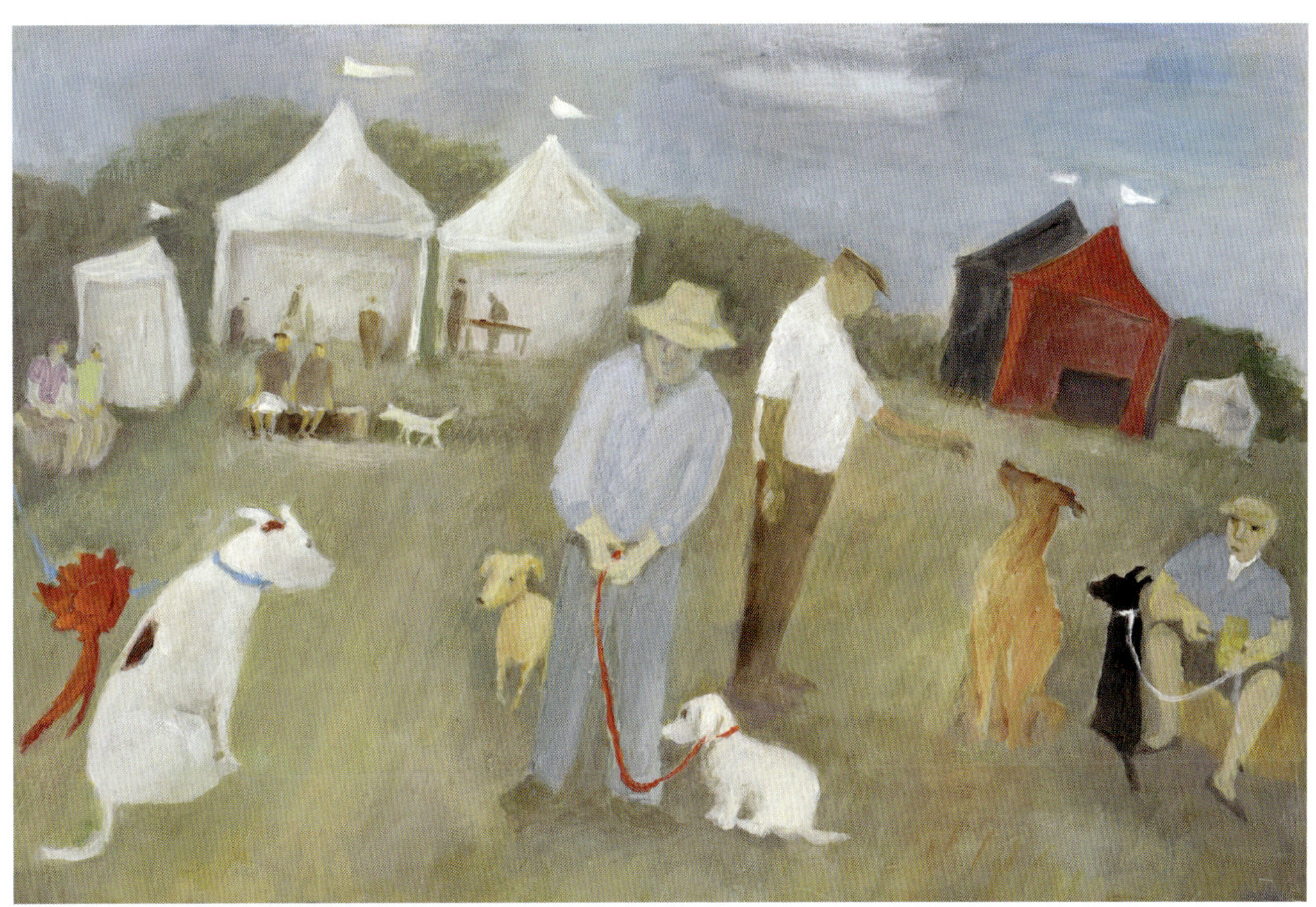

Best Friends
2015 · oil on board · 20.5 x 30.5 cm / 8 x 12 in

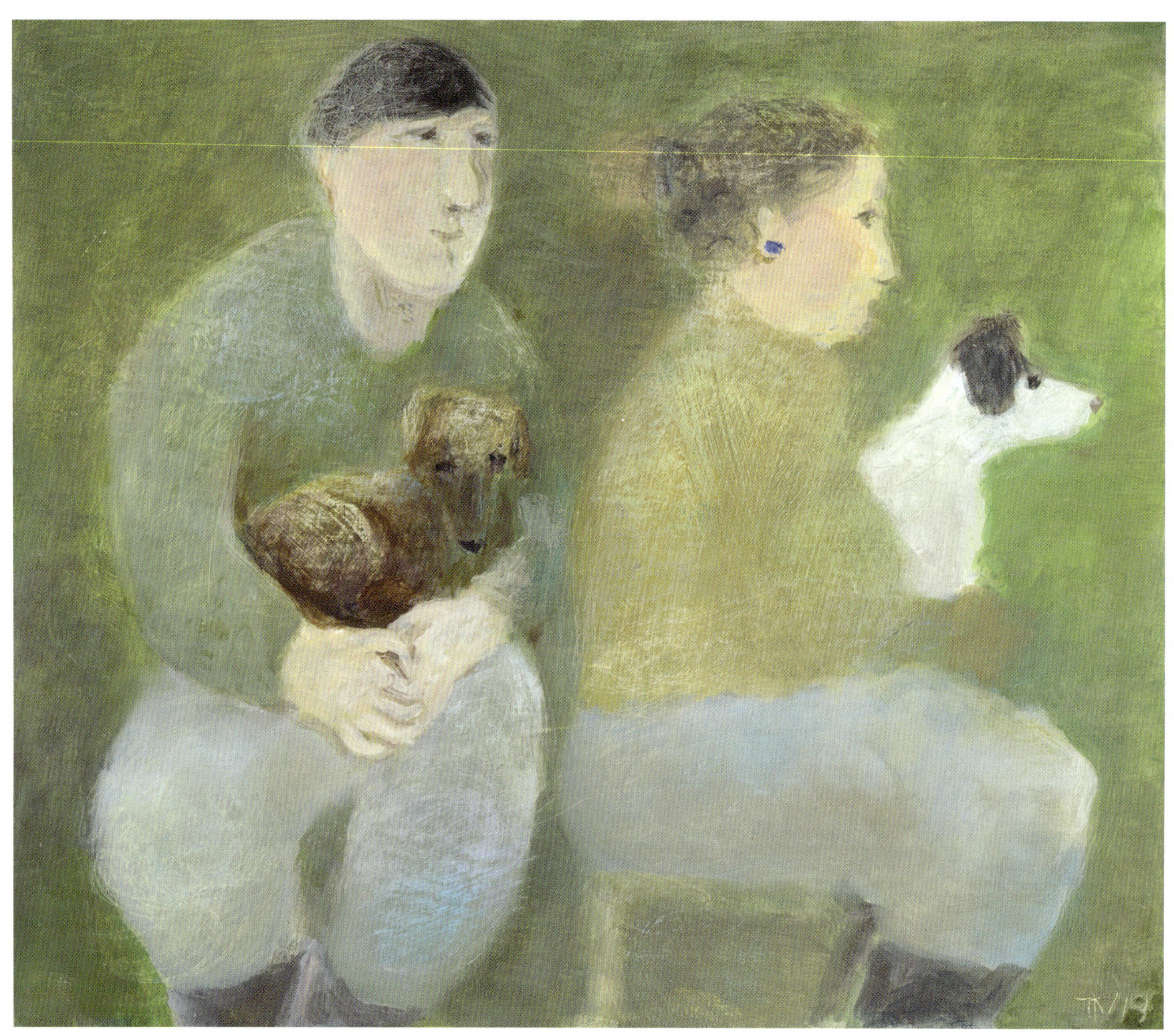

Keen Interest
2019 · oil on board · 18 x 20.5 cm / 7 x 8 in

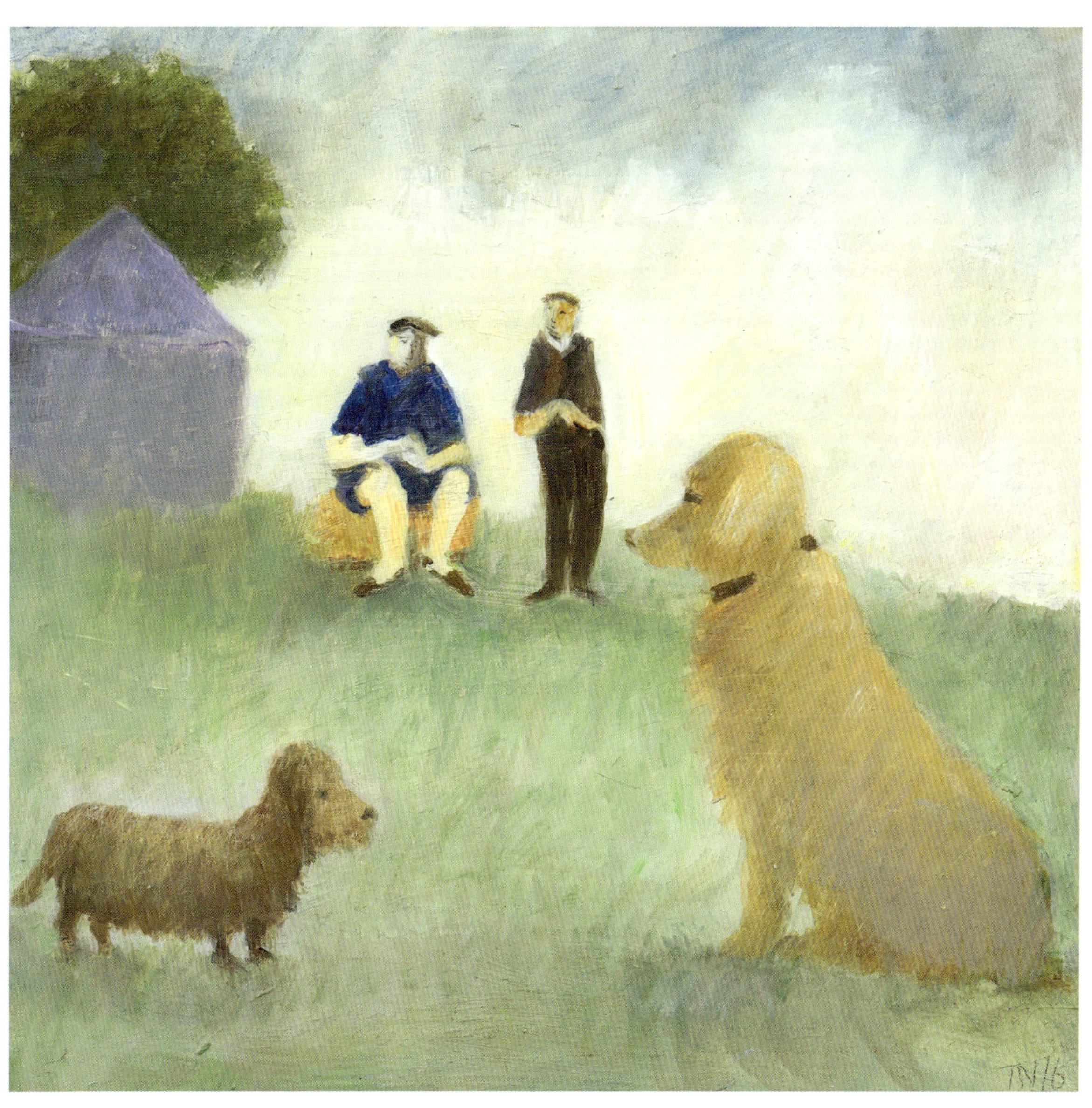

Judging
2016 · oil on board · 18 x 18 cm / 7 x 7 in

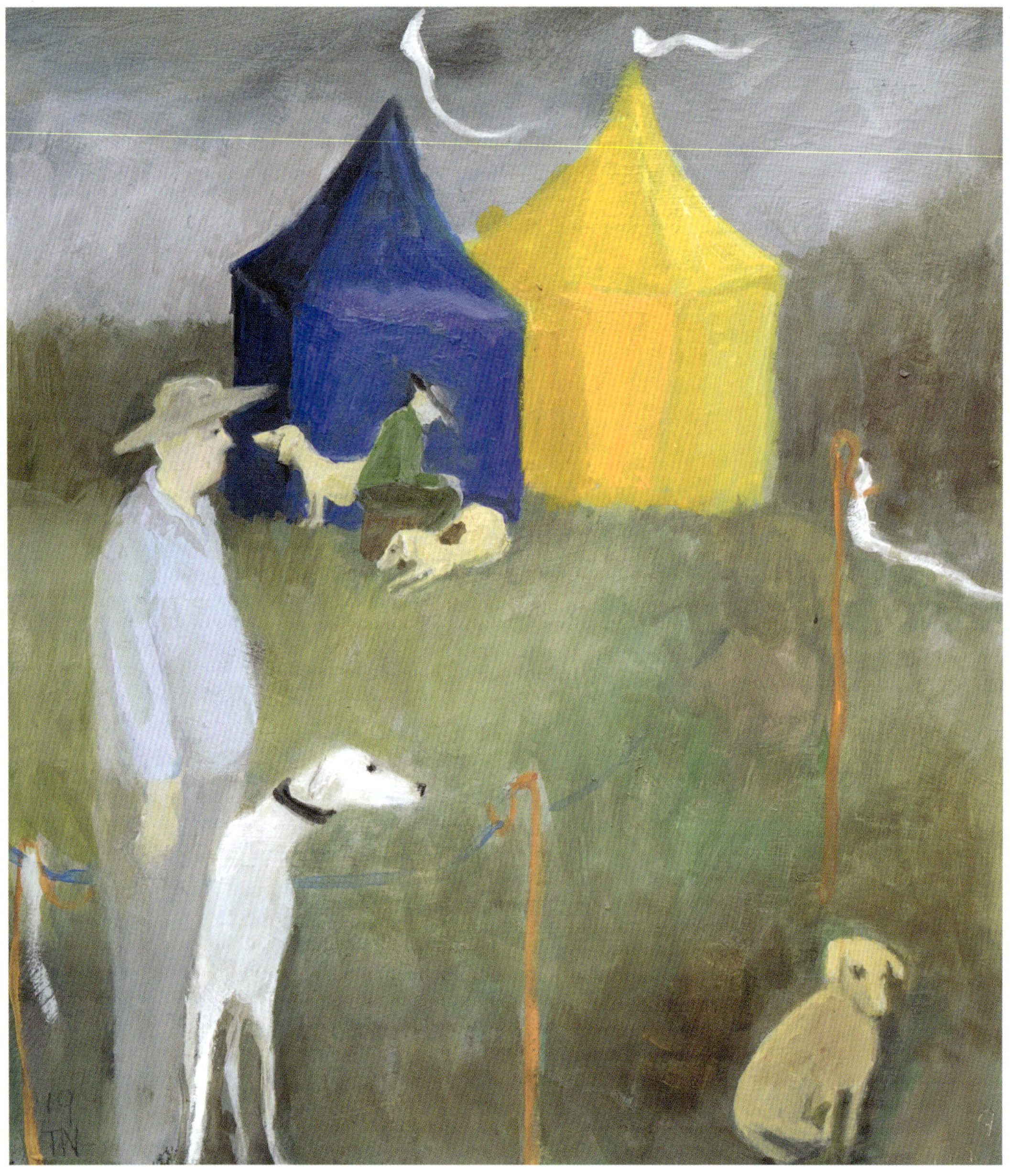

Best Bitch
2019 · oil on board · 19 x 16.5 cm / 7½ x 6½ in

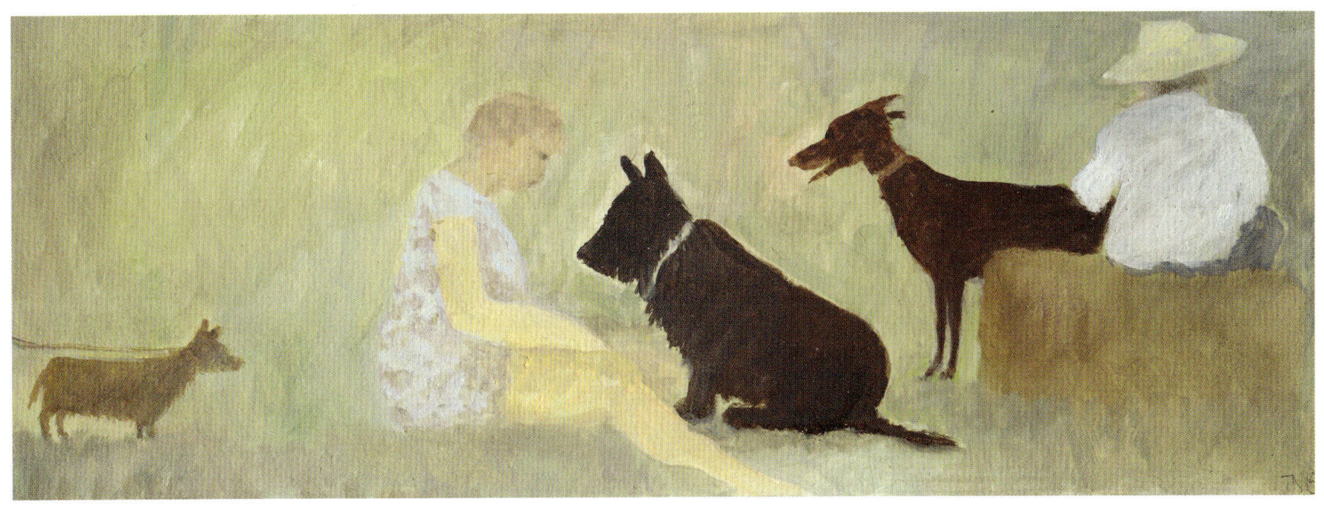

Variety
2015 · oil on board · 10 x 28.5 cm / 4 x 11¼ in

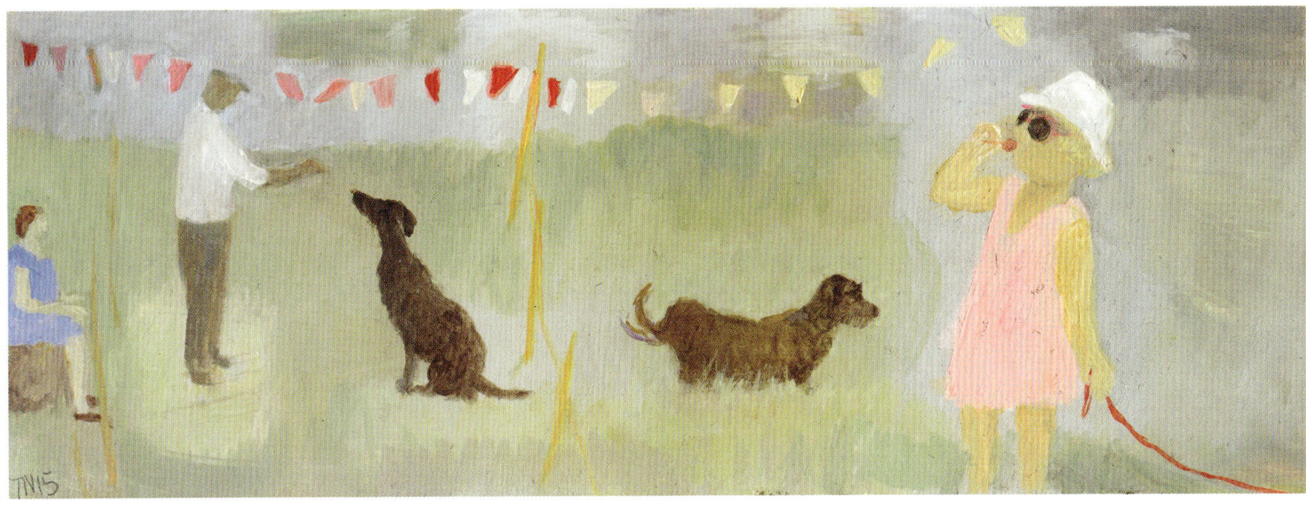

Treats
2015 · oil on board · 10 x 26.5 cm / 4 x 10½ in

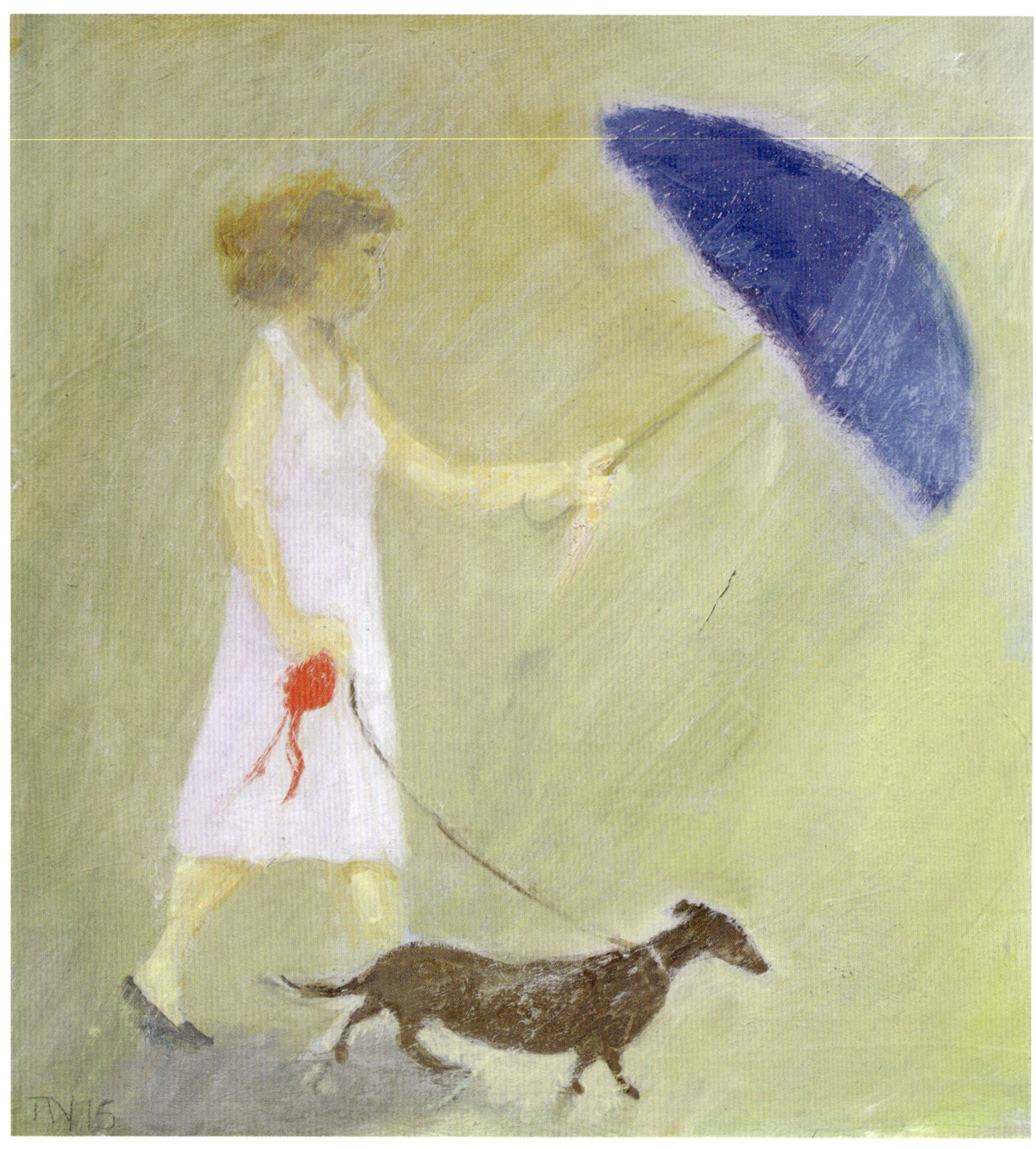

Shade for 'Best in Show'
2015 · oil on board · 17 x 15 cm / 6¾ x 6 in

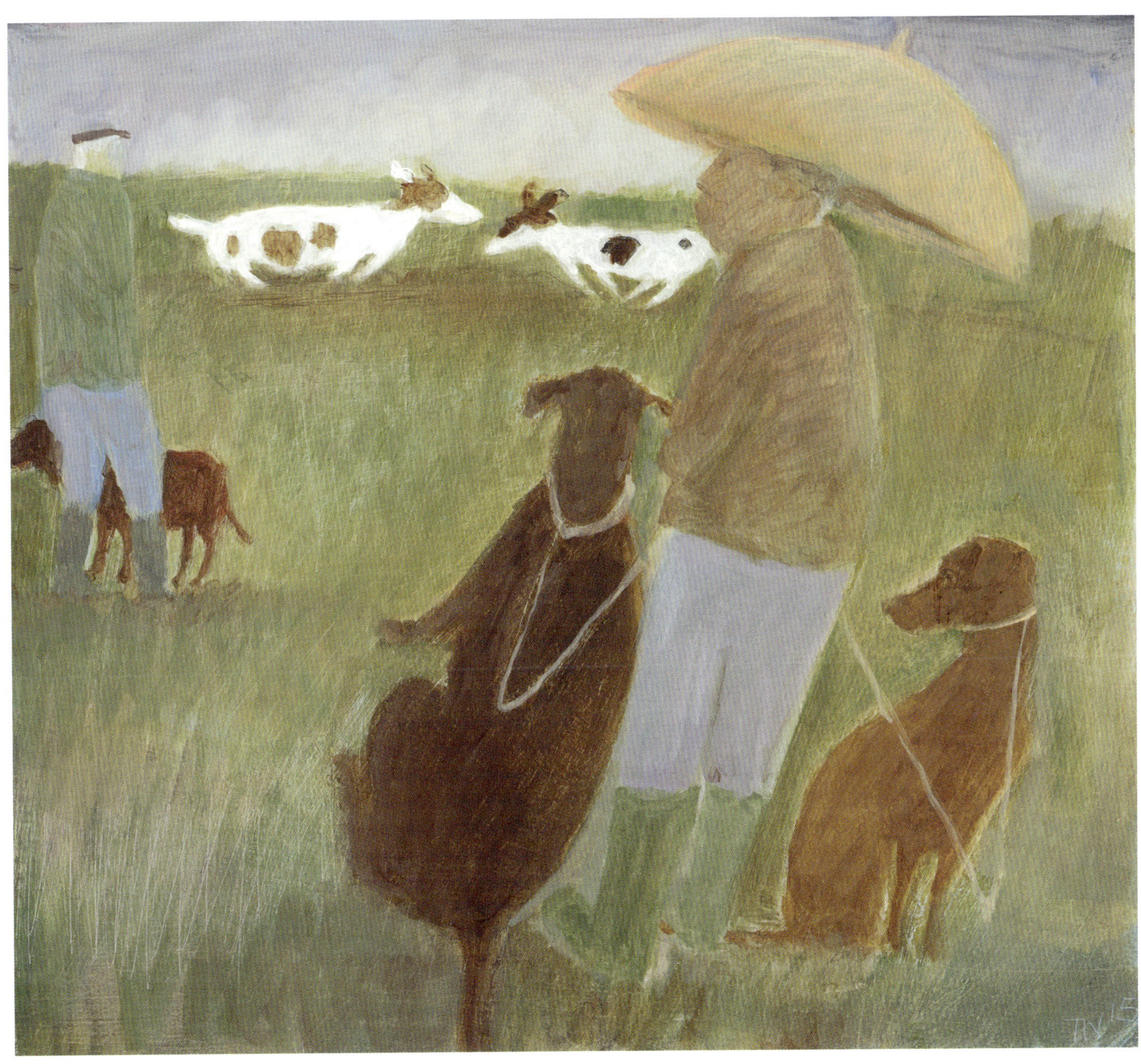

Terrier Racing
2015 · oil on board · 18.5 x 20.5 cm / 7¼ x 8 in

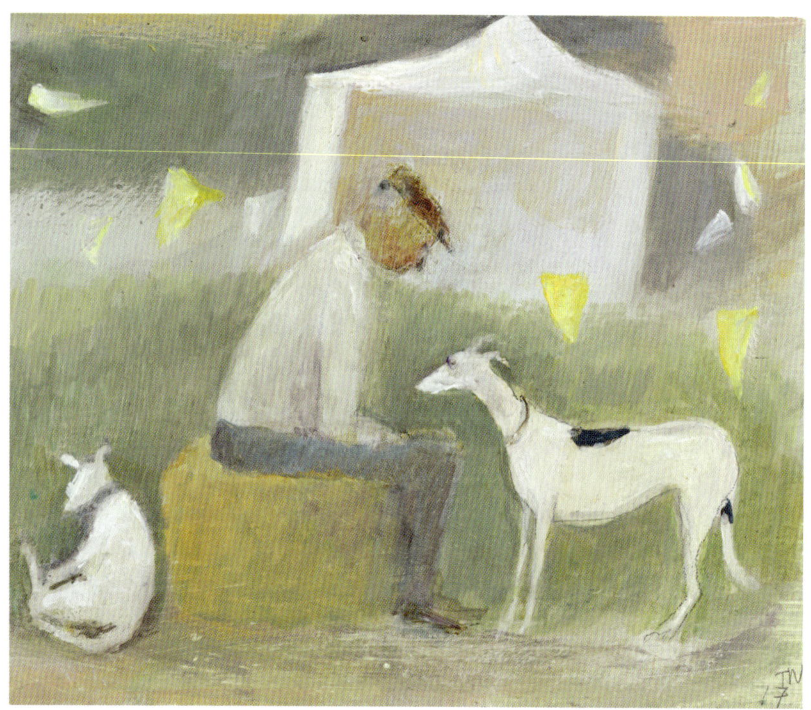

Understanding
2017 · oil on board · 10 x 11.5 cm / 4 x 4½ in

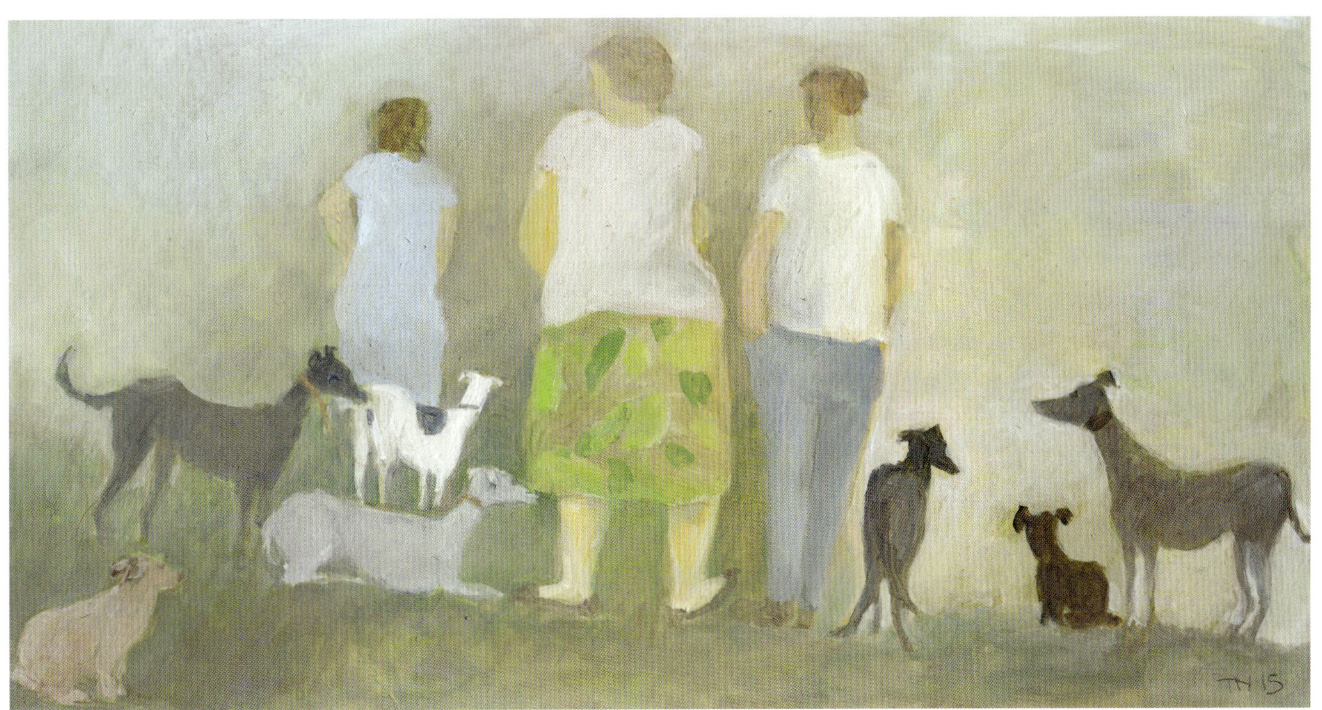

Watching the Show
2015 · oil on board · 13.5 x 25.5 cm / 5¼ x 10 in

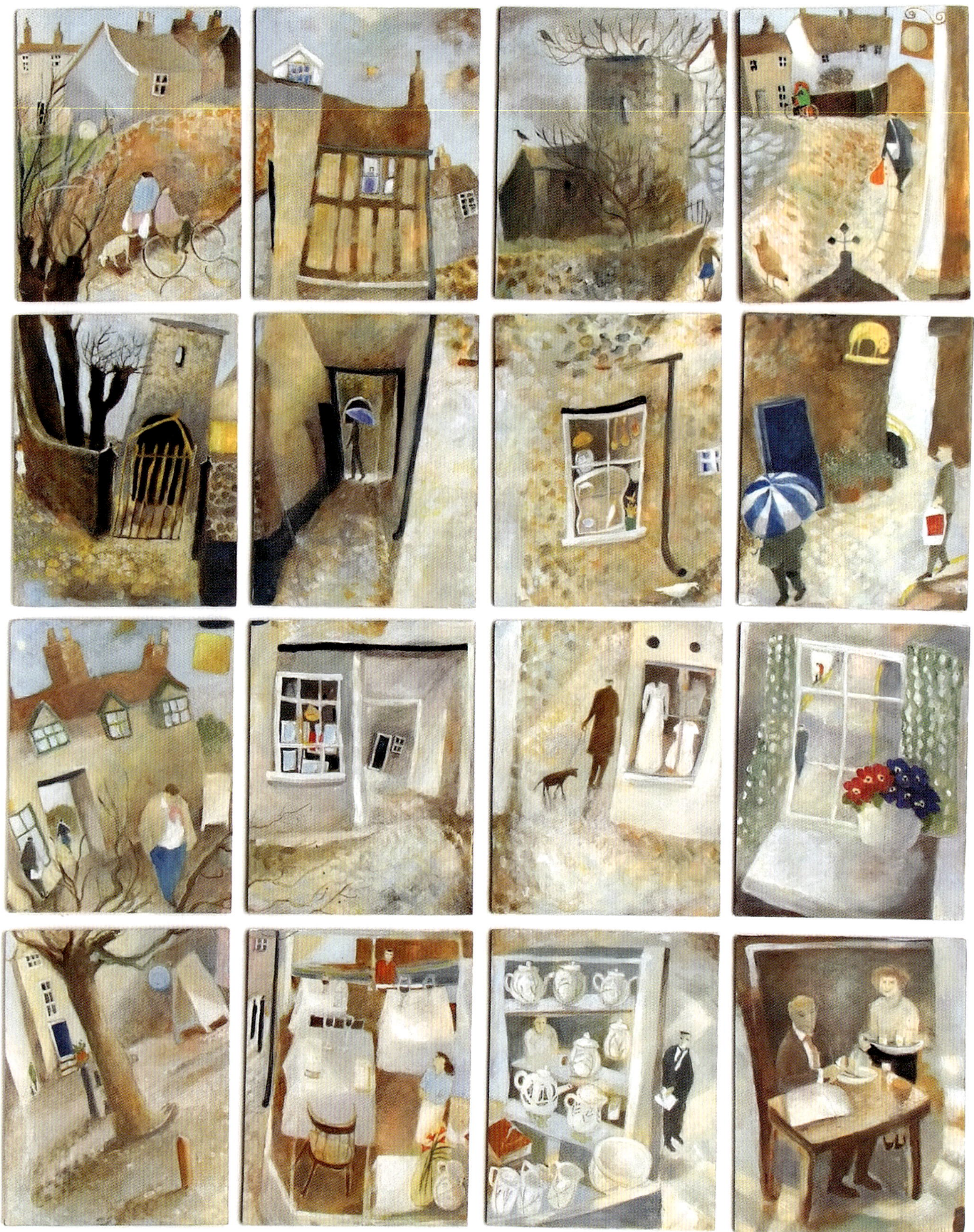

Old Norwich
2011 · oil on board · 25.5 x 20.5 cm (x 16) / 10 x 8 in (x 16)

8 · ELM HILL

Fake snow. Snow blows at me but it's the wrong season. It's coming from a machine and some people are wearing Victorian garb, mixed in with others in trendy clothes and standing amongst vans, silver boxes and cables — a film crew. I can't go to Elm Hill at the moment as the entrance to it is blocked to pedestrians because of the filming. But in my mind's eye I am imagining it as it appears in films — which it does, sometimes as a generalised backdrop for Dickensian streets.

NOTHING DISTURBING HERE

Elm Hill is Norwich's most picturesque street. As Pevsner and Wilson's guide to Norwich and the North-East says, 'There is not a single house in Elm Hill which could be disturbing.' Each house is wonderful in its oddness and history and all are different. There are doors that are used, and there are large, closed never-to-be-open doors; there are passageways, yards, places where the corners of the buildings have been taken off by carriages turning in, and a rabbit warren of underground passages that link cellars I'm told I can only imagine underneath the cobbles.

But Elm Hill is real too, not just a showpiece. It's lived in by residents and teddy bears, and is used by young men on their way to cafés, their arms round their laptops. It has shops of the interesting sort: a bookshop, an antique shop, a taxidermist who stuffs ravens and dresses mice by lamplight, and cafés. Cafés that are busy and cafés that are not. A teashop where you can sit in a yard on your own and drink in the past. In one café, women talk and older couples order the cheese scones. The café's fairly busy. It's 11 o'clock. There are crosswords to do on the tables. The sun only stops when people pass the window, and there is a Bob Dylan song in the background.

There's a shop that sells teddy bears. Wall to wall. Floor to ceiling, hundreds of glassy eyes staring at you. They have all kinds of names: Togs, Threads, Rags, Long Golden Curly, Long Golden Curly with Growl, Long Golden Curly with Brahms' Lullaby. It's such a nice shop, even if you are wary of teddy bears you might end up buying one.

COBBLES

The cobbles on Elm Hill are rather like a frozen beach. Difficult to walk on if you are wearing heels, but even if you aren't they could easily twist your ankle. Like brown eggs they have to be laid upright and not on their sides, because that's how they are stronger. That is why some of them are still here after all those wagons have trundled over them. Imagine the noise in the fifteenth and sixteenth centuries, when behind the frontages of shops and houses on this street, all kinds of businesses carried on, with their dirt and smells.

Many of the merchant houses on this street had quays on the river Wensum, which was a thoroughfare to Great Yarmouth and beyond. Stand in the now useful car park between the street and the river and look up at the big windows of some of the workshops located at the back of the houses. They were designed to let the light in for weavers who came from the Low Countries as religious refugees. They worked their trade weaving, Norwich being famous for its fine shawls, until their eyesight failed. They were called Strangers, and so we have Strangers' Hall. Between the merchants' houses and the river were the workers' homes. The divide was huge but the distance is not.

HENRY NINHAM'S ELM HILL

I go to the castle (Norwich Castle Museum and
Art Gallery), which is a few streets away from the
river up on a hill, home to the Norwich School of
Painters, the most famous being John Sell Cotman
and John Crome. There is an undated painting of
Elm Hill houses by Henry Ninham (1796–1874),
who was also part of that group. It shows the corner
of Elm Hill where Waggon and Horses Lane comes
in. Not much has changed. In the painting, a man
crosses with a long bundle of something, a woman
walks the other way, washing hangs from the
windows, the cathedral spire is in the distance.
I go back to my drawing on that corner; some
buildings are recognisable and a man is loading
roof tiles, balancing them on his shoulder and
holding them steady with his head; people pass,
the spire always in the distance.

ST PETER HUNGATE CHURCH –
OPEN TO SUN AND SOUND

This is a square black church on the corner before
you turn down Elm Hill. Today it's summer and
the north doors are open. Open to the medieval
view. Below is the Britons Arms (the oldest building in the street, the sort of place you would meet
an aunt for lunch), the outside of The Garth
(a medieval courtyard), and then on down to the
river. St Peter Hungate's garden is planted with
artichokes and cardoons, lavender and rosemary
– medieval plants. The church is now home to the
county's medieval glass collection. Light usually
enters through the stained colours; today it's
also let in through the door.

I went into the church one summer after-
noon, and music seemed to be coming from the
very building itself, as if held in its fabric since
medieval times. This came from a sound-sculpture
– 'Sihlabelela' – hosted by the church in 2019 and
created by Mira Calix. It features recordings of
fifty different people singing a refrain, coming
from tape players balanced on plinths, so as I walk
around the church I am carried by a raft of their
sound. I look up to the fragments of medieval glass
arranged in the windows. I find these fragments,
in amber and ultramarine lozenges of glass, more
valuable than if the complete window was there.

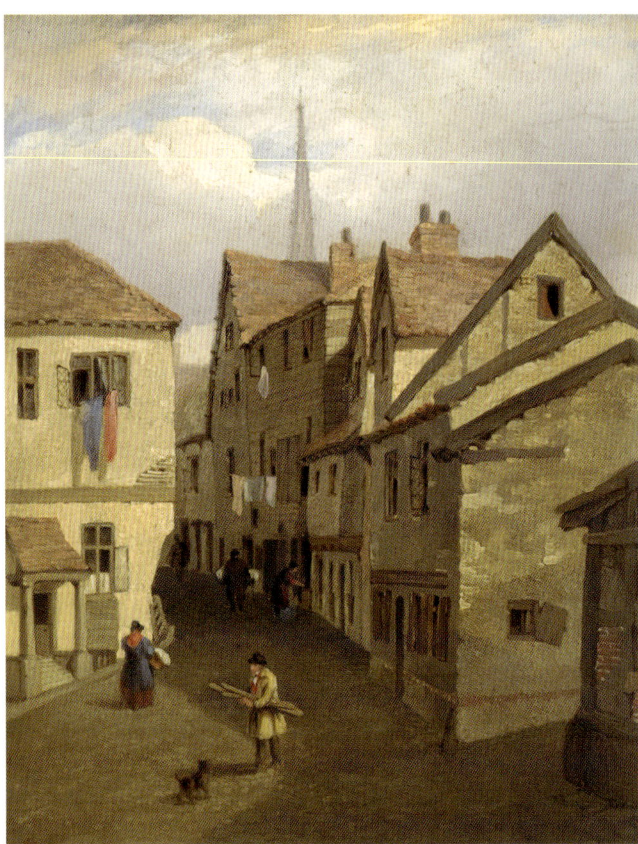

Henry Ninham · *Old Houses, Elm Hill, Norwich*
undated · oil on millboard · 23 x 18 cm / 9 x 7 in
Norfolk Museums Service (Norwich Castle Museum & Art Gallery)

The church's benches are against the wall, so the
floors can sing too, in the sunlight and the music.
The bench-ends are carved by apprentices, boys
who have not seen seals or griffons, so we have oak
carvings that look like mermaids, or griffons that
have bendy legs. Their heads are polished by years
of hands, and now by the sun. Sweet 3 pm.

OLD NORWICH

It used to have elm trees in the square. Due to
Dutch elm disease it now has a plane tree. The
Strangers who came from the Low Countries,
bringing their trades with them, also brought their
canaries, which is why the football team is called
the Canaries. There used to be a canary with copper
saucepans in a window overlooking the plane tree.
I've painted them, but now they have gone.

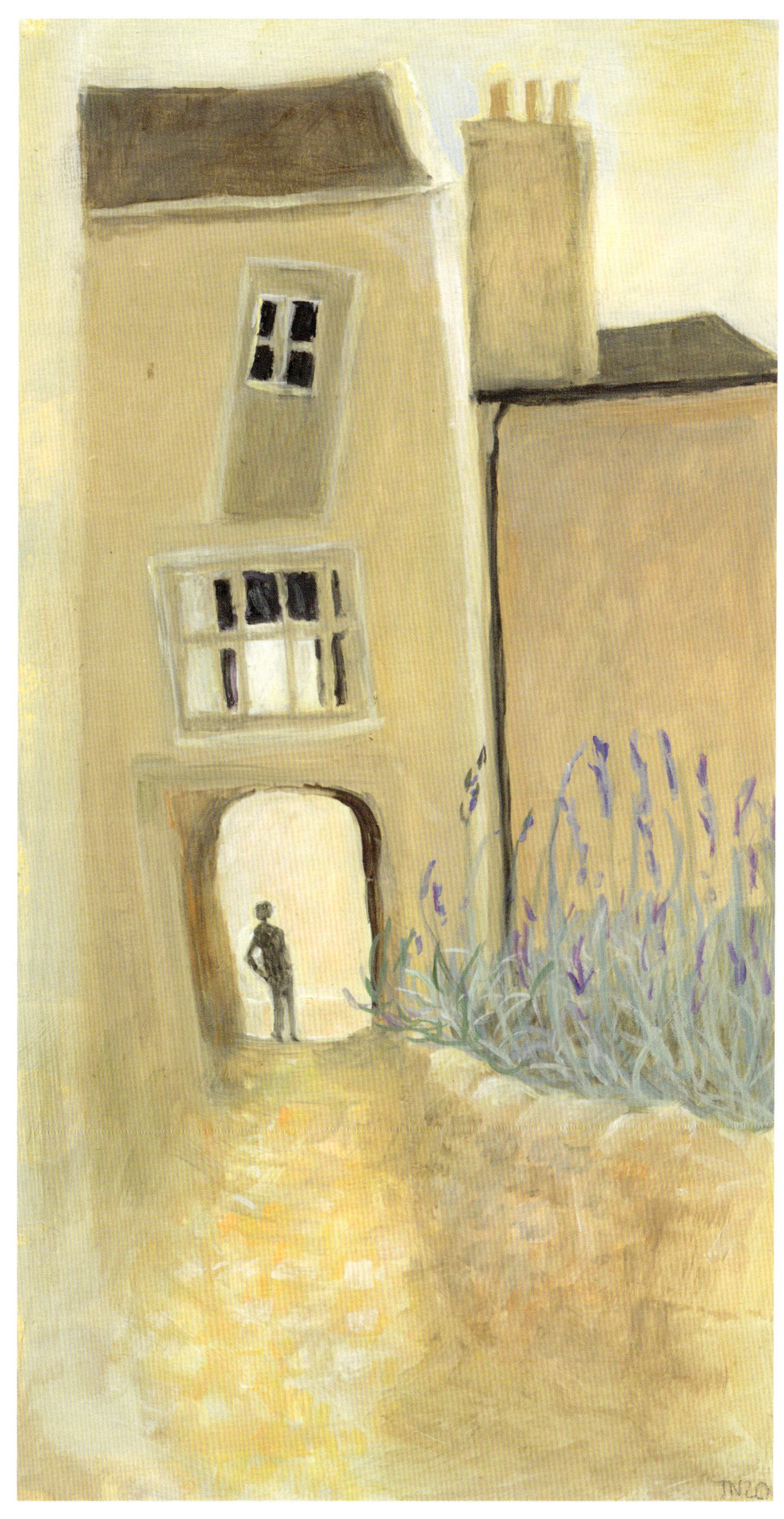

The Alley
2020 · oil on card · 26.5 x 14 cm / 10½ x 5½ in

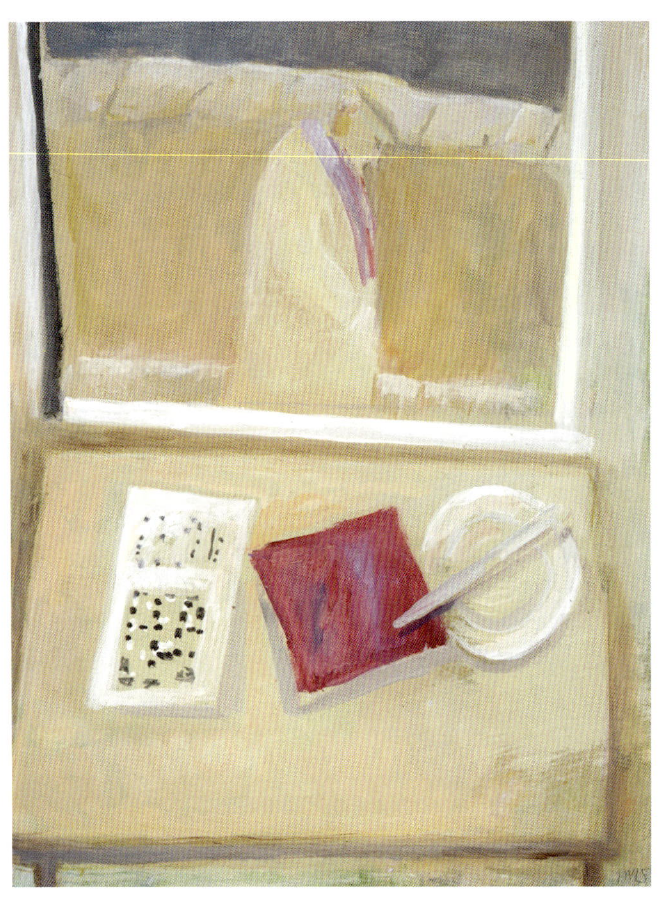

Crosswords
2015 · oil on board · 26.5 x 20.5 cm / 10½ x 8 in

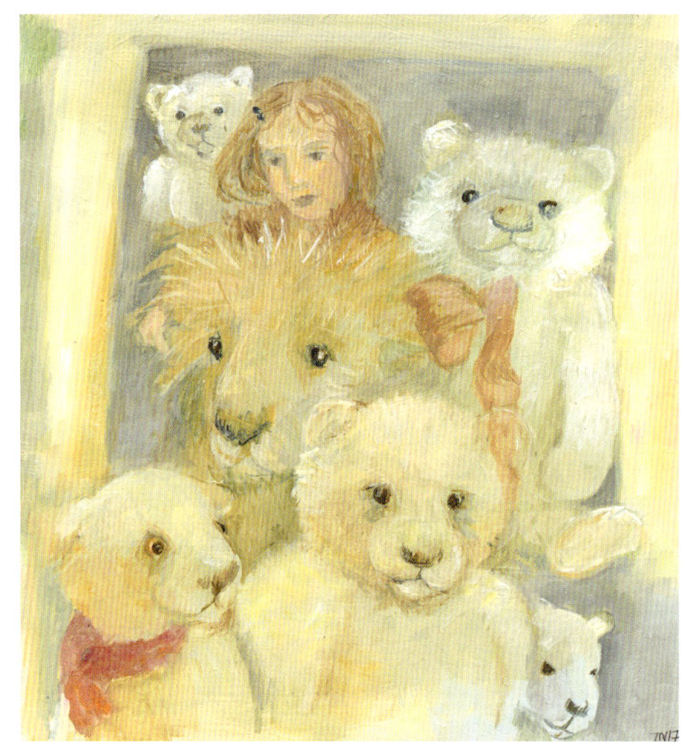

The Teddy Bear Shop
2017 · oil on card · 22 x 19.5 cm / 8¾ x 7¾ in

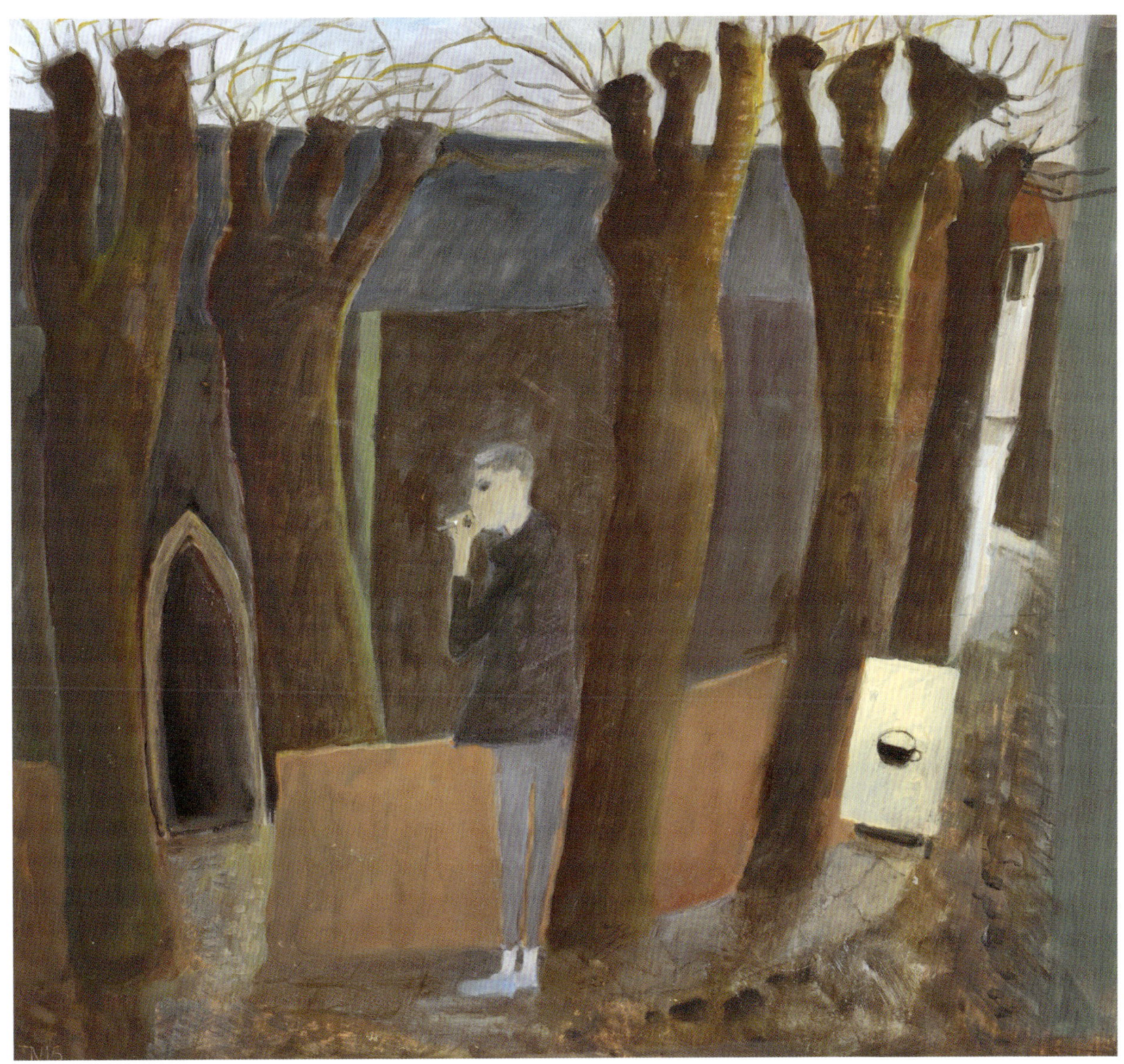

Man Smoking in January
2015 · oil on board · 33 x 35.5 cm / 13 x 14 in

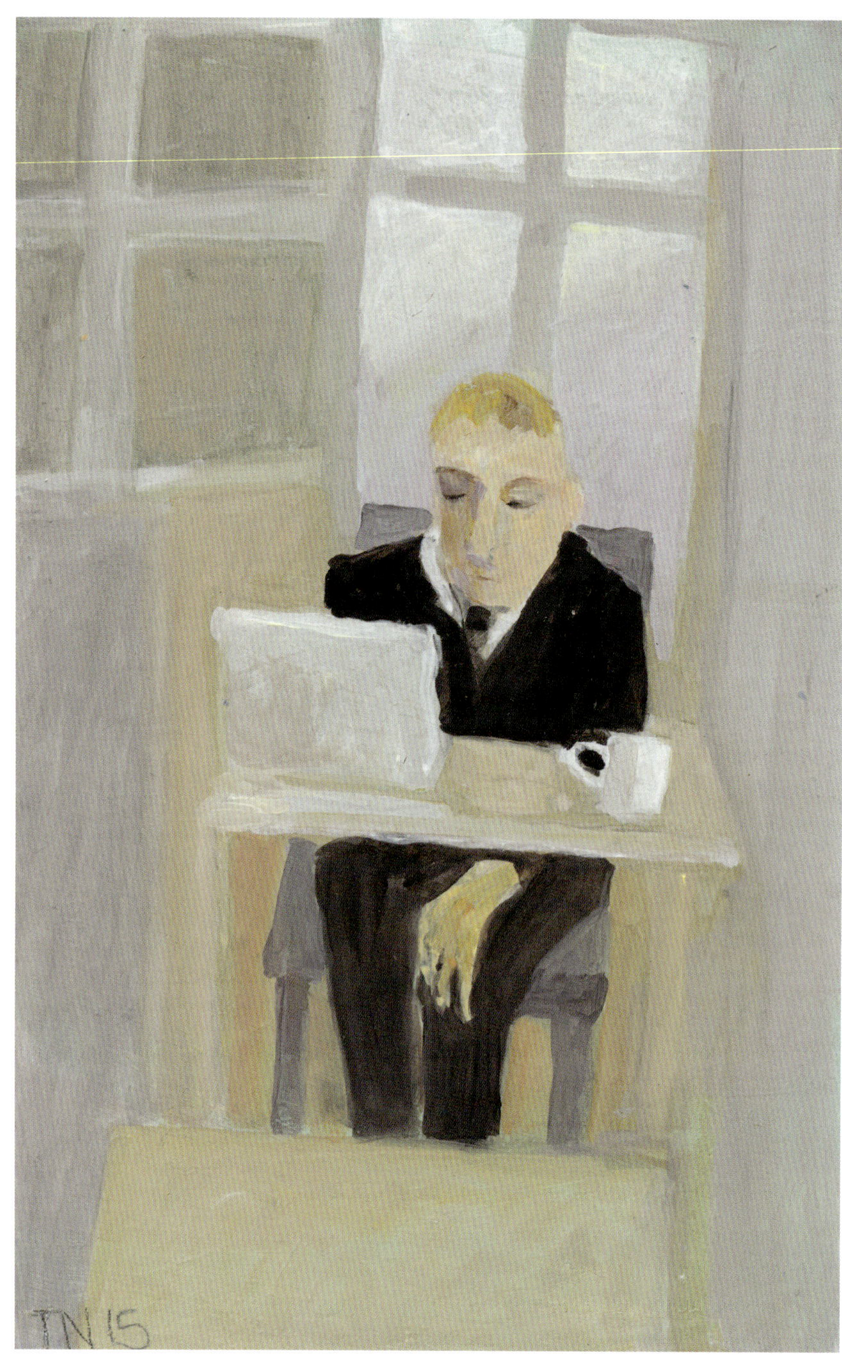

Man Working I
2015 · oil on board · 16 x 10 cm / 6¼ x 4 in

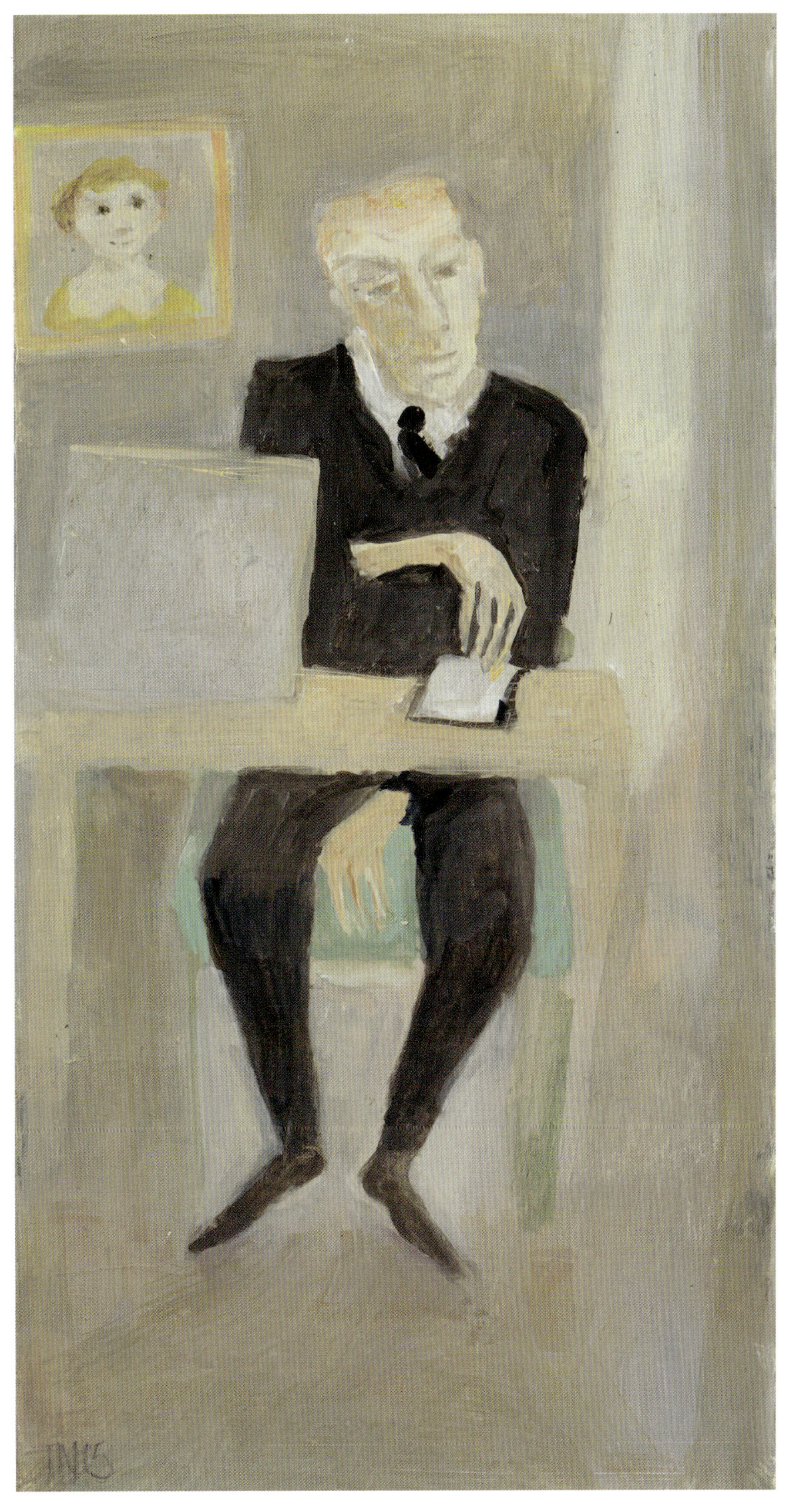

Man Working II
2015 · oil on board · 22 x 11.5 cm / 8¾ x 4½ in

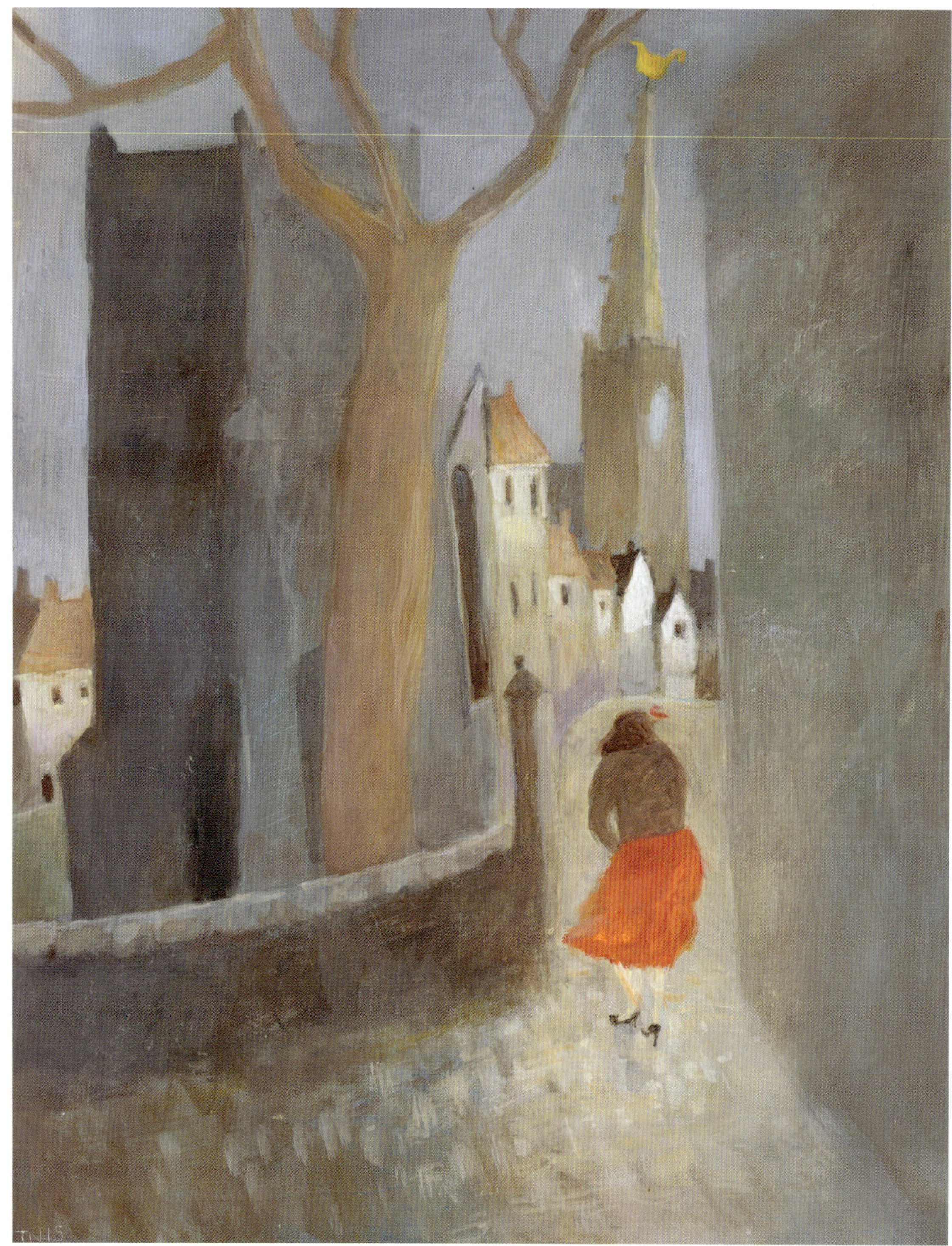

Cobbles and Heels
2015 · oil on board · 34.5 x 26 cm / 13½ x 10¼ in

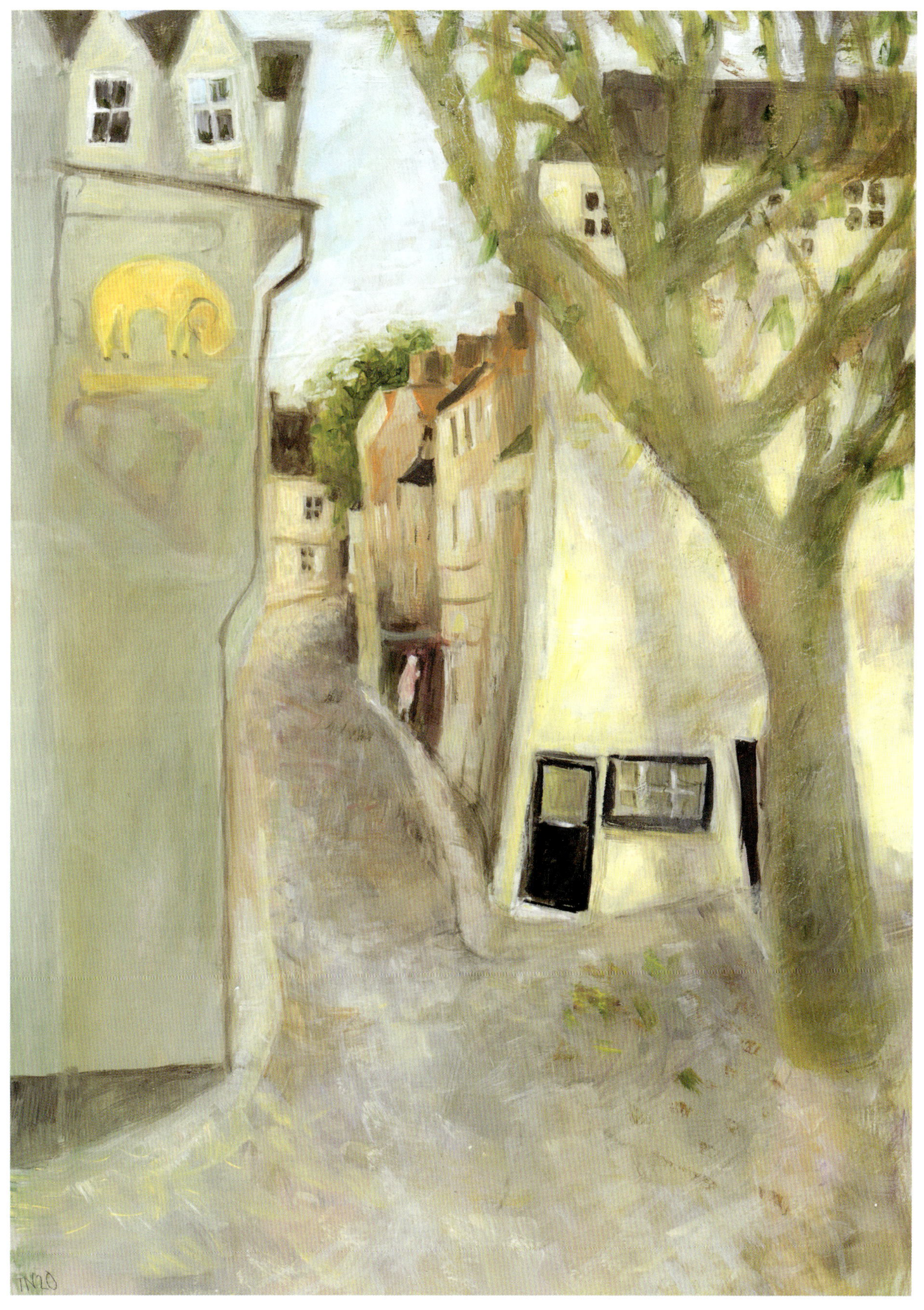

Some Elements of Elm Hill
2020 · oil on board · 40.5 x 29 cm / 16 x 11½ in

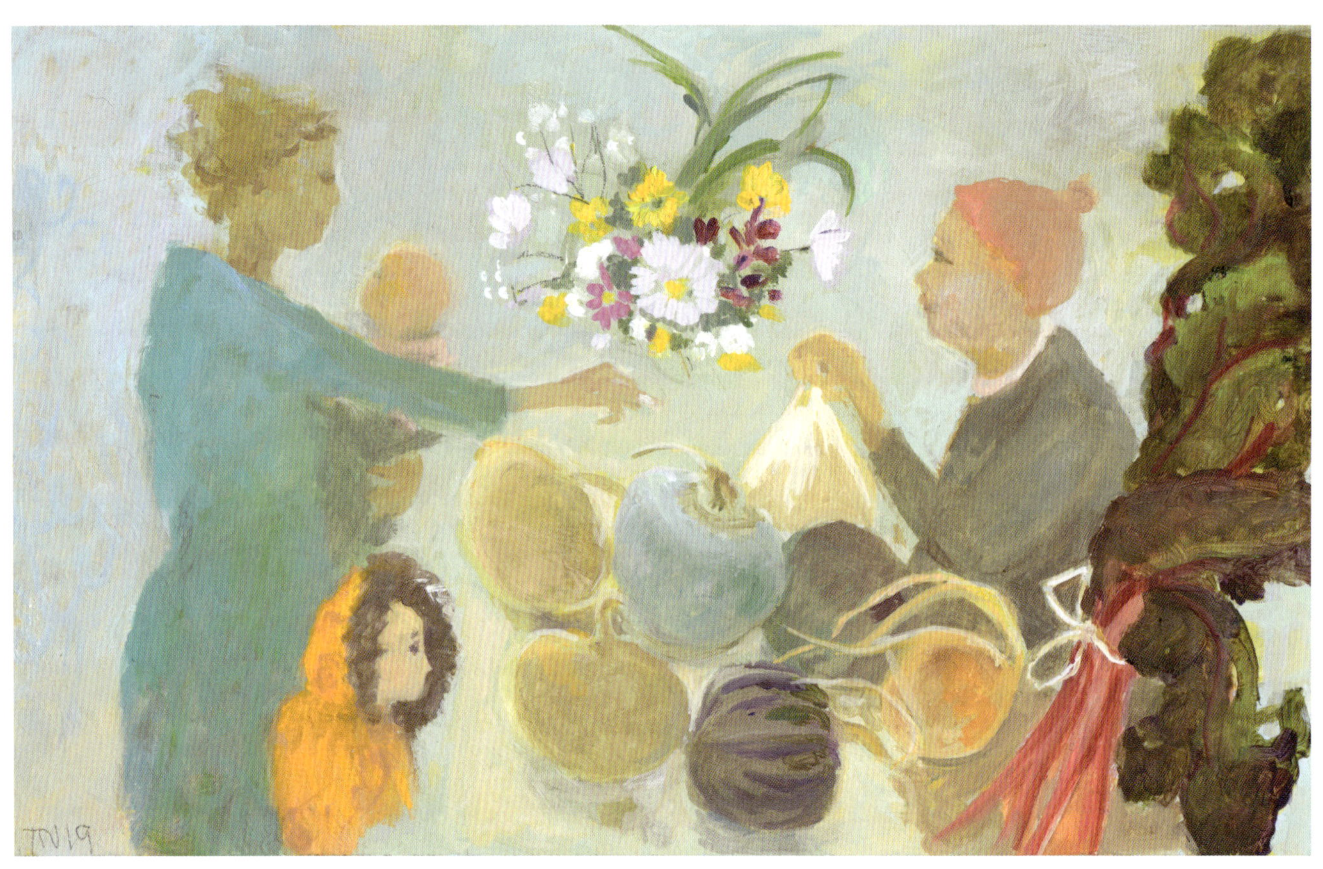

Transaction
2019 · oil on board · 12.5 x 20.5 cm / 5 x 8 in

The farmers' market is held in a large corrugated building with a concrete floor. It holds the cold. All items are bathed in a golden electric light, except those by the door where the vegetables look normal.

There's a sort of festival feeling as you arrive with your cash and bags ready. You don't know who you might meet, but you will know someone. Even the loos are like festival loos as you climb up the iron steps into a loo van that smells and sways.

A CARNIVAL OF PRODUCE

Unsquashable squashes — what a joy! Hard and sweet. Those blue-green hubbards, and the stripy Turk's turbans, the buttercups and the butternuts, the pattypans and the pumpkins and the large beige tromboncino, which starts as an edible squash then grows very big, turns beige and becomes something else. The woman standing behind them wears the most perfect pumpkin-orange jumper. It's her show.

Chocolate tomatoes and black radishes; white radishes hard and interesting. Jubilant radicchio. Expectant eyes of the stallholders. The apple man is still there with his rosy cheeks bobbing behind his apples. Sometimes he has pears, too, but they go quickly. Today he also has quinces.

Much tasting to be done. A line of all those pestos and pickles on little saucers and a plate of broken biscuits to dip as many times as you dare before you feel you have to buy a jar. Lime chutney wins, maybe because it's the strongest taste. The most delicious-smelling tempting bits of sausage, if you are not being a vegetarian, with appley, herby, leaky additions. The woman who makes that chocolate positions broken pieces of truffle enticingly just where your fingers linger, making them hard to resist. But be careful to get your tasting done in the right order: not the truffle before the soused herring and then the gin.

MAKING IT WORK

I know that I will romanticise my visit to the farmers' market. It's a bleak time for the country's economy, but here people put on the farmers' market and make it work. They turn up with their stalls and hopes and for the shoppers it's part of their lives. You don't just buy things; it's quite likely the items are local and you know something about them.

It's tough producing produce, packing it to certain standards, getting there early and standing around, often in the freezing cold, and then unloading the car to store everything in the garage when the morning is over. Somehow, it's that robust determination that feeds into the produce that spills out of our bags when we get home. How much better it is to cook supper after a farmers' market than a supermarket. A bit more pricy and a bit more effort and dirt; a lot more sense and a lot more taste.

I wonder about the stallholders' back stories. The people who make the jewellery: do they sit watching telly in the evenings, threading up the stones? The man whose dahlias have deep blue-green leaves: I listen carefully to the information he gives me about easy-draining soil and laying a plastic sack around the base dark-side up so they don't get too wet through winter and I can mulch over them in the spring. All I can do is to buy one and hope I don't let him and it down.

THE PERFORMANCE

The stalls are like little stage sets: different from one another but each one often all of a piece — the

produce, the fabrics, the people and the dog.
It's up to you to interact with them. There is
usually some banter. The wood-turner has made
quite a high stage and covered it in a red cloth.
The golden bowls shine out like lamps under
the artificial light. He appears at the back as
if he is the puppeteer. Even the stalls that sell
similar things are very different: mounds of
vegetables on some, one sweetheart cabbage
on another.

Everyone dresses for a farmers' market, in
layers which deepen as the winter progresses —
as do the conversations about what you have on.
But the back of the building is always chilly; it
does not get the sun and the cold also comes
from the chiller. They fry the bacon and make
it a café area with bunting. There are about six
tables, with tablecloths, lovely flowers, thick
white mugs and ketchup for the bacon baps.

Fortified, one finishes the rest of the market.
Honey man only sells honey. The honey pots
make two pyramids with the sun pouring through
them. I don't buy one as I don't want to spoil the
display. In the last bit, before I have to dodge past
the noisy generator to get out into daylight, is a
fridge. A small bottle of raw milk cream nestles
up to a large bottle of raw milk. I can't separate
them so they both come home with me.

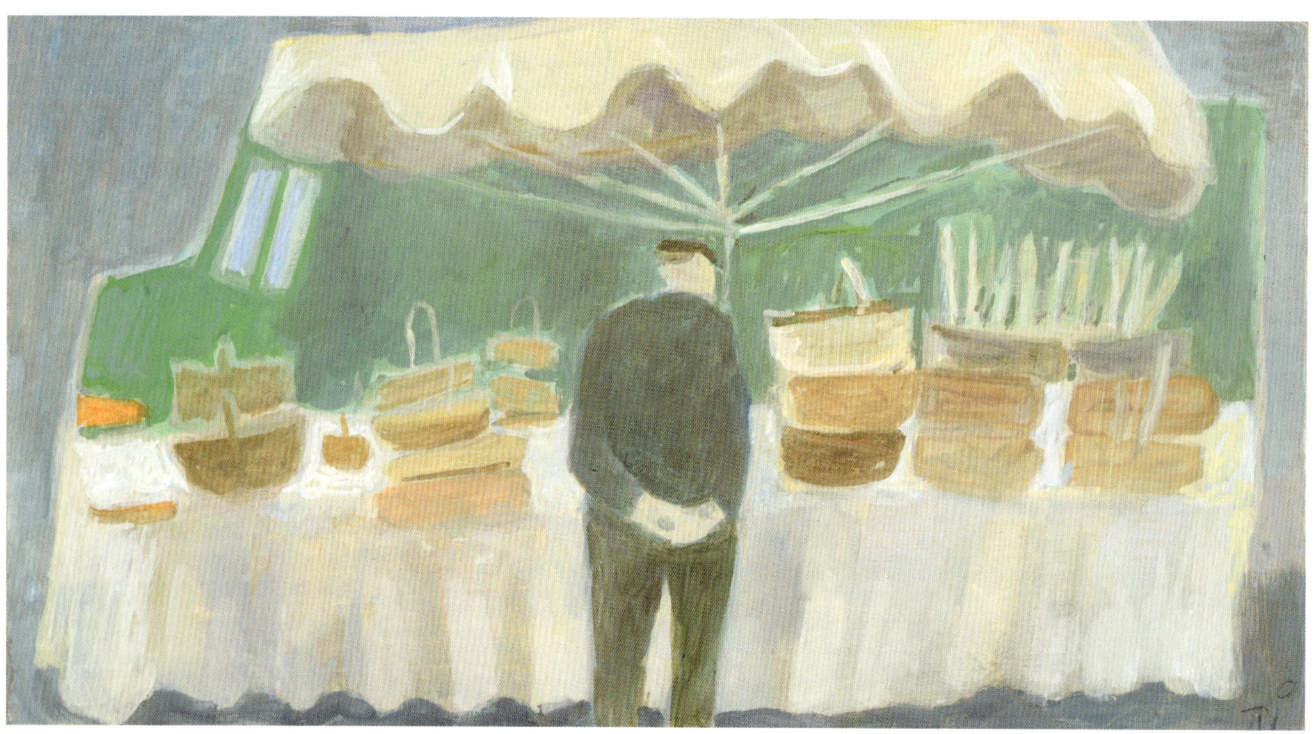

The Basket Van
2019 · oil on board · 11.5 x 20.5 cm / 4½ x 8 in

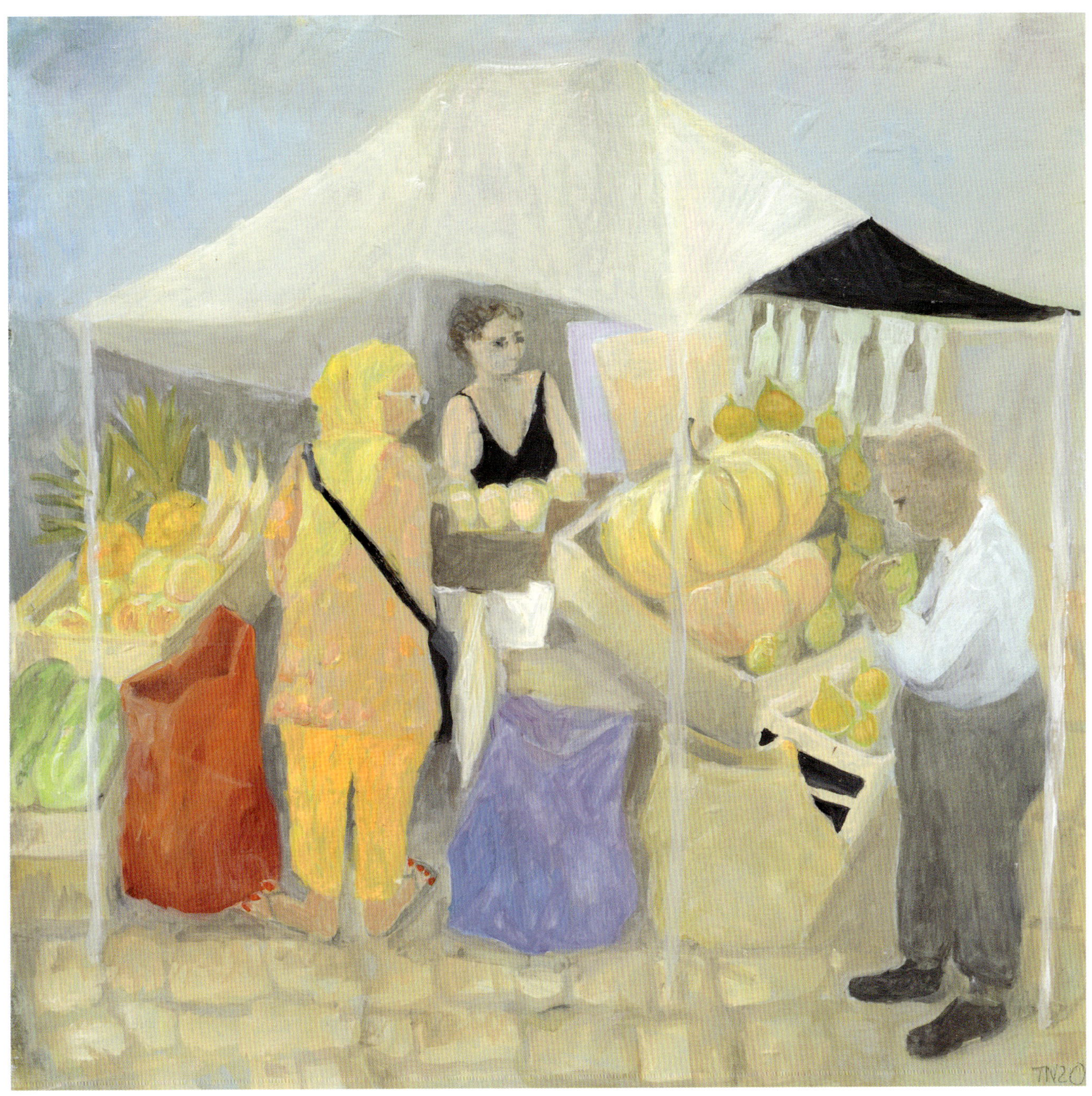

He Loved Pears
2020 · oil on board · 24 x 24 cm / 9½ x 9½ in

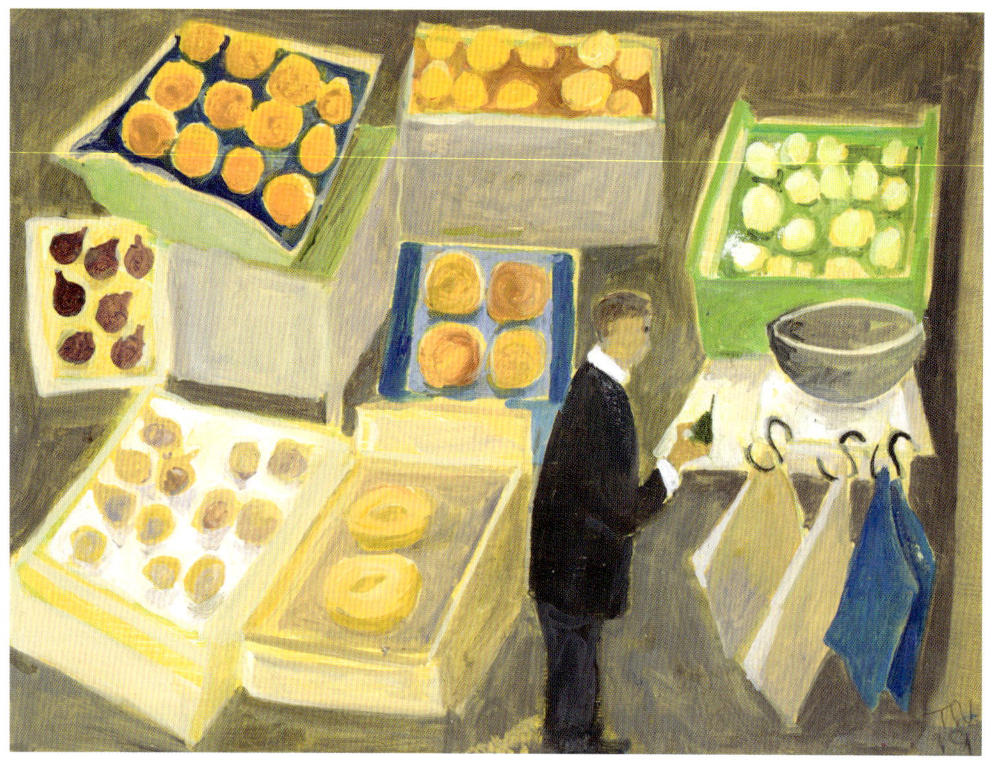

Choosing a Pear
2019 · oil on card · 14.5 x 19.5 cm / 5¾ x 7¾ in

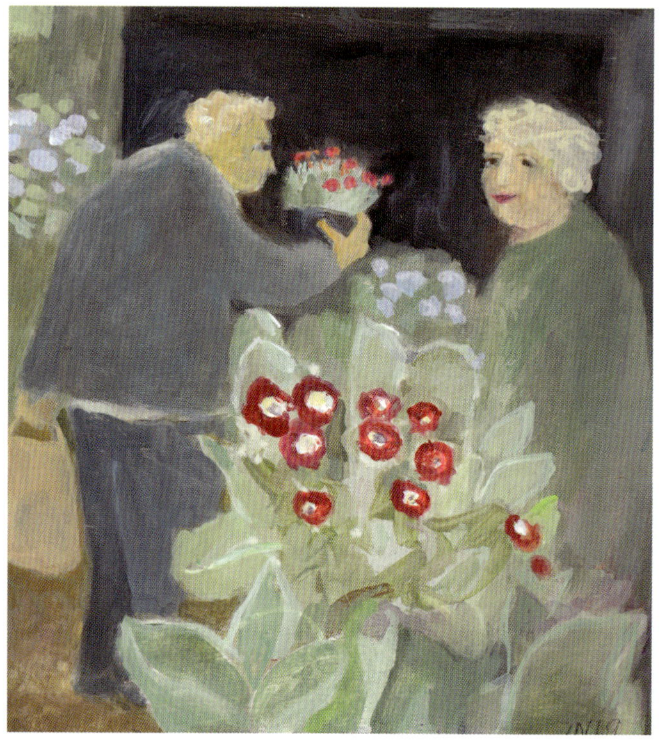

Smitten
2019 · oil on board · 14 x 12.5 cm / 5½ x 5 in

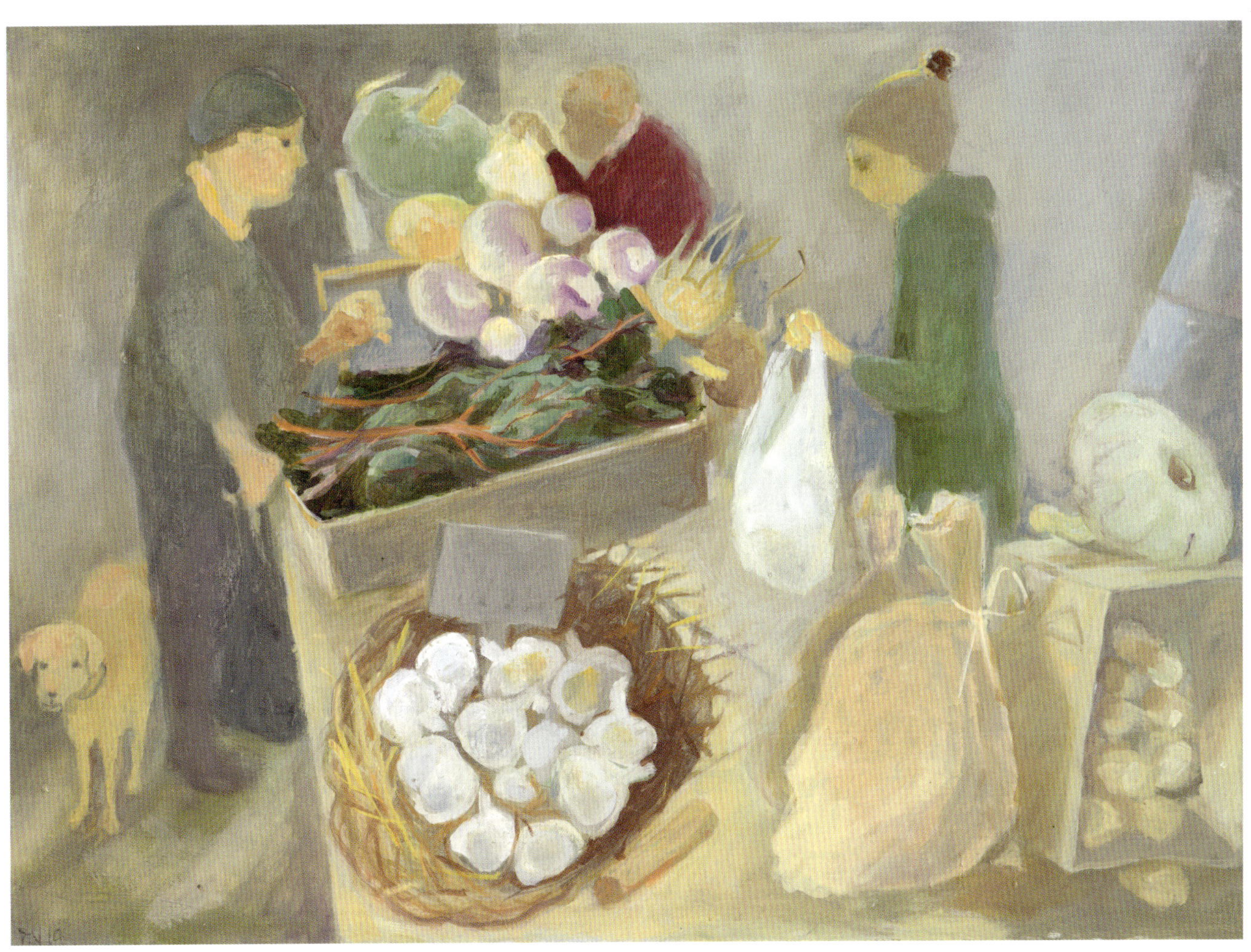

The Wonderful Veg
2019 · oil on board · 23 x 30.5 cm / 9 x 12 in

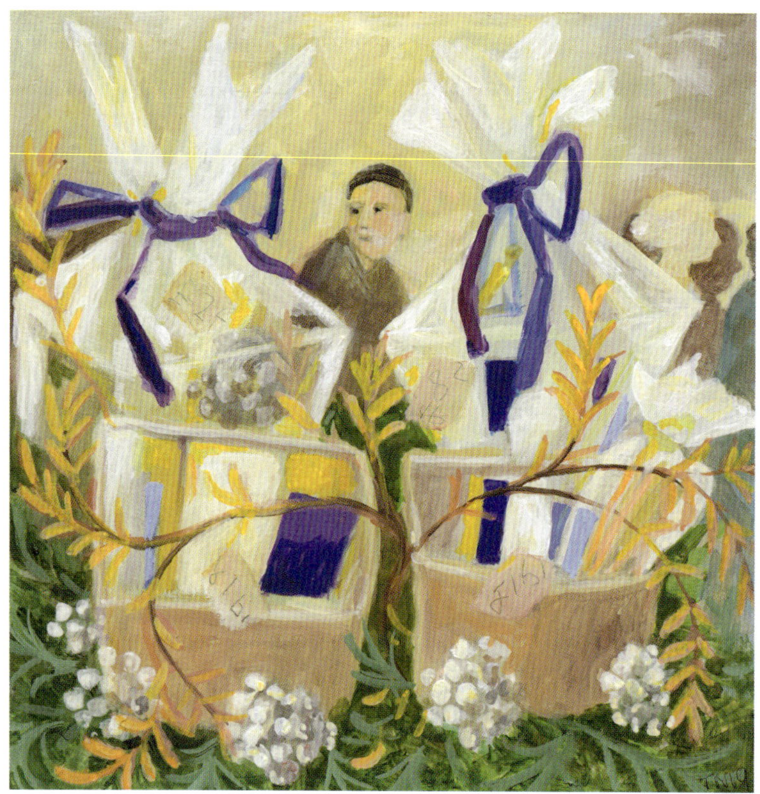

And His Mother's Present
2019 · oil on board · 19 x 18 cm / 7½ x 7 in

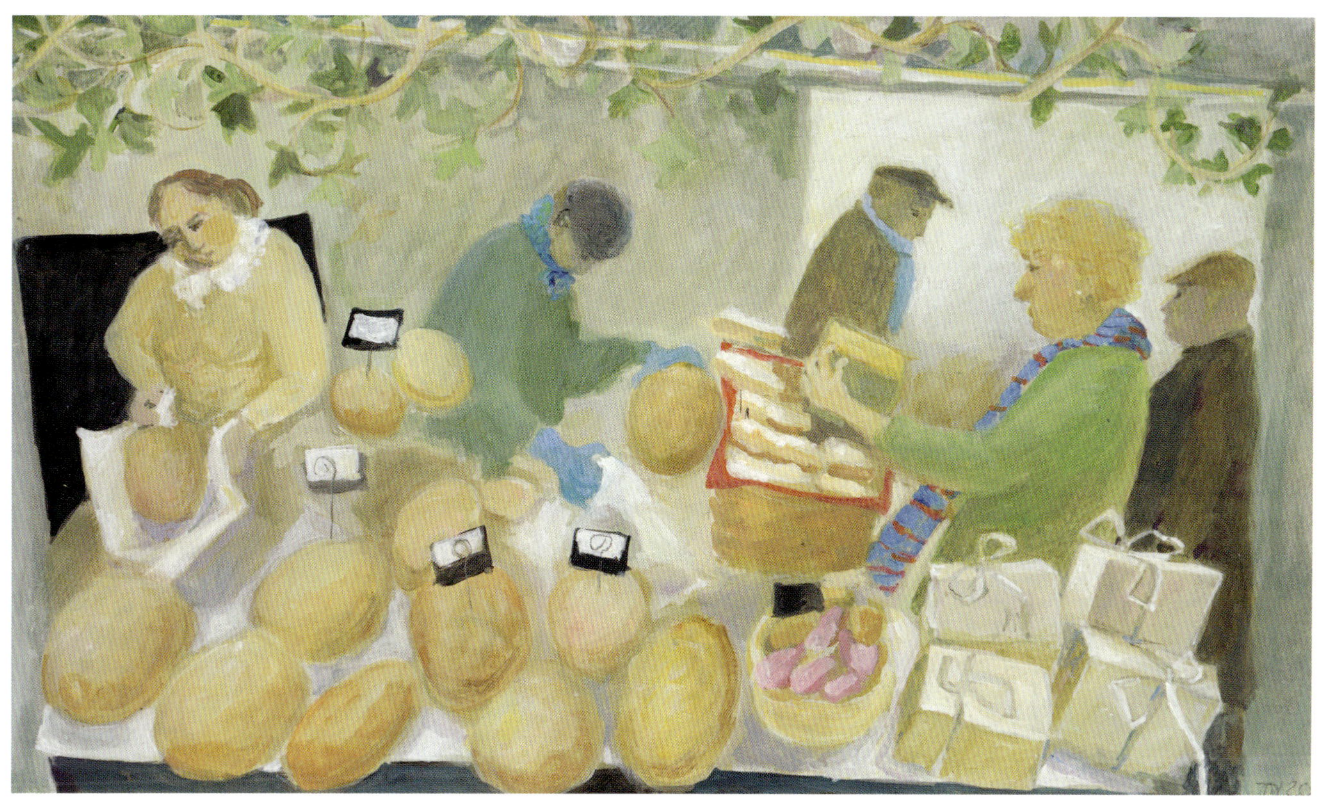

Breads and Cakes
2020 · oil on board · 19 x 32 cm / 7½ x 12½ in

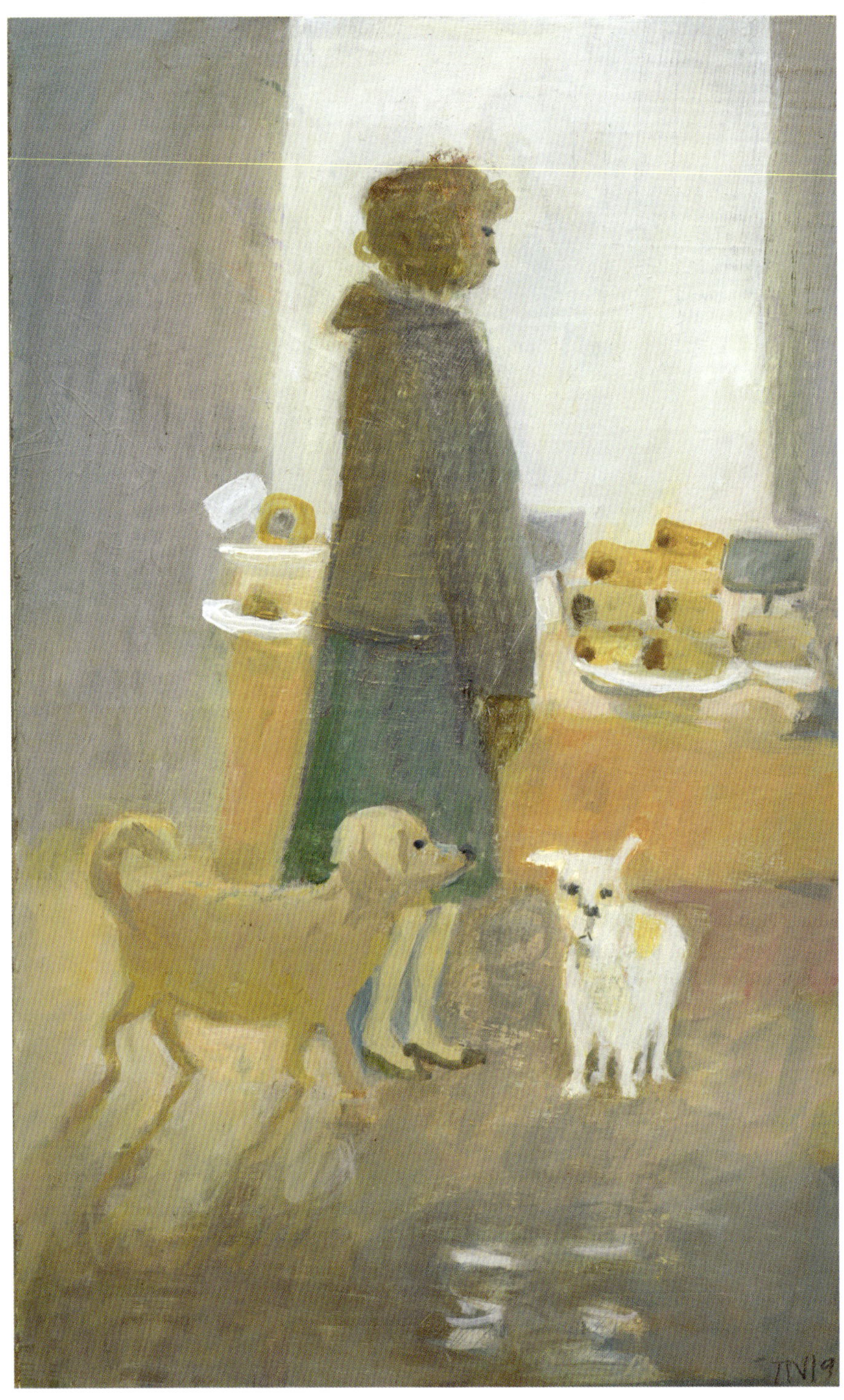

Sausage Rolls
2019 · oil on board · 19 x 11.5 cm / 7½ x 4½ in

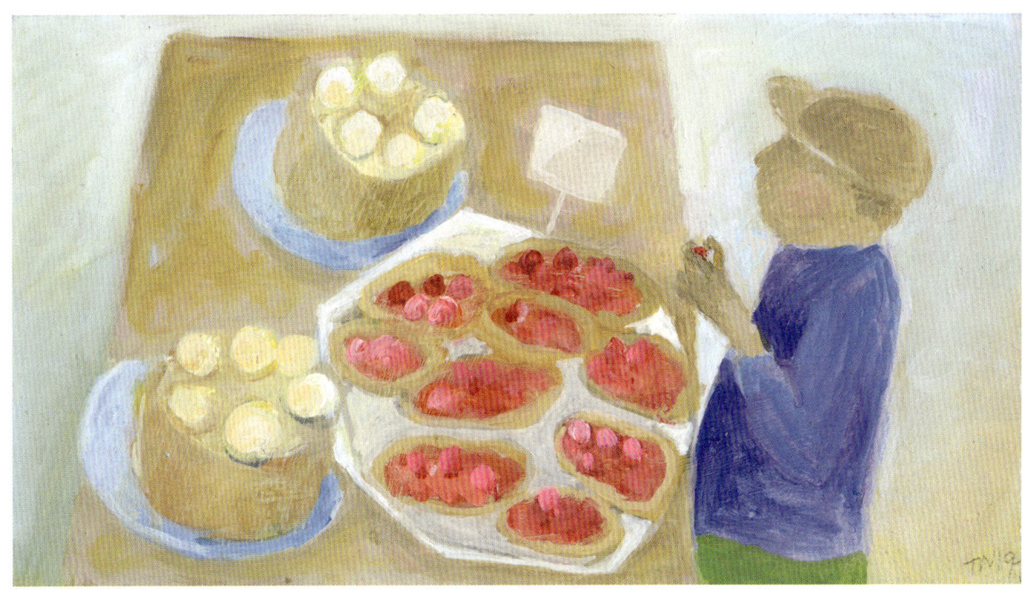

Tarts
2019 · oil on board · 8.5 x 14.5 cm / 3¼ x 5¾ in

Boiled Cake

12oz. marg.

12oz. 1½ 1½

{ 8 ozs dried fruit mixture
1½ cup milk
1 cup brown sugar
½ lb marg.

(1 cup is
Hartleys mug
size)

Put in pan and simmer gently until
the fruit is tender. Allow to cool
then add.

{ 2 beaten eggs
2 cups s/r flour.

Put in baking tin and cook in mod. oven
at nt 1½ hours.

Coconut delights

4½ ozs flour
2 oz porage oats
2 oz coconut
2 oz marg
4 oz sugar
pinch salt
1 desertspoon golden syrup
1 tablespoon boiling water
(½ teaspoon bicarb soda)

Mix all dry
ingredients.

Add melted marg
and syrups
Stir in soda dissolved
in boiling water.

Form into balls and press with finger
on to greased sheet.
Cook in gentle oven and take out
when pale golden brown.

10 · HOME

The Aga is the centre of the house. Traditionally cream, this one is navy. New ones can be pink; black is nice. The early ones were filled with anthracite. One coal scuttle full in the evening and that was it. It warmed the house (well, the kitchen), was used for all the cooking and did some hot water.

OUR AGA

We lived in a timbered farmhouse when we were growing up, which was cold. The Aga was central. The most important conversations seemed to be when someone had their back to the Aga. My sister and I used to take it in turns to sit on the cooler hot plate lid, feet on a stool, often reading. Our friends with younger children had to take the door off their bottom oven because the kittens like to get in there and the children would shut them in. After supper my father used to pull his chair out and put his feet in the oven.

'Boiled' Fruit Cake in the Aga

- *225 g dried fruit mixture*
- *350 ml milk*
- *150 g brown sugar*
- *225 g marg or butter*

Put it all in a big pan and simmer gently until the fruit is tender. Allow to cool, then add:

- *2 beaten eggs*
- *340 g self-raising flour*

Put in a baking tin and cook in the Aga's baking oven/moderate oven for about 1½ hours.

Mary

We had to move out of the way for cooking and endless tea-making. I have two Aga kettles, one from my parents and one from my grandparents. The kettles are lined with limescale and have survived them all. Toast is made in a wire tennis bat that slides under the hot plate lid — the toast comes out covered in squares.

Where there is toast, there may also be eggs. Lunch is often eggs. Omelette in summer, in the backyard with a glass of white; in winter scrambled with mustard; boiled for all the rest of the days. Good eggs are one of life's delights, yolks the colour of dandelions. Boil some water, make some toast, put eggs in water, don't wander off (I don't time them so this is important), spread toast thinly with marmite. Serve with strong tea and something to read.

THE STOVE

The wood-burning stove is another member of the family. When it's going it feels as if the house is in action too. It's a companion. Electricity is anonymous. Stoves have personalities and they can be difficult. We run this one on free wood when possible. People know we want wood, and just as we are running low a new lot often arrives in the garden.

I've learnt a lot about wood and the people who bring it. Deliveries vary: sometimes the garden is filled with fence panels, usually after a storm; they are good for kindling. Sometimes I get large bits with nails in that the chainsaw does not like. Once there was a small brown bag, so carefully packed with little pieces, as if for a doll, that it seemed a shame to burn it.

Wood warms you three times: collecting, cutting and burning. I have three sorts of wood: kindling, seconds and serious. This stove heats the room, the radiators and the hot water.

BIRDS

Watching the birds feeding in the garden is one of life's pleasures. It means you have to be at home regularly, have to be quiet and have to buy quite a lot of bird food.

Many people want to tell you the stories of their birds – either the special visitors like the four bullfinches that morning or the everyday antics of their birds. These are *their* birds because they observe them. So much better to sit with them if you can and watch their birds, the stories unfolding in shared comments. One couple I know told me of their extra-friendly robins. When I was there I met Mr and Mrs Robin, who appeared on cue. With another neighbour we watched a long-tailed tit with a short tail.

THINGS ON THE WINDOWSILL, THINGS ON THE WALLS

Books do furnish a room, but so do the little things we keep on our bookcases and windowsills. Little shrines to the past. The one Lego spaceship kept, the one painted stone, or a postcard of a forgotten place remain. The windowsills may change, the boy may have children of his own, the rest of the holiday is forgotten but a story is held in that object. New objects arrive and absorb our unfolding lives.

Paintings also furnish a home. When my paintings go from my walls the house feels emptier; ghost paintings of cobwebs remain. Looking at paintings in a gallery or museum is so different from having them at home. It's the one opposite where you sit at home where your eyes are drawn. How many times did your eye travel to that painting, over it and into it?

COMING HOME

In a way, the places in this book contain my life. And they are fluid – they have changed a lot since I started making the paintings shown in these pages. They do exist, but you won't find them as I do – you will find your own things here.

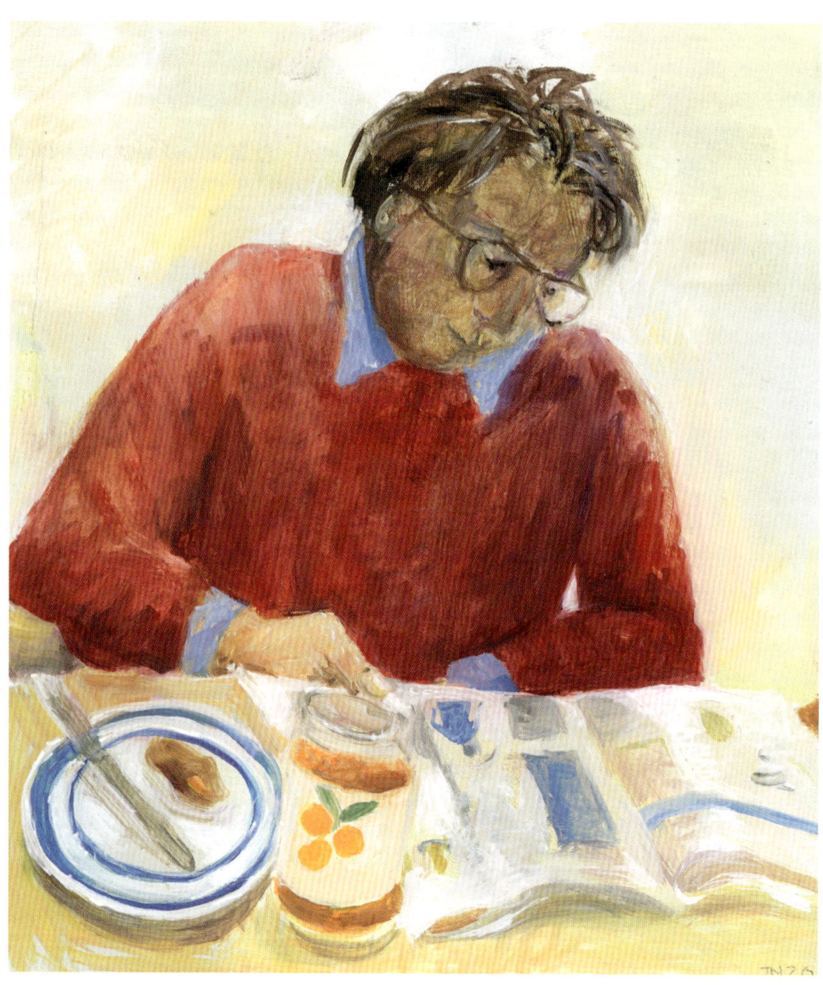

Football
2020 · oil on card
26.5 x 23 cm / 10½ x 9 in

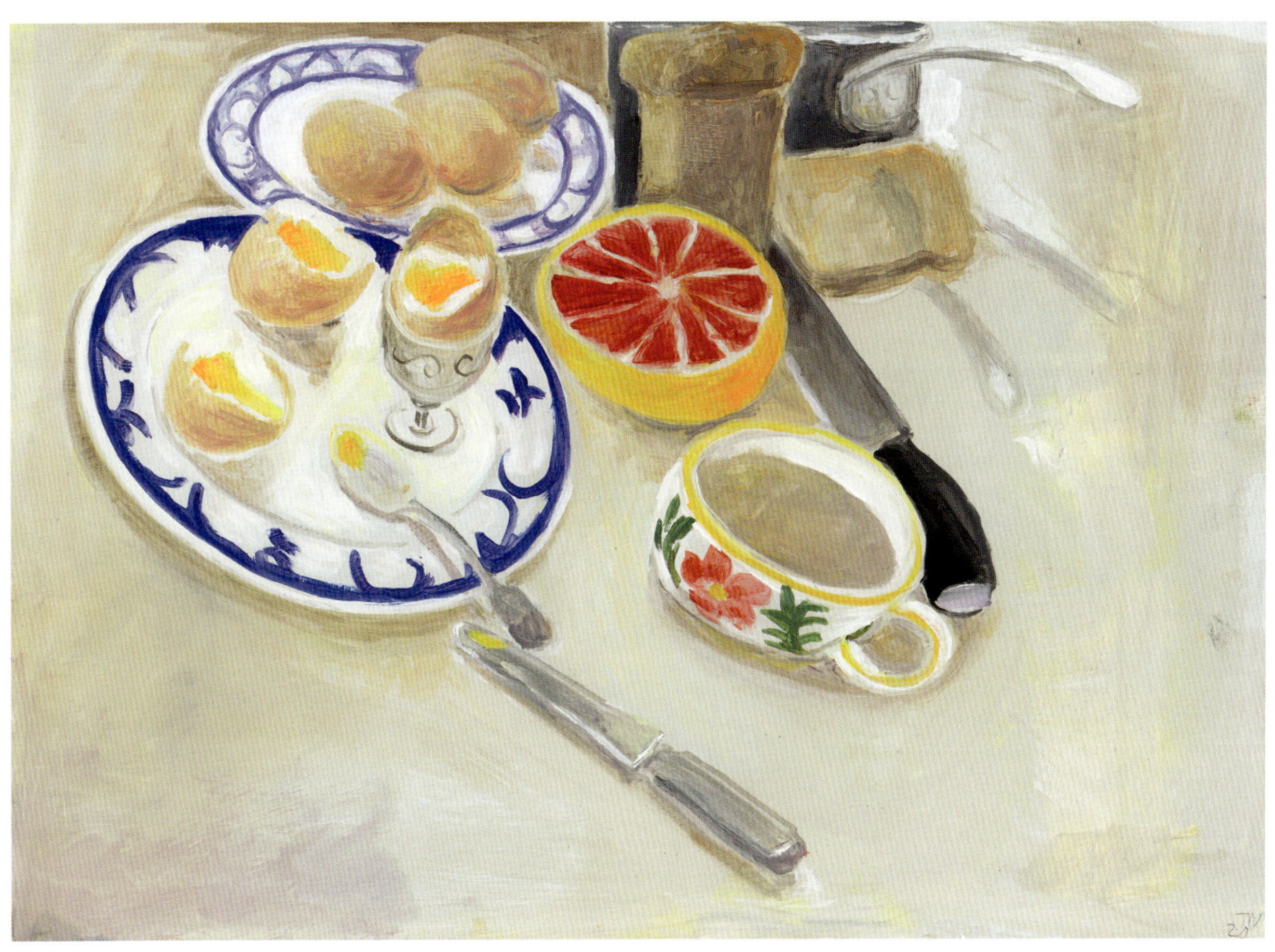

Boiled Eggs
2020 · oil on board · 26.5 x 37 cm / 10½ x 14½ in

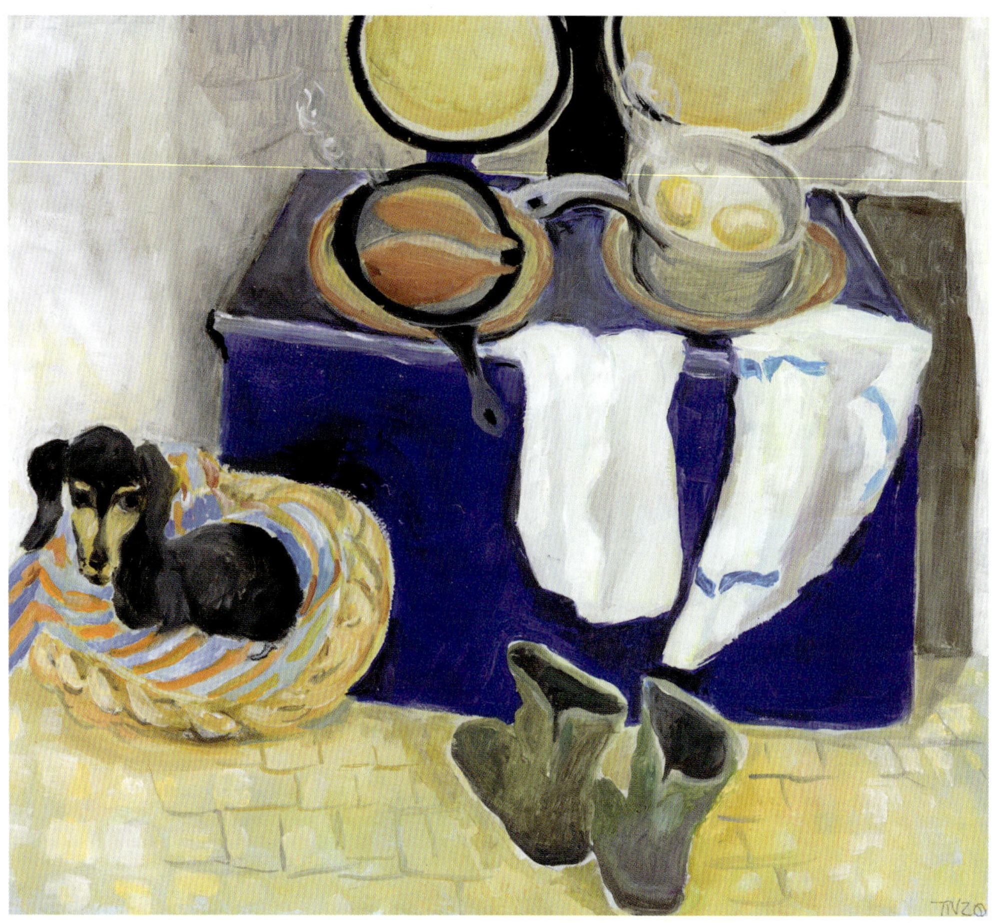

The Aga
2020 · oil on card · 28 x 30.5 cm / 11 x 12 in

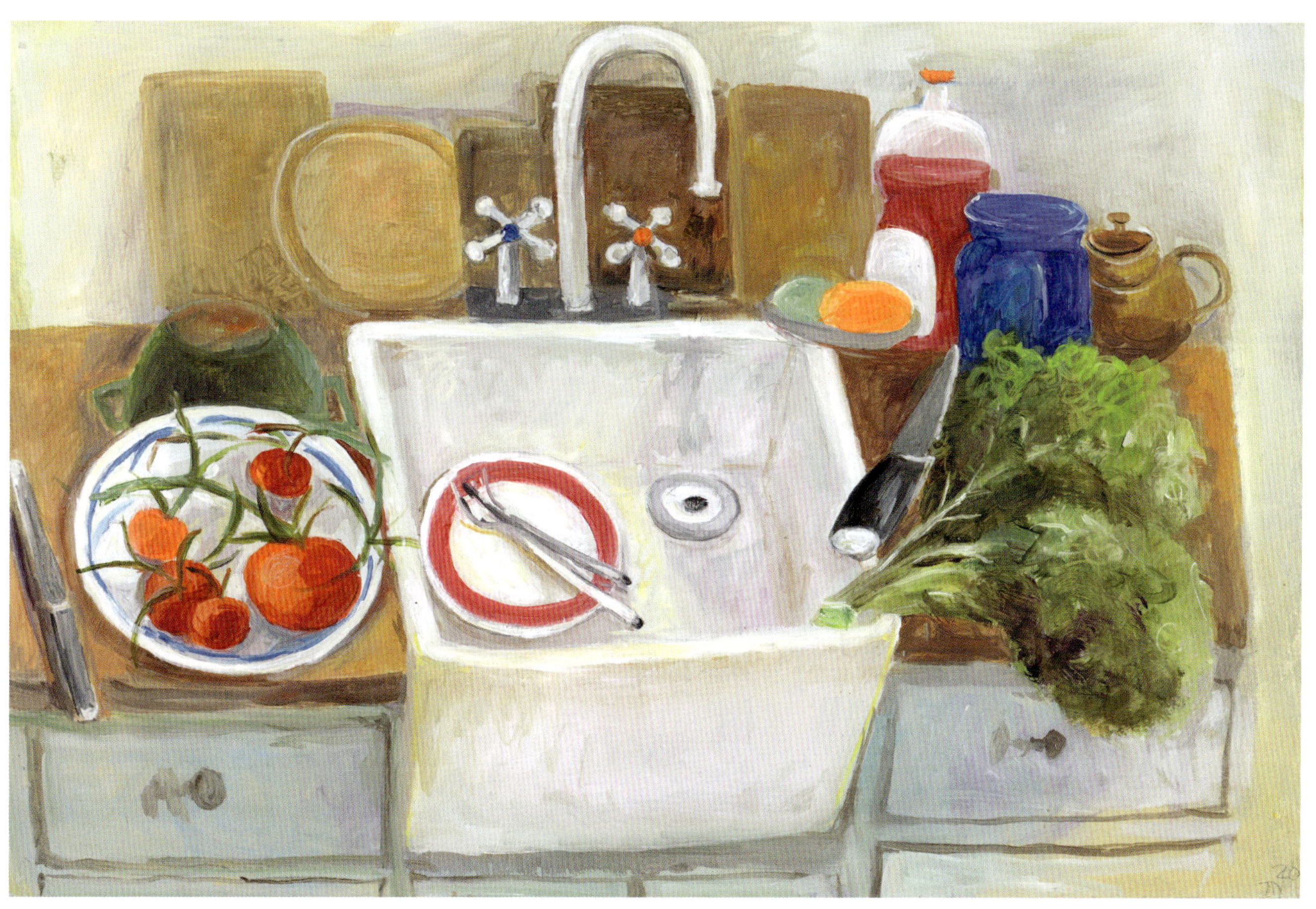

Kitchen Sink
2020 · oil on card · 28.5 x 42 cm / 11¼ x 16½ in

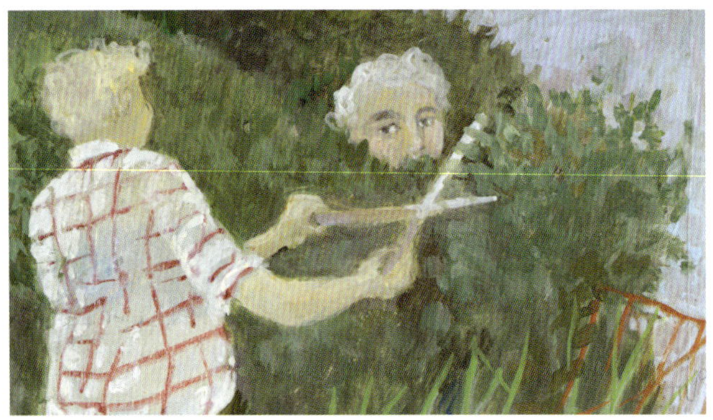

The Neighbour
2020 · oil on board · 7.5 x 12.5 cm / 3 x 5 in

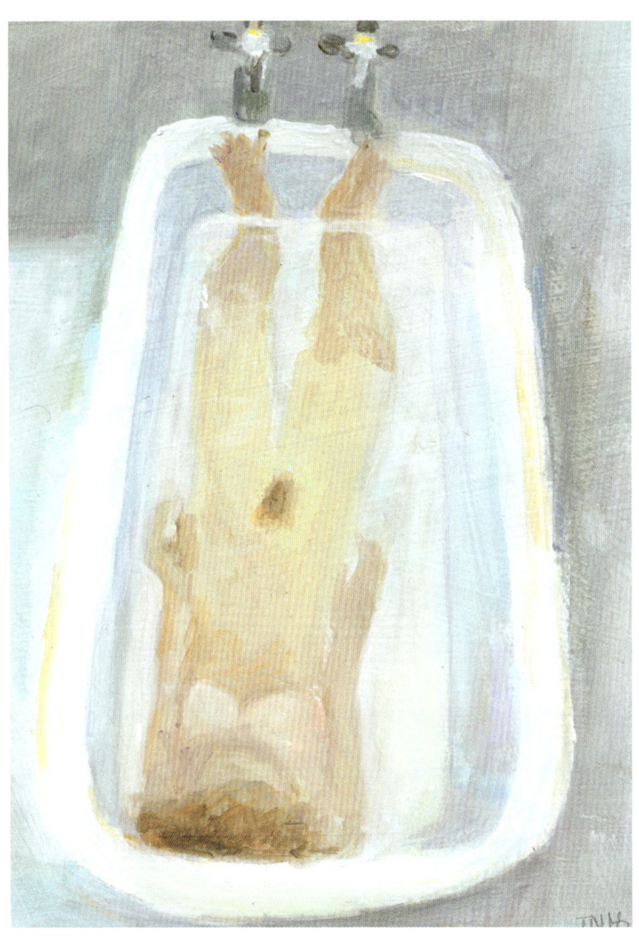

The Bath
2019 · oil on card · 18.5 x 12.5 cm / 7¼ x 5 in

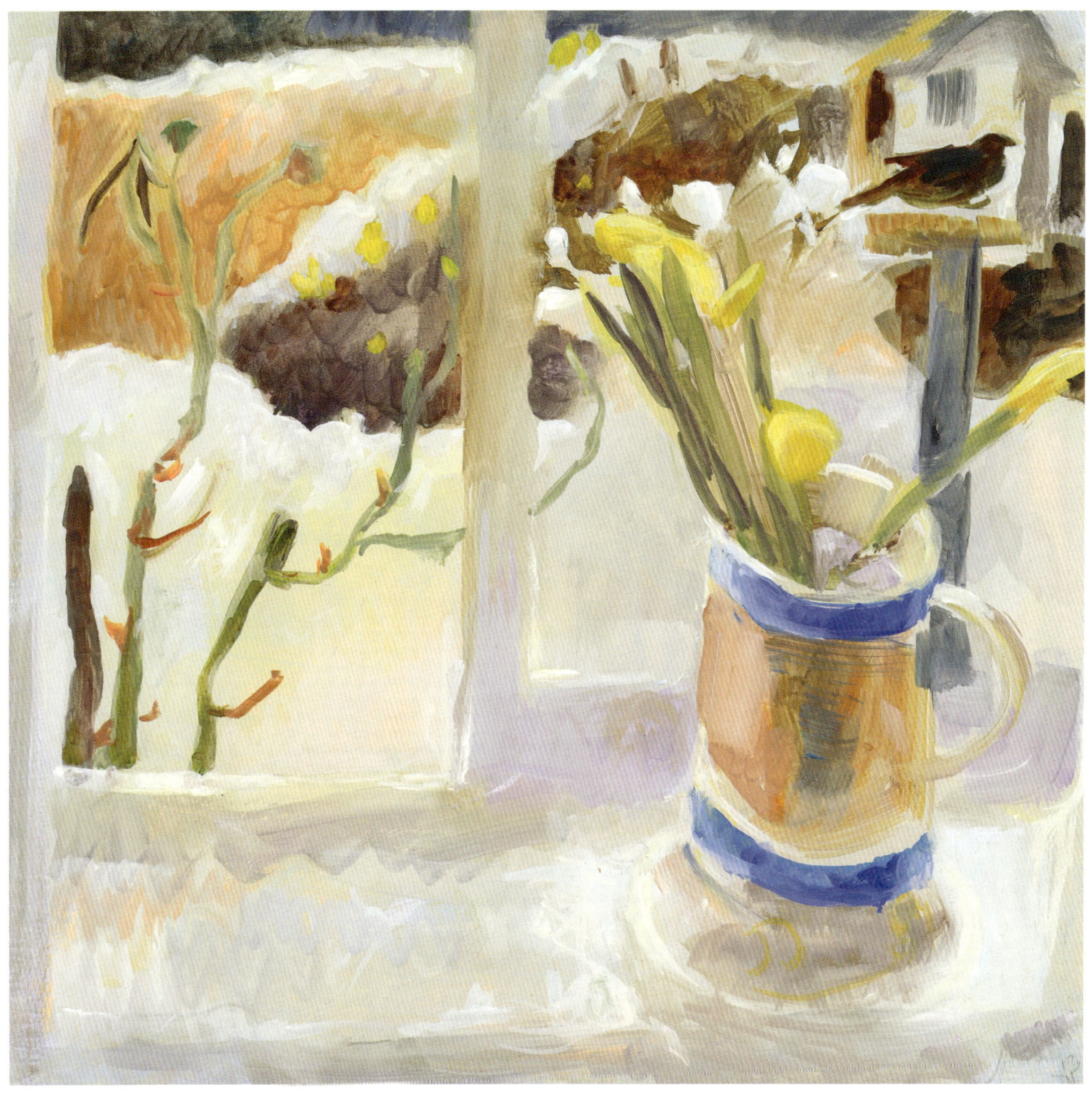

Snow in March
2013 · oil on board · 40.5 x 40.5 cm / 16 x 16 in

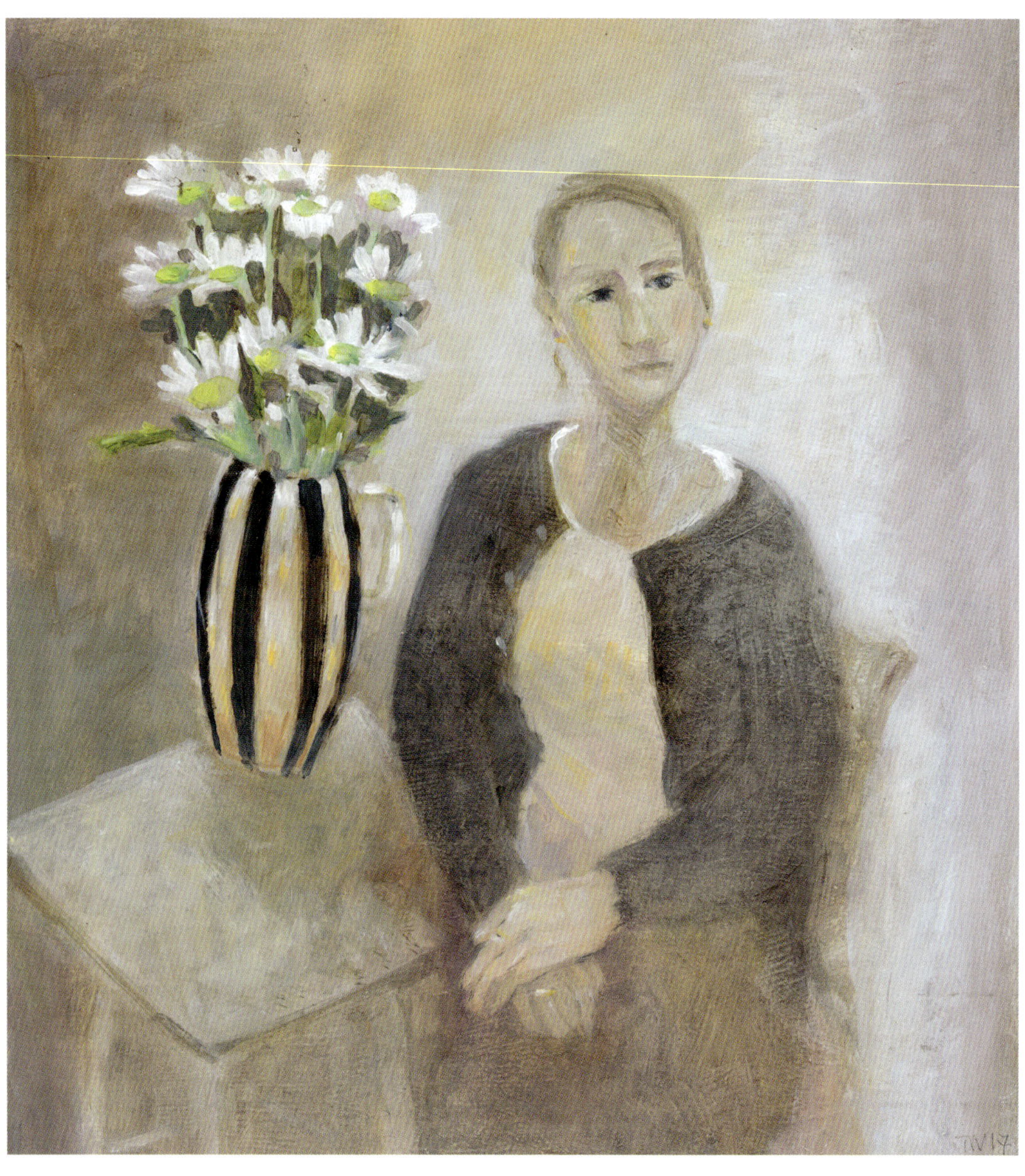

Visitor
2017 · oil on board · 20.5 x 18.5 cm / 8 x 7¼ in

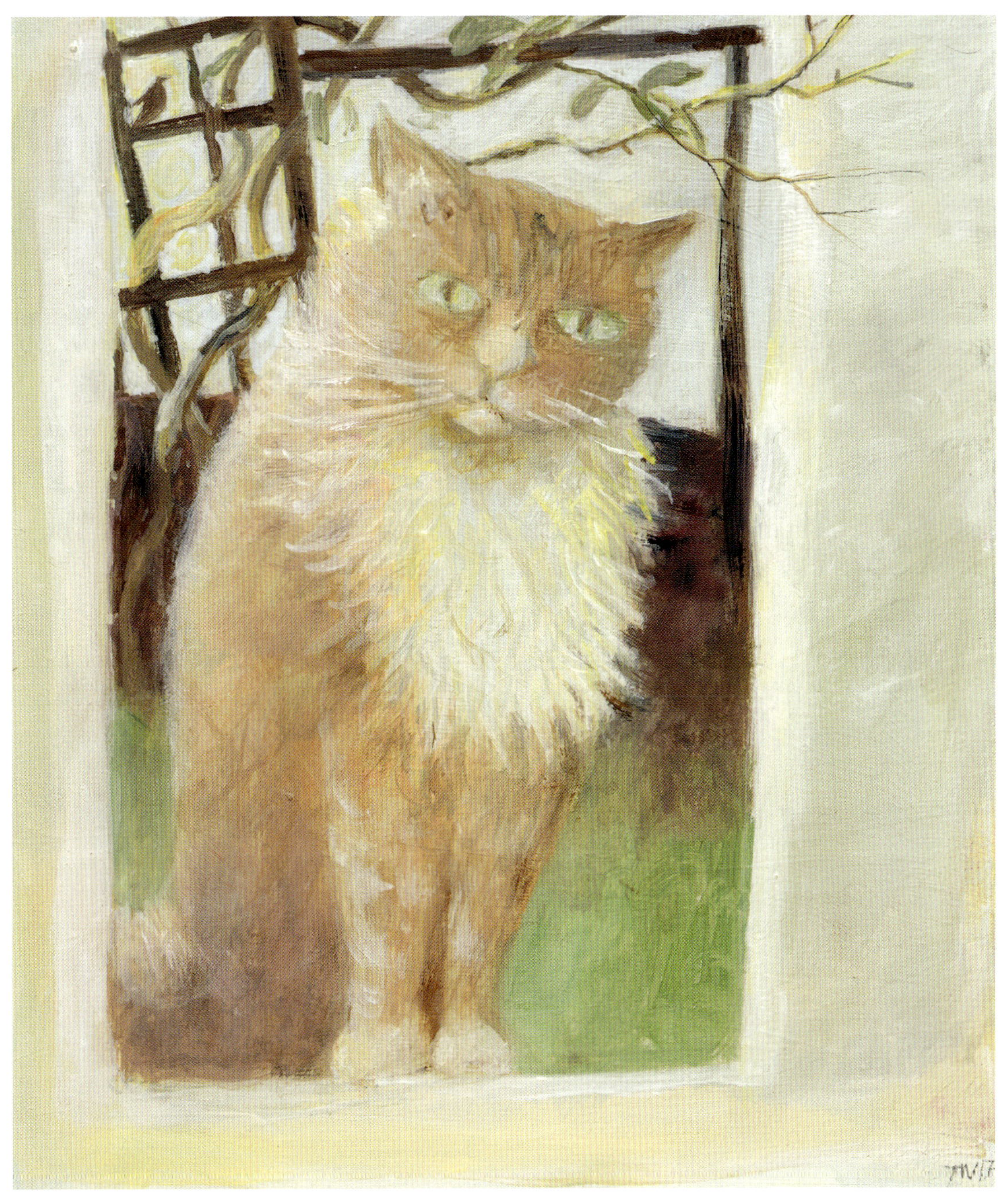

At the Window in the Morning
2017 · oil on card · 24 x 19.5 cm / 9½ x 7¾ in

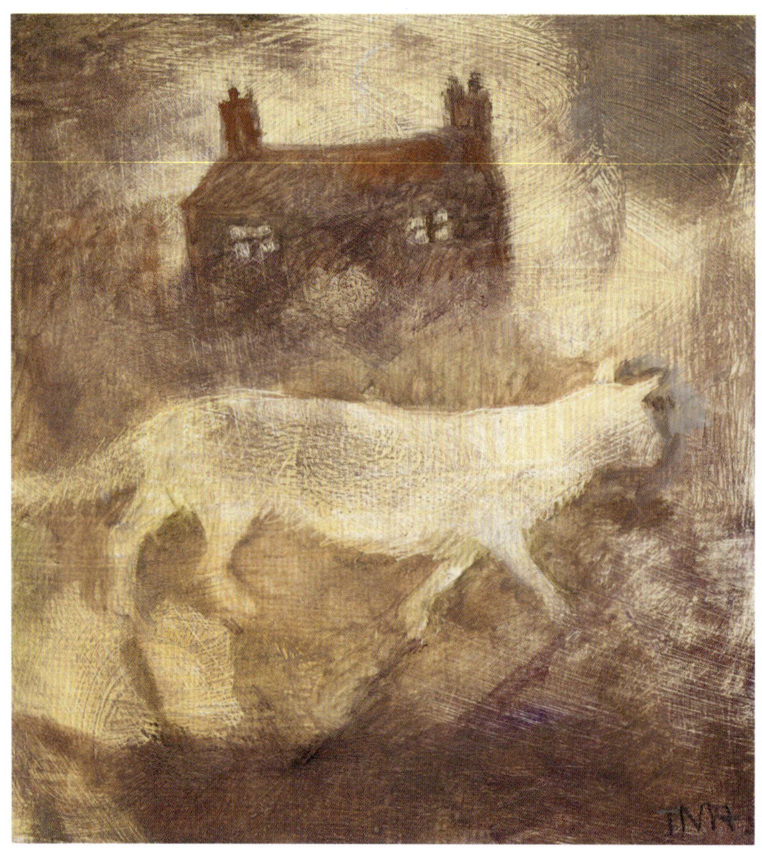

Out There
2017 · oil on board · 12 x 11 cm / 4¾ x 4½ in

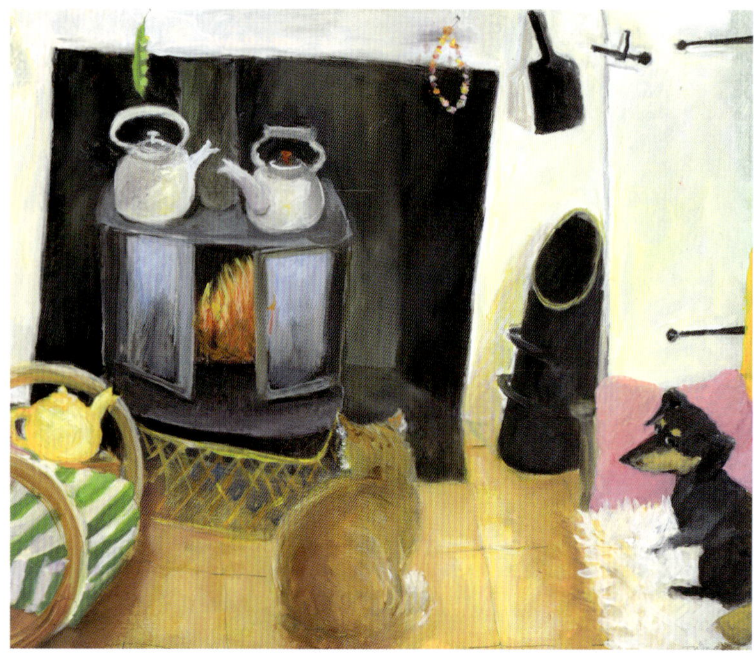

The Stove
2020 · oil on card · 23 x 26.5 cm / 9 x 10½ in

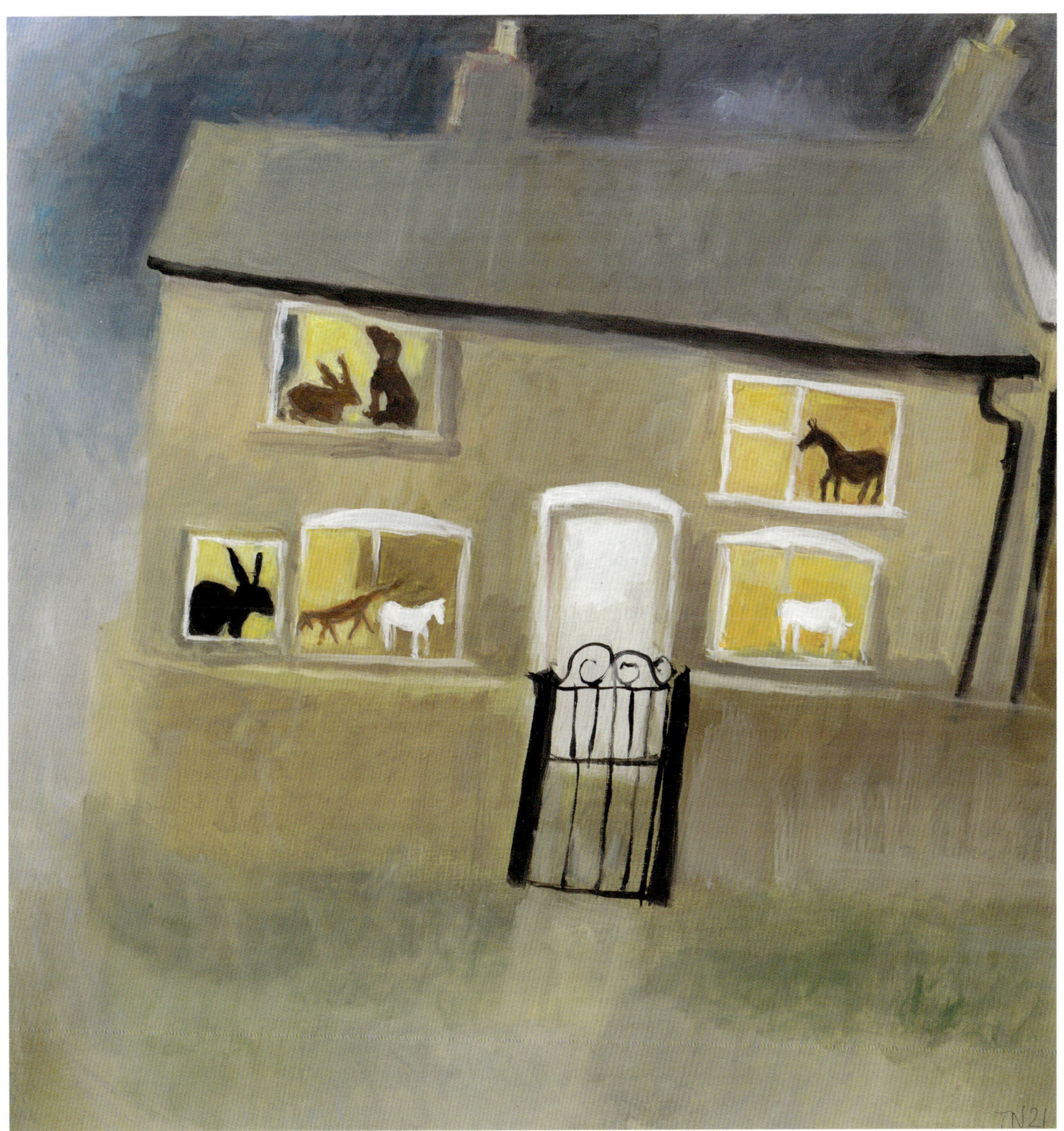

Teatime, January Evening
2021 · oil on board · 21 x 19.5 cm / 8¼ x 7¾ in

ACKNOWLEDGEMENTS

I would like to thank: Chris Bradley, Sarah and Alistair Carr, Ann Follows, Jason Gathorne-Hardy, Rose Higham-Stainton, Bob Jackson, Henry Jackson Newcomb, Rob Parfitt, Ken Skipper, Christine Smith, Telfer Stokes, Susan — and Nina and Pervy.

NOTES

INTRODUCTION: for Slater quote, see David Herbert (ed.), *The Operas of Benjamin Britten: The Complete Librettos Illustrated with Designs of the First Productions* (The Herbert Press, 1989), p. 99; Montagu Slater's libretto was inspired by George Crabbe's poem 'The Borough' (1810).

THE FENS: for Kingsley quote, see *Collection of British Authors*, vol. 829, 'Hereward the Wake by Ch. Kingsley' (Bernhard Tauchnitz, 1866), p. 15.

ST JAMES VILLAGE ORCHARD: the orchard's website is www.stjamesvillageorchard.org.uk; the Dunbar picture is at Manchester Art Gallery, see https://manchesterartgallery.org.

THE CATHEDRAL OF THE MARSHES: for Jefferies quote, see Richard Jefferies, *The Story of My Heart*, originally published 1883 (Constable and Company Ltd, 1947), p. 20; for the Thomas interview, see Christopher Southgate, *Theology in a Suffering World: Glory and Longing* (Cambridge University Press, 2018), p. 175 and note 71; for Blythe quote, see Ronald Blythe, *The Time by the Sea: Aldeburgh 1955–1958* (Faber and Faber, 2013), p. 103.

ELM HILL: for Pevsner and Wilson quote, see Nikolaus Pevsner and Bill Wilson, *Norfolk 1: Norwich and North-East*, The Buildings of England series (Yale University Press, 2002), p. 297.